*W*heat-Free

*R*ecipes & *M*enus

Delicious Dining Without Wheat or Gluten

Carol Fenster, Ph.D.

Wheat-Free

Recipes & Menus

Delicious Dining Without Wheat or Gluten

Carol Fenster, Ph.D.

Savory Palate, Inc.
8174 South Holly, Suite 404
Littleton, CO 80122-4004

Printed in the United States of America
First Printing, 1995
Second Printing, 1997

Although the author and publisher have exhaustively researched many sources to ensure the accuracy and completeness of the information in this book, we assume no responsibility for errors, inaccuracies, omissions, or any inconsistency herein. No information contained herein should be construed as medical advice or as a guarantee that individuals will tolerate foods prepared from recipes in this book.

Library of Congress Catalog Card Number 95-74983

ISBN 1-889374-05-9
(formerly 1-57502-049-1)

Wheat-Free Recipes and Menus: Delicious Dining without Wheat or Gluten by Carol Fenster, Ph.D.

SUMMARY
1. Wheat-free cookbook, wheat-free diet, wheat-free food, gluten-free diet,
2. Wheat intolerance, gluten intolerance, wheat sensitivity, wheat allergy, food allergy, asthma, gluten sensitive enteropathy, dermatitis herpetiformis

Cover design by Shaeffer Reagan Design, Denver, CO

For information or to order more copies, contact Savory Palate, Inc., 8174 South Holly, #404, Littleton, CO 80122-4004. (303) 741-5408 (Order form at back of book).

ACKNOWLEDGMENTS

The idea for this book came from my own need for a wheat-free diet. But the book was nurtured and supported by many people.

Special thanks to my testers and tasters. . . you gave me valuable input about the dishes in this book in terms of taste, texture, and appearance.

The people who reviewed this manuscript provided excellent feedback and offered many suggestions for improving the book. They include Jane Dennison-Bauer, Maura Zazenski, Nancy Carol Sanker, Ellen Speare, Brett Fenster, and Kay DuBois. Thanks to each of you.

My friend, Jean Yancey—an accomplished business woman in her own right—was a continual source of ideas, encouragement, and support. Thank you, Jean!

Finally, a very special thank you to Larry and Brett—my husband and son—who tasted the dishes, offered suggestions, and were very supportive, loving, and generous with their time. This book is dedicated to them and to the memory of my mother, who first introduced me to cooking.

What People Are Saying . . .

Many people have improved the quality of their dining by using recipes from the Special Diet Series by Savory Palate, Inc. Here's what they're saying about *Wheat-Free Recipes & Menus.*

• *Living on a limited diet should not limit the possibilities! This book provides great variety and best of all . . . great taste for our wheat-free lifestyle. Thanks to Carol for developing a pizza recipe that is cause for true celebration at our house!*
  – Nancy Carol Sanker, OTR, Fort Collins, CO

• *Finally! A wheat-free cookbook that's upbeat, informative and good.*
  – Maura Zazenski, Littleton, CO

• *Thanks to you I had the most delicious Thanksgiving dinner. I haven't enjoyed a meal like that in 9 years.*
  –Jennifer Roach, Colorado Springs, CO

• *Each time I make the White Bread, I'm thrilled with the texture and taste. It's the best I've ever made.*
  – Cecile Weed, Garden Grove, CA

• *Carol's recipes make it easy to serve others since the results are every bit as good as the wheat recipes.*
  - Lillian Stich, St. Cloud, MN

Table of Contents

PREFACE

Background

Why did I write a cookbook for wheat-sensitive persons? I, too, am wheat-sensitive. I cannot tolerate wheat because it causes nasal congestion and stuffiness, making me feel dull, groggy, and lethargic. I was plagued by chronic sinusitis for most of my adult life, but it wasn't until nearly 6 years ago that I officially began avoiding wheat. It wasn't easy.

I learned that it's very difficult to avoid wheat because it's everywhere! It's an ingredient in a wide variety of foods, including bread, cake, soup, pasta, sauces, and candy. Yes, candy—even licorice contains wheat flour! And, eating in restaurants or away from home presents obvious problems of not knowing exactly what's in the food.

Rather than give up wheat entirely, I tried eating only a little. However, the nasal congestion, stuffiness, and chronic sinusitis continued. Antibiotics treated the sinus infections, but did nothing to address the underlying cause of the sinusitis in the first place.

I decided to take complete control over what I ate. This meant lots of research into how I could prepare the same dishes I was accustomed to eating, while eliminating wheat as an ingredient. I learned which alternative flours were acceptable to wheat-sensitive persons and how these flours perform in various recipes.

At the same time, my research confirmed my suspicions that millions of other people must also avoid wheat. I wasn't alone! After eating wheat, some people just don't feel well. Others experience nasal stuffiness, a bloated feeling, intestinal distress, and even anaphylactic reactions. People with celiac sprue must completely avoid wheat because of the gluten it contains. Clearly, there are many of us who must avoid wheat. The important thing is to recognize and admit to ourselves that we cannot continue to eat wheat and expect to feel good. So, I — and millions of others—have changed our eating patterns.

Today, my diet is wheat-free and I feel wonderful. And I'm eating the same dishes I once ate—but they're made without wheat or gluten. This book shows you how to adopt a wheat and gluten-free diet so you, too, can feel better—and still eat the dishes you want.

Additional Information

Check your local book store, health food store, and library for books on wheat and gluten sensitivities. Ask about local support groups for people with food allergies. These groups are a rich source of information about learning to live with food sensitivities and celiac sprue. The following groups provide more information:

Food Allergy Network (FAN)
4744 Holly Avenue
Fairfax, VA 22030-5647
(800) 929-4040
(703) 691-3179

Celiac Sprue Association/USA
PO Box 31700
Omaha, NE 68131-0700
(402) 558-0600; (402) 558-1347 - FAX
celiacusa@aol.com

National Jewish Center for Immunology
    and Respiratory Medicine
1400 Jackson Street
Denver, CO 80206
(800) 222-5864 (Lung Line)
(303) 388-4461

Gluten Intolerance Group of No. America
PO 23053
Seattle, WA 98102-0353
(206) 325-6980
gig@accessone.com

Asthma and Allergy Foundation of
    America
1125 15th Street, N.W., Suite 502
Washington, D.C. 20005
(800) 7ASTHMA (Help Line)
(202) 466-7643

Celiac Disease Foundation
13251 Ventura Blvd., Suite 3
Studio City, CA 91604-1838
(818) 990-2354; (818) 990-2379 - FAX
http://www.celiac.org/cdf

INTRODUCTION

Who Is This Book For?
This cookbook is for people who can't eat wheat or gluten. Whatever the reason for eliminating wheat from your diet—and there are many, many reasons—you must adjust your approach to dining.

Wheat and gluten-sensitive persons can eat almost all of the dishes they once ate. The secret is to prepare those dishes using alternative ingredients. This book shows you how by:

- **identifying ingredients needed for wheat-free and gluten-free cooking**

- **providing recipes for a wide variety of flavorful dishes that either eliminate flour or use alternative flours and other ingredients that don't contain wheat or gluten**

- **providing menus to help in meal planning so once you've selected an entree, you'll know what other dishes will taste good and look good with that dish**

The basic principle behind wheat and gluten-free cooking is:

Remove the wheat. Replace it with alternative ingredients and a few special preparation techniques.

For those with additional food sensitivities, see the Appendix for guidelines on using substitutes for dairy, eggs, and refined sugar.

Why Is It Important to Learn Wheat-Free Cooking?
Many of you have already learned how to incorporate wheat-free flours and grains into your diet. If not, you may be

continuing to eat wheat-laden foods—or, you may beliminating crucial food groups from your diet in order to avoid wheat. The United States Department of Agriculture (USDA) recommends that we eat 6-11 servings of the food group that includes bread, cereal, and pasta. This book provides recipes so that you can eat a wide variety of foods—using wheat-free, gluten-free flours and grains—from this food group.

What Kind of Recipes Are In This Book?

Wheat is omitted in all recipes and menus. Alternative flours—readily available at health food stores or by mail-order—are used instead. Barley, oats, kamut, spelt, and rye are excluded because their gluten aggravates some people. In many recipes, amaranth and quinoa are offered as substitutes for the rice flours. Celiacs, please consult your physician about amaranth and quinoa.

Wherever possible, unnecessary fats, oils, and sugars are removed in recipes—without sacrificing flavor and texture. In addition, animal fats are used very sparingly. Most recipes use olive oil or canola oil, but you may your favorite oil. Butter is used occasionally, primarily for flavor. *However, this is not meant to be a low-fat or low calorie cookbook.*

Recipes for many family favorites are included (for example, Meat Loaf and Chicken Noodle Soup). But there are also recipes for contemporary cuisine, emphasizing the lighter, fresh-ingredient approach—often with a Southwestern touch. I've incorporated a wide variety of foods for you to choose from.

All recipes were tested in my kitchen as well as the kitchens of my recipe-testers. We used a variety of appliances. I used an electric Jenn-Aire range, oven, and microwave while my testers used other brands, including a gas range. All of us achieved consistently successful results.

How This Book Is Organized

I recommend that you read pages 1 through 8 in the Introduction first. They'll give you an overview of cooking without wheat or gluten, the ingredients you'll need, and some basic tips. Also, read pages 10-12 for more specifics on baking bread with wheat and gluten-free flours. See the Appendices for more information, including guidelines for cooking without dairy, eggs, or sugar.

Approximate nutritional analyses are offered using calculations from the USDA. This information includes calories, fat, percent of fat, protein, carbohydrate, sodium, and cholesterol **per serving**, unless noted otherwise. Your exact nutrient intake may vary, however, due to ingredients used, size of portions, and number of portions consumed. It's best to check with your dietitian or nutritionist about your nutrient intake.

Approximate preparation times are given for each recipe. These times include assembling and baking or cooking the recipe and are meant to help organize your efforts during meal planning and preparation. Of course, preparation times may vary.

Starting on page 253, you'll find menus in a variety of categories—fish, poultry, and beef—as well as special categories such as Quick & Easy Dinners, Meatless Meals, and Southwestern Menus. These menus give you wheat and gluten-free ideas about what to serve with the main dish.

In the Appendices, you'll also find information about alternative flours including measurements to use when substituting other flours for wheat flour, what to use in place of wheat flour as a thickening agent, and how the different flours perform in various baking situations. There is also a list of prepared foods that are often hidden sources of wheat or gluten and a list of Mail-Order Sources that carry wheat-free and gluten-free flours, grains, and other ingredients.

Successful Wheat-Free Cooking
Always read through the entire recipe before mixing the ingredients. This helps you do several things:

- make sure all the required ingredients are on hand to avoid a last minute trip to the store

- know the order in which ingredients are added

- notice any unusual or unique directions

Follow the recipe exactly the first time you make it. Then, if you want to modify it to better suit your individual taste, you'll have a "frame of reference" to guide you. All of us have our own personal preferences in food, so feel free to experiment.

When you're ready to cook, assemble all ingredients on one side of the counter. As you add that ingredient, place the container or box on the other side of the counter. That way, if you're interrupted or accidentally lose your place in the recipe, you'll know what you've already added to the recipe and won't leave out or duplicate ingredients.

A very useful resource is the *Cooperative Gluten-Free Products Listing* published by the Celiac Sprue Association. It lists products that are wheat and gluten-free and is a very useful tool. Take it with you when you go grocery shopping so you know which brands are gluten-free. See Celiac Sprue Association on page viii.

Recipes to Prepare and Keep on Hand

Keeping these items on hand makes your wheat and gluten-free cooking more efficient because these dishes are used in other recipes. I've provided the page numbers for easy reference.

Recipe	How To Use
Chocolate Wafer Cookie - 112	Great as quick dessert or as crust for Easy Chocolate Cheesecake.
Pasta - 69	Make several batches of spaghetti, fettucini, noodles, etc. Freeze. Use in Beef and Chicken Paprika's, Fettucine Alfredo, Beef Stroganoff or Beef Burgundy.
Pretzels - 40	Store these in an air-tight container for quick snacks. Or, crush for an unusual pie crust.
Spaghetti Sauce - 157	Use in Spaghetti & Meatballs or Eggplant Parmesan or as sauce for Pizza.
Vanilla Wafers - 118	Freeze. Use to make a crumb crust for a pie or cheesecake.
White Bread - 30	Keep on hand for toast, sandwiches, and bread crumbs.
Yellow Cake - 102	Top with fresh fruit and whipped cream for a quick dessert. Or, use in Yogurt Breakfast Trifle or Boston Cream Pie.
Yogurt Cheese - 165	Store in refrigerator and use to "cream" sauces. Replaces sour cream in some recipes such as Pastry Crusts.

SETTING UP A WHEAT-FREE PANTRY

In addition to the usual fruits, vegetables, canned goods, and staples you keep on hand, the following page lists ingredients that are necessary for wheat and gluten-free cooking—but that you may not ordinarily keep in your pantry.

As you assemble your wheat-free, gluten-free pantry, you'll be amazed at how often wheat occurs in the most unexpected places. To help you in this area, see Hidden Sources of Wheat and Gluten in the Appendix for a partial list of such foods.

If you can't find the ingredients locally, see the Index for Mail-Order Sources.

WHEAT AND GLUTEN-FREE PANTRY

Ingredient	What It Does
Ascorbic Acid	Acid helps leavening process.
Baby Foods -- Applesauce, Apricots, Bananas, Pears, Prunes	Partial replacement for fats and oils. Provides moisture and binds ingredients together in cakes, cookies, breads.
Baking Powder (cereal free)	Leavens baked goods.
Baking Soda	Leavens baked goods. Combine with cream of tartar to make baking powder.
Cream of Tartar	Neutralizes baking soda. Mix 1 part baking soda with 2 parts cream of tartar to make baking powder.
Dry Milk Powder	Protein boosts yeast activity in breads and other baked goods.
Egg Replacer	Replaces eggs and leavens and stabilizes baked goods.
Extracts (gluten-free) such as vanilla, almond, butter	Flavor boost in desserts, baked goods.
Flours (gluten-free) white rice, brown rice, bean, potato starch, tapioca, and cornstarch or arrowroot.	Replaces wheat flour. See Wheat-Free Flours in Appendix for flour characteristics and uses.
Gelatin powder (unflavored)	Binds ingredients together in some baked goods and desserts.
Gum -- xanthan -- guar	Substitutes for gluten and acts as a stabilizer, emulsifier, and suspension agent so dough rises well. Also thickens. Use in baked goods.
Soy Lecithin (granules or liquid)	Softens the loaf and improves texture of bread. Granular and liquid versions measure the same.
Yeast (gluten-free)	Leavening for bread, baked goods.
Yogurt	Provides additional moisture in baking. Thickens and creams sauces. Used to make Yogurt Cheese (See Index).
Cooking spray (gluten-free)	Use in place of oil to sauté. Prevents baked goods from "sticking" to pan.
Vinegar (gluten-free)	Use cider, wine, or rice vinegar. Strengthens yeast dough to rise better.

So . . . when I make these recipes, how will the food taste?
Each recipe in this book had to pass strict tests in terms of taste
and appearance. In addition to kitchen-testing each and every
recipe myself, I conducted several tasting sessions in my home,
in other people's homes, and for professional groups. I also
teach cooking classes at local health food stores nationwide.

In each and every case, tasters gave the greatest compliment of
all: **none of them guessed that the food was free of wheat
and gluten, or they couldn't believe it even when I told
them.**

Hopefully, you've read the preceding pages and you're now
looking forward to preparing some of the wheat-free, gluten-
free recipes in this book and once again enjoying the dishes you
want to eat. Good luck and happy cooking!

NOTE: For those of you with additional food sensitivities, you
will be interested in my newest book. *Special Diet Solutions:
Healthy Cooking Without Wheat, Gluten, Dairy, Eggs, Yeast, or
Refined Sugar* (ISBN 1-889374-00-8), $15.95) is designed for
those with multiple food sensitivities. Each wheat and gluten-
free recipe has directions for further modifying the recipe to
also exclude dairy . . . or eggs . . . or refined sugar. . . or all
three. There is also a special yeast-free bread section.

BREADS

YEAST BREADS
Breadsticks 13
Bruschetta 14
Dilly Bread* 15
Fennel Bread* 18
Focaccia 20
French Bread 22
Hamburger Buns* 23
Pizza Crust 24
Pretzels 40
Pumpernickel Bread* 25
Raisin Bread* 27
Russian Black Bread* 29
White Bread* 30

QUICK BREADS
Boston Brown Bread 32
Cheese Biscotti 33
Corn Bread 34
Corn Tortillas 35
Crackers 39
Flour Tortillas 36
Sopaipillas 37
Spoon Bread 42
Yorkshire Pudding 38

BREAKFAST BREADS
(Yeast & Quick)
Bagels 49
Baked Doughnuts 45
Banana Bread 50
Blueberry-Lemon Muffins 47
Raspberry Muffins 48
English Muffins 16
Buttermilk Biscuits 51
German Pancakes 52
Pancakes 52
Popovers 38
Scones 41
Waffles 54
   Blue Corn Waffles 55
   Corn Waffles 55

Yeast bread recipes have been updated—they're faster because they have just one rising, instead of two.

* Recipes make one 1-pound loaf. For **free** conversion of these recipes to 1 1/2 or 2 pound loaves for your bread machine, send your name and address to Savory Palate, 8174 S. Holly, #404, Littleton, CO 80122

Bread is the staple of life. And this section has recipes for many mouth-watering, wheat-free ways to enjoy it. Such as Focaccia, Hamburger Buns, Scones, Popovers, and the traditional White Bread.

But wait, you're thinking . . . *will I like breads made without wheat or gluten?*

Non-wheat breads are not like wheat breads
Breads made with non-wheat flours may look, taste, and smell slightly different from those made with wheat flours. Several reasons account for these differences.

First of all, breads made from wheat-free, gluten-free flours look different because these flours do not have the right kinds of proteins to form the gluten framework that holds leavening gases. As a result, these non-wheat breads may not be as large in volume or as light in texture as wheat breads. However, you will quickly come to appreciate the texture of these breads.

Second, wheat-free, gluten-free flours may taste slightly different because our taste buds have been conditioned over the years to associate the "wheat" taste with bread. In other words, we've learned to expect the taste of wheat in bread. I recently tasted a wheat flour tortilla (after a long abstinence) and was amazed at my palate's ability to distinguish the taste of wheat.

Finally, the aroma we commonly associate with *wheat* breads is somewhat diminished because we're not using wheat. Be sure to check the Wheat-Free Flours section in the Appendix to see how to use alternative flours—especially the garbanzo/fava bean flour which is a wonderful addition to our repertoire of flours.

In this section, you'll find recipes that make non-wheat breads closely resemble wheat breads. These recipes use ingredients that help improve the volume, texture, flavor, and aroma of non-wheat breads. For example, vinegar helps yeast rise and develops flavor (which, in turn, strengthens aroma), xanthan gum lends structure to help trap leavening gases, and Egg Replacer improves the texture of breads.

New advances in technology, such as bread machines, take much of the guesswork out of bread making. With program-mable machines, some experimentation may be required in this book's recipes to achieve the right settings. My Welbilt (on light setting) warms the ingredients for 20 minutes, mixes 10 minutes, rests 5 minutes, kneads 15 minutes, rises 25 minutes, punches down then rises again 54 minutes. It bakes for 40 minutes. Total time is 2 hours and 50 minutes. If you wish to program your machine for one rise, eliminate the second rising of 54 minutes. My recipes make 1-pound loaves. (See page 9 for ordering bread recipes for 1 1/2 or 2-pound loaves.)

Secrets to success when baking wheat-free breads
A combination of wheat and gluten-free flours produces a better texture than single flours. For example, brown rice flour combined with potato starch and tapioca flour is not as grainy.

Measure flours and other dry ingredients this way: Spoon the the flour into a measuring cup or spoon, but don't pack it down. Using the straight edge of a knife or a spatula, level the flour even with the top of the measuring cup or spoon.

Smaller recipes (those containing 2 cups of flour or less) are easier to adapt to wheat-free flours. Recipes containing cake flour are especially easy to adapt since they don't depend upon gluten for their structure.

Non-wheat flours require more leavening to compensate for their lack of elasticity. As a general rule, use at least 25% more baking soda or baking powder than you would use in a wheat version. However, I usually don't increase yeast in yeast breads.

Dissolve the leavening agent in liquid portion of recipe before adding to the rest of the ingredients. This helps the bread rise.

Adding protein—such as cottage cheese, dry milk powder, or eggs—helps improve the structure of yeast breads.

Bake the breads at lower temperatures for longer periods of time.

Bake the breads in smaller loaves or pans (5 x 2 1/2-inch rather than 9 x 5-inch) for a better texture and more even baking.

These recipes were developed or adapted at 5000 feet altitude, but are not necessarily altitude-sensitive. If you're baking at 7,500 or 10,000 feet, no changes are usually required. At sea level, you may need to adjust recipes using these guidelines:

- increase baking powder or baking soda by 1/4 to 1/2 (If using acidic ingredients such as sour milk or buttermilk, no adjustments are needed.)
- increase rising times for yeast breads by 30 minutes
- increase each cup of sugar by 2-3 tablespoons
- decrease liquid by 3-4 tablespoons per cup of liquid
- decrease oven temperature by 25 degrees

Source: These tips come from the Colorado State University Cooperative Extension Bulletin 530A, 1985, and my personal baking experiences with wheat-free flours.

Breadsticks

These breadsticks taste great with a Spaghetti & Meatballs dinner (See Index). You can experiment by adding different herbs to the dough or sprinkling the breadsticks with your favorite Italian spices.

1 tablespoon gf dry yeast
1/2 cup brown rice flour
1 tablespoon dry milk powder or non-dairy milk powder
1/2 cup tapioca flour
2 teaspoons xanthan gum
1/2 cup grated Parmesan cheese (cow, rice, or soy)
1/2 teaspoon salt
1 teaspoon gf onion powder

1 teaspoon unflavored gelatin powder
2/3 cup warm water (105°)
1/2 teaspoon sugar or honey
1 tablespoon olive oil
1 teaspoon cider vinegar
1 egg white, beaten to a foam
1 teaspoon Italian seasoning
cooking spray

Preheat oven to 400 degrees for 5 minutes, then turn off.

In medium mixer bowl while oven is preheating, blend the yeast, flours, dry milk powder, xanthan gum, Parmesan cheese, salt, onion powder, and gelatin powder on low speed of electric mixer. Add warm water, sugar (or honey), olive oil, and vinegar. Beat on high for 3 minutes. Dough will be soft and sticky. (Bread machine is not recommended.)

Place dough in large, *heavy-duty* plastic freezer bag that has 1/2-inch opening cut diagonally on one corner. (This makes a 1-inch circle.) Coat a large baking sheet with cooking spray. Squeeze dough out of plastic bag onto sheet in 10 strips, each 1-inch wide by 6 inches long. For best results, hold the bag of dough upright as you squeeze, rather than at an angle. Spray breadsticks with cooking spray, then sprinkle with herb seasoning.

Place in warmed oven to rise for 20-30 minutes. Leaving breadsticks in oven, turn oven to 400 degrees and bake until golden brown, about 15-20 minutes. Switch position of baking sheet halfway through baking to assure even browning. Cool on wire rack. When cool, store in airtight container.

Preparation Time = 1 hour, 15 minutes. Serves 10 (one breadstick each).
Calories 93 (27% from fat); Fat 3g; Prot 4g; Carb 13g; Sod 260mg; Chol 3mg.

Bruschetta

Use the French Bread (See Index) as the basis for this recipe. Feel free to experiment with your own versions of toppings.

1 loaf gf French Bread	1/2 teaspoon salt
cooking spray	1/4 cup grated Parmesan
1 garlic clove, minced	cheese (cow, rice, or soy)
1 tablespoon extra virgin	2 tablespoons fresh parsley,
olive oil	finely chopped

Diagonally slice the French Bread into 8 pieces. Coat a large skillet or grill with cooking spray. Over medium heat, cook each bread slice for 2 minutes on each side or until golden brown.

Arrange on serving plate.

Mix together the minced garlic, olive oil, and salt. Use a pastry brush to coat top side of each bread slice with oil mixture. Sprinkle with Parmesan cheese and parsley.
Preparation = 10 minutes. Serves 4 (2 slices per serving).
Calories 72 (60% from fat); Fat 5g; Prot 3g; Carb 4g; Sod 396mg; Chol 4mg.

TOPPINGS TO SPREAD ON GRILLED BREAD SLICES
1. Combine 1/4 cup Yogurt Cheese (See Index), 1 teaspoon lemon juice, 1/4 teaspoon oregano, and 1/2 teaspoon olive oil.
2. In food processor, puree together 3/4 cup ripe black olives, 1 clove garlic, 1/8 teaspoon dried thyme, 1 teaspoon dried basil, and 1 teaspoon olive oil.

Dilly Bread

This is my grandmother's recipe which was passed down from my mother to me. I've modified it for wheat-free flours. The cottage cheese improves the structure of wheat-free breads. Note the smaller yeast amounts for the bread machine version.

1 teaspoon sugar or honey
1/4 cup water
gf dry yeast (see below)
1 cup low-fat cottage cheese
2 eggs at room temperature
1 tablespoon sugar or honey
1 tablespoon canola oil
1 teaspoon cider vinegar
1 1/4 cups brown rice flour
1/2 cup potato starch flour

1/4 cup tapioca flour
1 tablespoon dried minced onions
1 tablespoon dried dill weed
1 tablespoon dill seed
1/4 teaspoon baking soda
1/2 teaspoon salt
2 teaspoons xanthan gum
1 teaspoon unflavored gelatin
   powder
cooking spray

HAND METHOD: Combine **1 tablespoon** yeast, 1 teaspoon sugar, and 1/4 cup warm water (105°). Set aside 5 minutes or until yeast is foamy. Warm cottage cheese to room temperature.

Combine cottage cheese, eggs, sugar, canola oil, and vinegar in large mixer bowl. Beat until well blended. Add yeast mixture.

Combine dry ingredients in another bowl. Add to egg mixture, 1/2 cup at a time and beat slowly. Scrape sides of bowl continually and continue beating until dough is stiff. Place in 2 small pans (7 x 3-inch) that are coated with cooking spray. Let rise until double in size.

Preheat oven to 350 degrees. Bake for 35 minutes or until loaves sound hollow if tapped. Remove bread from pans; cool on rack. Makes 2 small loaves.

BREAD MACHINE. Follow bread machine instructions. I combine dry ingredients, using **1 1/2 teaspoons dry yeast**. Pour into bread machine. Combine liquid ingredients (water at room temperature) and pour over dry ingredients in bread machine. Set controls and bake.

Preparation = 3 hours. Serves 12. Makes one 1-pound loaf.

Calories 150 (19% from fat); Fat 3g; Prot 8g; Carb 22g; Sod 249mg; Chol 44mg.
Brown Rice Substitute (not for celiacs): 1 cup quinoa flour and 1/4 cup amaranth.

English Muffins

I had never made English Muffins before, so I was pleasantly surprised to find how easy these are, even with wheat-free flours. English Muffins are great toasted for breakfast or as the basis for Eggs Benedict (See Index).

2 tablespoons gf dry yeast
1 tablespoon sugar
1 1/4 cups warm water (105°)
2 cups white rice flour
2 cups tapioca flour
1/3 cup brown rice flour
2/3 cup dry milk powder or non-dairy milk powder*
3 teaspoons xanthan gum

1 tablespoon unflavored gelatin powder
1 teaspoon salt
1/4 cup canola oil
4 large egg whites at room temperature
1 tablespoon yellow cornmeal
cooking spray

Dissolve yeast and sugar in water. Let foam 5 minutes.

In large mixer bowl, combine flours, dry milk powder, xanthan gum, gelatin powder, and salt. Blend on low, then add canola oil and egg whites. Mix well. Add yeast mixture and beat on high for 3 minutes. Arrange muffin rings on baking sheet that is sprayed with cooking spray and dusted with cornmeal.

(To make aluminum foil rings, take 1 foot of foil and fold in half, lengthwise, again and again, until 1-inch high. Secure ends together with masking tape). Spray rings with cooking spray.

Divide dough into 12 equal pieces and press into each ring. Cover and let rise in a warm place for about 50 minutes.

Preheat oven to 350 degrees. Bake the muffins for 15 minutes or until lightly browned. With spatula, turn the muffins (tins and all) over and bake another 10 minutes or until lightly browned.

Remove English muffins from cookie sheets to cool. When rings are cool enough to handle, remove muffins from rings. Preparation = 1 1/2 hours. Serves 12. Makes 12 English muffins.

Calories per muffin: 260 (19% from fat); Fat 5g; Prot 7g; Carb 45g; Sod 219mg; Chol 1mg.

* Depending on the consistency and density of the non-dairy milk powder, you may need to use less than 2/3 cup. Start with 1/2 cup and add if necessary, 1 tablespoon at a time, until the dough reaches desired consistency. Some experimentation may be required and, depending on the type of non-dairy milk powder used, the muffins may not rise as high.

Salt is added to foods to improve flavor, but it also affects the chemistry and structure of baked goods. For example, salt helps control and slow the yeast fermentation so that the bubbles of carbon dioxide and moisture produced by the yeast are more uniform in size. However, too much salt can seriously inhibit yeast activity.

Fennel Bread

This is a very moist, very dense bread that tastes great in sandwiches. Try it plain, toasted, or in grilled sandwiches such as a Reuben. Note the smaller yeast amount in the bread machine version.

gf dry yeast (see below)
3 tablespoons brown sugar
1 cup warm water (105°)
1 1/2 cups brown rice flour
1/3 cup potato starch flour
1/3 cup tapioca flour
1 teaspoon salt
2 teaspoons xanthan gum
1 teaspoon unflavored gelatin powder
1 tablespoon fennel seeds

1 tablespoon flax seeds (optional)
1/3 cup dry milk powder or non-dairy milk powder
1/4 teaspoon soy lecithin
2 teaspoons Egg Replacer
2 large eggs, lightly beaten
3 tablespoons canola oil
1 teaspoon cider vinegar
1 tablespoon molasses
cooking spray

HAND METHOD: Combine **1 tablespoon yeast**, 2 teaspoons of the brown sugar, and water and set aside to let yeast foam, about 5 minutes.

In large mixer bowl, combine flours, salt, remainder of sugar, xanthan gum, gelatin powder, fennel and flax seeds, dry milk powder, lecithin, and Egg Replacer. In separate bowl, combine eggs, canola oil, vinegar, and molasses.

With mixer on low speed and using regular beaters (not dough hooks), add egg mixture to dry ingredients and blend. Blend in yeast mixture, increase speed to high, and beat for 2 minutes.

For smaller loaves, coat three small pans, 5 x 2 1/2-inches, with cooking spray. Divide dough among pans. Place in warm place to rise for 45-60 minutes or until doubled in bulk.

For one large loaf, use 9 x 5-inch pan coated with cooking spray and let dough rise until double in bulk.

Preheat oven to 350 degrees. Bake small loaves for 25-30 minutes, large loaf for 40-50 minutes—or until tops are nicely browned.

BREAD MACHINE: Use **1 1/2 teaspoons dry yeast**. Follow your bread machine instructions. I combine dry ingredients and add to bread machine, making sure kneader is in place. Combine liquid ingredients (water at room temperature). Pour carefully over dry ingredients in bread machine. Set controls and bake.

Preparation = 3 hours. Serves 10. Makes one 1-pound loaf.

Calories 211 (24% from fat); Fat 6g; Prot 13g; Carb 27g; Sod 267mg; Chol 43mg.
Brown Rice Substitute (not for celiacs): 1 cup amaranth flour and 1/2 cup quinoa flour.

Focaccia

Focaccia is a cross between pizza and rustic flat bread. It's fairly easy to make and the dough is especially forgiving. At serving time, dip it in flavored olive oil or spaghetti sauce—just like the Italian restaurants!

1 1/2 teaspoons gf dry yeast
3/4 cup warm water (105°)
1 teaspoon sugar
1 cup brown rice flour
1/4 cup potato starch flour
1/4 cup tapioca flour
1 1/2 teaspoons xanthan gum
1 teaspoon unflavored
   gelatin powder
1 teaspoon dried rosemary
1/2 teaspoon gf onion powder

3/4 teaspoon salt
2 large eggs
2 tablespoons olive oil
1/2 teaspoon cider vinegar
1 tablespoon cornmeal (optional)
TOPPING
1 teaspoon Italian seasoning
1/4 teaspoon salt
1 tablespoon olive oil
cooking spray

Dissolve sugar in warm water. Sprinkle yeast into water and stir until yeast dissolves. Set aside to foam, about 5 minutes.

Combine flours, xanthan gum, gelatin powder, rosemary, onion powder, and salt in a small mixer bowl. Whisk eggs, olive oil, and vinegar into the dissolved yeast and stir the mixture into the flour. Beat dough with mixer for 2 minutes, using a spatula to keep stirring down the dough on the mixer beaters. The dough will be soft and sticky

Transfer dough to 11 x 7-inch nonstick pan coated with cooking spray and cornmeal. Sprinkle with Italian seasoning, salt and olive oil. Cover with aluminum foil and let rise in warm place for 30 minutes.

Preheat oven to 400 degrees. Bake for 15 minutes.
Preparation = 1 hour. Serves 4 (large pieces).
Calories 200 (20% from fat); Fat 5g; Prot 6g; Carb 34g; Sod 381mg; Chol 71mg.

ALTERNATIVE TOPPINGS

HERB: Combine 1/2 teaspoon dried rosemary, 1/2 teaspoon dried sage, 1/2 teaspoon dried thyme, 1/4 teaspoon black pepper, and 2 tablespoons Parmesan cheese.

SUN-DRIED TOMATO AND OLIVE: 1/4 cup chopped sun-dried tomatoes in oil, 1/4 cup chopped black olives, and 1/4 cup chopped onion sautéed until translucent in 1 teaspoon olive oil.

PESTO: Puree the following in food processor just until smooth, leaving a bit of texture: 1 cup fresh basil leaves, 1 garlic clove, 1/2 cup pine nuts. With motor running, slowly drizzle in 1/4 cup olive oil through feed tube. Add 1/4 cup Parmesan cheese and a dash of freshly ground black pepper.

French Bread

I've updated this favorite—it's faster and has a crispier crust because it goes directly into a 425° oven without any rising time.

2 tablespoons gf dry yeast
1 1/2 cups warm water (105°)
1 tablespoon sugar
2 cups white rice flour
1/2 cup potato starch
1/4 cup tapioca flour
2 teaspoons xanthan gum
1/4 cup dry milk powder or
   non-dairy milk powder

1 3/4 teaspoons salt
2 teaspoons Egg Replacer (optional)
3 tablespoons canola oil
3 large egg whites, lightly beaten
1 teaspoon cider vinegar
2 tablespoons cornmeal (optional)
milk or eggs for brushing (optional)
cooking spray

Dissolve the sugar in the warm water, then stir in the yeast. Set aside to foam for 5 minutes.

Coat baking pans or French-loaf shaped pans with cooking spray. Dust with cornmeal (if using). Preheat oven to 425 degrees.

In bowl of heavy-duty mixer, combine flours, xanthan gum, dry milk powder, salt, and Egg Replacer (if using). Blend on low speed of mixer.

Add yeast mixture to flour mixture. Still on low speed, blend in oil, egg whites, and vinegar. Beat on high speed for 2 minutes. Dough will be somewhat soft.

Spoon onto prepared pans, shaping the dough into two French-loaf shapes on a baking sheet or in French-bread pans. Brush with milk or beaten eggs, if desired, for glossier crust.

Place immediately into preheated oven and bake for approximately 30 minutes, or until bread is nicely browned.

Remove bread from pans and cool on wire rack. Makes 2 loaves.

Preparation = 45 minutes. Serves 12.

Calories: 190 (18% from fat); Fat 4g; Prot 5g; Carb 35; Sod 335mg; Chol 0mg.

Hamburger Buns

If you've eaten hamburger patties without a bun for so long that you've forgotten what a real hamburger tastes like, this recipe will help refresh your memory. These buns freeze beautifully.

1 1/2 teaspoons gf dry yeast
1 teaspoon sugar or honey
1 cup brown rice flour
1/4 cup potato starch
1/4 cup tapioca flour
1 1/2 teaspoons xanthan gum
1 teaspoon unflavored gelatin
  powder

1 tablespoon gf onion flakes
3/4 teaspoon salt
1/4 teaspoon soy lecithin (optional)
3/4 cup warm water (105°)
2 tablespoons canola oil
2 large eggs
1/2 teaspoon cider vinegar

Combine yeast, sugar, flours, xanthan gum, gelatin powder, onion, salt, and lecithin in a small mixer bowl. Add warm water, oil, eggs, and vinegar to the flour mixture. Beat dough with electric mixer on high (using regular beaters, not dough hooks) for 2 minutes. The dough will be soft and sticky.

Transfer dough to eight English muffin rings (or aluminum foil rings—see page 16) on baking sheet. Rings and sheet should be coated with cooking spray. Cover with aluminum foil and let rise in warm place for 30 minutes or until desired height.

Preheat oven to 400 degrees. Bake for 15-20 minutes or until tops are golden brown. Cool 5 minutes, then remove buns from rings. Lightly toasting the cut side of bun before serving produces a crispy texture. Makes 8 buns.

Preparation = 1 hour. Serves 8.
Per bun:
Calories: 170 (26% from fat); Fat 5g; Prot 3g; Carb 29g; Sod 290mg; Chol 45mg

Variation: For an herb-flavored bun, add 1 teaspoon rosemary leaves (crushed) and 1/2 teaspoon Italian herb seasoning.

Pizza Crust

This crispy pizza crust tastes so delicious that my guests did not know it was wheat-free—and then couldn't believe it when I told them at the end of the meal! Use any topping you like, but see the Index for a delicious fat-free Pizza Sauce.

1 tablespoon gf dry yeast
2/3 cup brown rice flour
1/2 cup tapioca flour
2 tablespoons dry milk powder
  or non-dairy milk powder
2 teaspoons xanthan gum
1/2 teaspoon salt
1 teaspoon unflavored gelatin
  powder

1 teaspoon Italian seasoning
2/3 cup warm water (105°)
1/2 teaspoon sugar
1 teaspoon olive oil
1 teaspoon cider vinegar
cooking spray

Preheat oven to 425 degrees. In medium mixer bowl using regular beaters (not dough hooks), blend the yeast, flours, dry milk powder, xanthan gum, salt, gelatin powder, and Italian seasoning on low speed. Add warm water, sugar, olive oil, and vinegar. Beat on high speed for 3 minutes. (If the mixer bounces around the bowl, the dough is too stiff. Add water if necessary, one tablespoon at a time, until dough does not resist beaters.) The dough will be soft.

Put mixture into 12-inch pizza pan or on baking sheet (for thin, crispy crust), 11 x 7-inch pan (for deep dish version) that has been coated with cooking spray. Liberally sprinkle rice flour onto dough, then press dough into pan, continuing to sprinkle dough with flour to prevent sticking to your hands. Make edges thicker to contain the toppings.

Bake the pizza crust for 10 minutes. Remove from oven. Spread pizza crust with your favorite sauce and toppings. Bake for another 20-25 minutes or until top is nicely browned. Preparation = 40 minutes. Serves 4.

Calories 180 (20% from fat); Fat 4g; Prot 4g; Carb 32; Sod 279mg; Chol 0mg.

Pumpernickel Bread

This bread is thick, dense and filling. It makes great sandwiches—try it in your next Reuben. Note the smaller yeast amount for the bread machine version.

gf dry yeast (see below)
1 cup water
2 tablespoons brown sugar
1 cup brown rice flour
1/2 cup potato starch flour
1/2 cup tapioca flour
3 teaspoons caraway seeds
2 teaspoons flax seeds (optional)
1 teaspoon instant coffee powder
1/2 teaspoon onion powder
2 teaspoons xanthan gum
1 teaspoon unflavored gelatin
  powder

1 teaspoon salt
6 tablespoons dry milk
  powder or non-dairy milk
  powder
2 teaspoons Egg Replacer
  (optional)
1 tablespoon cocoa
2 large eggs at room
  temperature
2 tablespoons canola oil
2 tablespoons molasses
1 teaspoon cider vinegar
cooking spray

HAND METHOD: Combine **1 tablespoon yeast**, warm water (105°) and 2 teaspoons of the brown sugar in small bowl. Set aside to foam, about 5 minutes.

In large mixer bowl using regular beaters (not dough hooks), combine remaining dry ingredients (including remaining brown sugar) and blend on low speed.

Combine eggs, oil, molasses, and vinegar and combine with yeast mixture after yeast has begun to foam.

With mixer on low speed, add liquid to dry ingredients. Once liquid is incorporated, increase mixer speed to high and beat for 2 minutes.

For small loaves, coat three 5 x 2 1/2-inch loaf pans with cooking spray. Divide dough among pans and put in warm place to rise for 45-60 minutes, or until doubled in bulk.

Preheat oven to 350 degrees. Bake loaves for 25-30 minutes. For large loaf, coat an 8-inch pie plate with cooking spray and place dough in it. Let rise about 35-40 minutes or until doubled in bulk. Bake for 40-50 minutes.

BREAD MACHINE: Reduce yeast to **1 1/2 teaspoons**. Follow your machine instructions. I combine dry ingredients and add to bread machine. Then I combine liquid ingredients (water at room temperature). Pour carefully over dry ingredients in bread machine. Set controls and bake.

Preparation = 3 hours. Serves 10. Makes one 1-pound loaf.

Calories 178 (23% from fat); Fat 5g; Prot 6g; Carb 29g; Sod 246mg; Chol 43mg. Brown Rice Substitute (not for celiacs): 1/2 cup amaranth flour and 1/2 cup quinoa flour.

Raisin Bread

This makes a wonderful breakfast bread—eat it plain, or with butter, jam, or cream cheese. Note different yeast amounts for bread machine versus hand version.

gf dry yeast (see below)
1 cup water
1 teaspoon sugar
1 1/3 cups brown rice flour
1/2 cup potato starch flour
1/4 cup tapioca flour
1 teaspoon xanthan gum
1 teaspoon unflavored gelatin powder
1/3 cup dry milk powder or non-dairy milk powder
1/4 teaspoon soy lecithin

1 teaspoon salt
2 tablespoons brown sugar, packed
1 teaspoon cinnamon
2 large eggs, lightly beaten
3 tablespoons canola oil
1 teaspoon cider vinegar
1/4 cup applesauce or pureed prunes (prune baby food)
1/2 cup raisins
cooking spray

HAND METHOD: Dissolve 1 teaspoon sugar in warm water (105°). **Add 1 1/2 tablespoons yeast** and let foam 5 minutes.

Combine flours, xanthan gum, gelatin, dry milk powder, lecithin, salt, brown sugar, and cinnamon in large mixer bowl.

Using regular beaters (not dough hooks), blend on low. Add eggs, canola oil, vinegar, and applesauce (or prunes) and mix well. Add water-yeast mixture and thoroughly blend on low speed. Beat on high speed for 2 minutes. Stir in raisins.

Spoon dough into three 5 x 2 1/2-inch pans that have been coated with cooking spray. (You may bake the dough in a 9 x 5-inch pan, but the texture is better when baked in smaller pans.) Let the dough rise in a warm place until it is doubled in bulk, approximately 45 minutes to an hour.

Preheat oven to 400 degrees. Bake the small loaves for about 20-25 minutes; large loaves require about 45 minutes. If breads are browning too quickly, cover with foil for remainder of baking time. Remove from pan. Cool on wire rack.

BREAD MACHINE: Use **1 1/2 teaspoons dry yeast**. Follow bread machine instructions. I combine dry ingredients and add to bread machine. Combine liquid ingredients (water at room temperature). Pour carefully over dry ingredients in bread machine. Set controls and bake. Add raisins following machine instructions.

Preparation = 3 hours. Serves 10. Makes one 1-pound loaf.

Calories 214 (25% from fat); Fat 6g; Prot 6g; Carb 35g; Sod 245mg; Chol 43mg. Brown Rice Substitute (not for celiacs): 1 cup amaranth flour and 1/3 cup quinoa flour.

Russian Black Bread

A dark, hearty bread that makes a great sandwich with tuna salad or smoked meats—or a Reuben. Note the different yeast amount for bread machines.

gf dry yeast (see below)
1 teaspoon sugar or honey
1 cup water
1 cup brown rice flour
1/2 cup potato starch flour
1/2 cup tapioca flour
2 teaspoons fennel seeds
2 teaspoons flax seeds
2 teaspoons gf instant coffee powder
1/2 teaspoon gf onion powder
2 teaspoons xanthan gum

1 teaspoon salt
1 teaspoon unflavored gelatin powder
2 teaspoons Egg Replacer
6 tablespoons dry milk powder or non-dairy milk powder
2 tablespoons cocoa powder
2 large eggs at room temperature
2 tablespoons canola oil
1 teaspoon cider vinegar
1/4 cup dark molasses
cooking spray

HAND METHOD: Combine **1 tablespoon yeast**, warm water (105°), and sugar in small bowl. Set aside to foam, about 5 minutes.

In large mixer bowl, combine remaining dry ingredients and blend on low speed. Use regular beaters, not dough hooks.

Combine eggs, oil, vinegar, and molasses and combine with water-yeast mixture after yeast has begun to foam. With mixer on low speed, add liquid to dry ingredients. Once liquid is incorporated, increase mixer speed to high and beat for 2 minutes.

For small loaves, coat three 5 x 2 1/2-inch loaf pans with cooking spray. Divide dough among pans and put pans in warm place to rise for 45-60 minutes, or until doubled in bulk.

Preheat oven to 350 degrees. Bake loaves for 25-30 minutes. For large loaf, place dough in 8-inch pie plate coated with cooking spray. Let rise 45 minutes to an hour, or until doubled in bulk. Bake 40-50 minutes.

BREAD MACHINE: Use **1 1/2 teaspoons dry yeast**. Follow bread machine instructions. I combine dry ingredients and add to bread machine. Then, I combine liquid ingredients (water at room temperature). Pour carefully over dry ingredients in bread machine. Set controls and bake.

Preparation = 3 hours. Serves 10. Makes one 1-pound loaf

Calories 178 (22% from fat); Fat 5g; Prot 6g; Carb 29g; Sod 246mg; Chol 43mg. Brown Rice Substitute (not for celiacs): 1 cup amaranth flour.

White Bread

This is the trusty standby. You'll want to keep a loaf of this bread on hand at all times because you'll use it so often—for sandwiches, toast, bread crumbs, and so on. Note the different amounts of yeast for the hand versus bread machine versions.

gf dry yeast (see below)
1 cup water
2 tablespoons sugar or honey
1 1/2 cups white rice flour
1/2 cup potato starch
1/4 cup tapioca flour
2 teaspoons xanthan gum
1 teaspoon salt

1/3 cup dry milk powder or
    non-dairy milk powder
1/4 teaspoon soy lecithin
1 teaspoon Egg Replacer
2 large eggs, lightly beaten
3 tablespoons melted butter
1 teaspoon cider vinegar
cooking spray

HAND METHOD: Combine **1 tablespoon dry yeast**, 2 teaspoons of the sugar, and warm (105°) water. Set aside to let yeast foam, about 5 minutes.

In large mixer bowl using regular beaters (not dough hooks), combine flours, xanthan gum, salt, remainder of sugar, dry milk powder, lecithin, and Egg Replacer. In separate bowl, combine eggs, melted butter, and vinegar.

With mixer on low speed, add egg mixture to dry ingredients and blend. Blend in water-yeast mixture, increase speed to high and beat for 2 minutes.

For smaller loaves, coat three small pans, 5 x 2 1/2-inches, with cooking spray. Divide dough among pans and place in warm place to rise for 45-60 minutes or until doubled in bulk. For one large loaf, use 9 x 5-inch pan coated with cooking spray and let dough rise until double in bulk, about 45-60 minutes.

Preheat oven to 350 degrees. Bake small loaves for 25-30 minutes; large loaf for 40-50 minutes, or until nicely browned. BREAD MACHINE: Use **1 1/2 teaspoons dry yeast**. Follow bread machine instructions. I combine dry ingredients and add to bread machine. Then, I combine liquid ingredients (water at room temperature). Pour carefully over dry ingredients in bread machine. Set controls and bake.

Preparation = 3 hours. Serves 10. Makes one 1-pound loaf.
Calories 193 (24% from fat); Fat 5g; Prot 5g; Carb 31g; Sod 283mg. Chol 52mg.

Boston Brown Bread

Very, very easy to make—a lot like the famous bread from Boston, only you bake this bread rather than steam it. It's great alone or spread with low-fat cream cheese.

1 cup brown rice flour
1/3 potato starch
1/4 cup soy flour
1/4 cup cornmeal
1/4 cup brown sugar, packed
1 teaspoon baking soda
1/2 teaspoon xanthan gum
1 teaspoon unflavored gelatin powder
1/2 teaspoon ground cinnamon
1/4 teaspoon ground allspice
1/4 teaspoon salt

1/4 teaspoon ground ginger
1/4 teaspoon ground cloves
1/2 cup raisins
1 cup buttermilk (or 1 table-spoon cider vinegar plus enough non-dairy milk to equal 1 cup)
1 large egg, lightly beaten
1/4 cup molasses
1/2 teaspoon vanilla extract
2 tablespoons canola oil
cooking spray

Preheat oven to 350 degrees. Coat three small nonstick baking pans, each 5 x 2 1/2-inches, with cooking spray.

Stir first 13 ingredients (brown rice flour through cloves) together in large bowl. Add raisins and mix well. In another bowl, combine buttermilk, egg, molasses, vanilla, and oil. Stir into bread mixture with spatula. Divide batter among prepared pans.

Bake for 30 minutes. Remove bread from pans and cool on rack.

Preparation = 45 minutes. Serves 6.

Calories 250 (20% from fat); Fat 6 g; Prot 6g; Carb 46g; Sod 272 mg; Chol 28 mg
Brown Rice Substitute (not for celiacs): 1/2 cup amaranth flour and 1/2 cup quinoa flour

Cheese Biscotti

This is a variation of the traditional sweet biscotti. Serve these crisp, cheesy strips with soups or salads.

1 1/4 cups brown rice flour
1/2 cup potato starch
1/4 cup tapioca flour
1/4 teaspoon salt
1 teaspoon xanthan gum
1 teaspoon baking powder
2 tablespoons sugar
1 teaspoon dried rosemary, crushed
1/2 cup low-fat sour cream (or sour cream alternative)

2 tablespoons olive oil
1/4 cup corn syrup
3 large egg whites
1/2 cup grated Swiss or sharp cheddar cheese (or soy cheese)
2 teaspoons Parmesan cheese (cow, rice, or soy)
1 1/2 cups sunflower seeds
2 teaspoons dried chives
cooking spray

Preheat oven to 350 degrees. Lightly coat a baking sheet with cooking spray.

In food processor, combine flours, salt, xanthan gum, baking powder, sugar, and rosemary. Process with on/off pulses until mixture resembles coarse meal.

Lightly beat together sour cream, olive oil, corn syrup, egg whites, Swiss and Parmesan cheeses in another bowl. Pour the egg mixture evenly over dough in food processor and pulse the machine on and off about 20 times to moisten dough.

Form dough into ball, working sunflower seeds and chives into the dough while shaping it.

Divide dough in half and shape each half into log about 12 inches long and about 2 inches wide and 1/2-inch thick.

Bake about 20 minutes, or until dough is browned at edges. Remove from oven and cool for 5 minutes. Leave the oven on. With a sharp knife (an electric knife works well here), cut each log on the diagonal into about 3/4-inch thick slices. Arrange slices (cut side down) on the baking sheet and return sheet to the oven. Bake another 5-7 minutes, or until the biscotti start to brown. Transfer biscotti to wire rack for cooling. Dust with additional Parmesan cheese, if desired. Makes about 2 to 2 1/2 dozen biscotti.

Preparation = 1 1/4 hours. Serves 10. (3 biscotti each)

Calories 319 (43% from fat); Fat 15g; Prot 10g; Carb 36g; Sod 141mg; Chol 6mg.

Corn Bread

I like to serve Corn Bread with Mexican or Southwestern meals. This version is very easy to assemble and the recipe is very forgiving.

1/4 cup brown rice flour
2 tablespoons tapioca flour
2 tablespoons potato starch
1/2 teaspoon xanthan gum
1/2 cup yellow cornmeal
2 tablespoons grated Parmesan cheese (cow, rice, or soy)
2 tablespoons sugar or honey
1/2 teaspoon baking powder

1/4 teaspoon baking soda
1/4 teaspoon salt
1 large egg
3/4 cup buttermilk (or 2 teaspoons cider vinegar plus enough non-dairy milk to equal 3/4 cup)
2 tablespoons canola oil
cooking spray

Preheat oven to 375 degrees. Coat an 8 x 4-inch or 8 x 8-inch pan with cooking spray. Set aside.

In medium bowl, combine flours, xanthan gum, cornmeal, Parmesan cheese, sugar, baking powder, baking soda, and salt. Make a well in center. Set aside. In another bowl, beat egg, buttermilk, and canola oil until well blended. Add egg mixture all at once to dry mixture, stirring just till moistened.

Bake for 20-25 minutes, or until top is firm and edges are lightly browned. Serve warm.

Preparation = 35 minutes. Serves 4.

Calories 173 (34% from fat); Fat 7g; Prot 5g; Carb 24g; Sod 246mg; Chol 38mg.

Corn Tortillas

Absolutely wonderful!. These tortillas are especially easy with a tortilla press (under $20 in kitchenware departments). Electric versions actually press and fry the tortilla. Or, roll tortilla between sheets of waxed paper or plastic wrap with rolling pin.

2 cups corn flour   **1 1/4 cups warm water**
   (not cornmeal))

In a bowl, combine corn flour and warm water. Blend mixture until it forms a smooth ball. Divide the dough into 12 equal pieces and shape into balls. Cover to prevent drying out.

Cut 24 pieces of waxed paper, each about 7 inches square. Put 1 square of the waxed paper on the bottom half of a tortilla press. Place a ball of dough slightly off center, toward the edge opposite the handle. Place another piece of waxed paper on top of the dough. Lower the top of the press and press down firmly on the lever. This makes a tortilla about 6 to 6 1/2-inches in diameter. Remove the tortilla, keeping it between the two squares of waxed paper and stack on a plate. Continue with remaining dough.

To fry, heat griddle or electric skillet over high heat until it is hot. Holding tortilla in left hand, peel off top layer of waxed paper with right hand—starting with side nearest left wrist—and pulling paper up toward the ceiling. Carefully invert the tortilla onto the griddle. Wait 3 seconds, then peel off remaining waxed paper. ***Do not leave waxed paper on tortilla for longer than 3 seconds because it will permanently cook into the tortilla.*** Cook tortilla about 2 minutes on each side until it looks dry and

has golden flecks on it. Transfer cooked tortilla to plate to cool between sheets of waxed paper. Cook remaining tortillas. Refrigerate in resealable plastic bag. Makes 12. Reheat to serve. Preparation = 30 minutes. Serves 6 (2 tortillas per serving).
Calories 141 (9% from fat); Fat 2g; Prot 3g; Carb 30g; Sod 8mg; Chol 0mg.

Flour Tortillas

This is a Santa Fe tortilla which is thicker and somewhat less pliable than the purchased kind. Tortillas are best when warm.

1/2 cup boiling water
1/2 teaspoon soy lecithin
1/2 teaspoon honey
1/4 cup evaporated skim milk (or non-dairy milk minus 1 table-spoon)
1 1/2 teaspoons canola oil

1 cup brown rice flour
1/2 cup potato starch
1/4 cup arrowroot
1 teaspoon salt
1 teaspoon cream of tartar
1/2 teaspoon baking soda

Add lecithin and honey to boiling water, stirring until lecithin is dissolved. Cool for 10 minutes. Add milk and oil. Meanwhile, sift together flours, arrowroot, salt, cream of tartar, and baking soda. Stir in liquid mixture to form a soft ball.

Lightly flour a countertop or pastry board; knead the dough for 1 minute. Cut in 4 balls, cover tightly, and chill for 2 hours.

Between heavily floured sheets of waxed paper or plastic wrap, roll each ball into a 7-8-inch circle, adding flour to prevent sticking. Remove waxed paper. In electric frying pan over high heat, cook each tortilla on both sides until brown speckles form. Wrap in foil immediately. Serve warm. Preparation = 30 minutes. (Excludes chill time) Makes 4.
Calories per tortilla: 266 (11% from fat); Fat 3g; Prot 5g; Carb 53g; Sod 643mg; Chol 1mg.

Sopaipillas

Sopaipillas "puff" better if you cut them in triangles at least 3-4 inches in size and gently press the "puffed" portion of the dough into the hot oil as it fries. Serve with honey or powdered sugar.

1 tablespoon gf quick-rising
     dry yeast
3/4 cup warm water (105°)
1 tablespoon sugar
1 teaspoon cider vinegar
2 cups brown rice flour
3/4 cup potato starch

1/4 cup tapioca flour
2 teaspoons xanthan gum
1/2 teaspoon salt
1 tablespoon canola oil
1 large egg white
2 tablespoons warm water (105°)
vegetable shortening for frying

Dissolve 1 teaspoon of the sugar in warm water and stir in yeast until thoroughly mixed. Let foam for 5 minutes.

Combine flours, remaining sugar, xanthan gum, and salt in large mixing bowl. Add cider vinegar to yeast mixture, then add to flour mixture along with oil and egg white. Blend with electric mixer on low, adding 2 tablespoons of warm water to form a thick but soft dough. Beat dough on high for 1 minute. Cover; let rise in a warm place about 1 hour or until doubled. Roll out to 1/4-inch thickness on board or countertop that is lightly floured with rice flour. Cut into 3 to 4-inch triangles.

In a deep 3 to 4-quart pan, heat 2 inches of oil to 350 degrees on a deep-frying thermometer. (An electric fryer works well because the temperature is controlled). Drop triangles of dough into hot oil, flat side down. When bread puffs, gently push portion where bubble is developing into hot oil to help sopaipillas puff evenly. Cook until pale gold, turning several times (1 to 2 minutes total cooking time). Remove with slotted spoon and drain on paper towels. Serve with honey or powdered sugar. Makes about 18 sopaipillas.

Preparation = 1 1/2 hours. Serves 9 (2 sopaipillas per serving).
Calories per sopaipilla: 206 (12% from fat); Fat 5g; Prot 5g; Carb 40g; Sod 129mg; Chol 0mg.

Popovers

My tasters raved about these popovers, commenting that they were "beautiful" and "delicious". The secret is to get the baking pan piping hot before adding the batter and then baking the popovers at very high temperatures. A popover tin (with narrower and deeper molds) also helps, but you can use your traditional muffin tin or custard cups.

4 eggs at room temperature
3/4 cup skim milk (cow, soy, rice, or nut)
1 tablespoon canola oil
2/3 cup white rice flour

1/4 cup potato starch
1 tablespoon tapioca flour
1/2 teaspoon salt
cooking spray

Preheat oven to 450 degrees. Put eggs, milk, and canola oil in blender and blend thoroughly. Add flours and salt and blend until thoroughly mixed.

Place a 6-muffin tin or 6 custard cups in oven while it is preheating. Just before pouring batter in tins, remove tins from oven and spray with cooking spray.

Fill tins or custard cups about half full of batter. Bake for 20 minutes at 450 degrees, then reduce heat to 350 and continue baking for 15 minutes or until sides of muffin are rigid to the touch. Do not open the oven until popovers are done because this may cause them to collapse. Serve warm.

Calories 119 (20% from fat); Fat 3g; Prot 3g; Carb 20; Sod 194mg; Chol 1mg.

Preparation = 45 minutes. Serves 6.

YORKSHIRE PUDDING: Pour 1 teaspoon of hot meat drippings into each cup of mold. Add popover batter and bake as directed above. Serves 6.

Calories 158 (40% from fat); Fat 7g; Prot 3g; Carb 21g; Sod 217mg; Chol 5mg.

NOTE: This recipe was developed for altitudes above 5000 feet. For lower altitudes, reduce eggs to 3.

Crackers

These great crackers travel well and can be frozen.

1/4 cup bean flour*
1/4 cup potato starch
1/4 cup sweet rice flour
1/2 teaspoon xanthan gum
1/4 teaspoon baking soda
1/2 teaspoon salt
1/2 teaspoon gf onion powder
2 tablespoons Parmesan cheese (cow, rice, or soy)
2 tablespoons soft butter or oleo (room temperature)
1 tablespoon honey or pure maple syrup
3 tablespoons toasted sesame seeds
2 tablespoons milk (cow, rice, soy, or nut)
1 teaspoon cider vinegar cooking spray

Preheat oven to 350 degrees. Spray a baking sheet with cooking spray.

In a medium mixing bowl, combine the flours, xanthan gum, baking soda, salt, onion powder, and Parmesan cheese. Add the butter and honey and mix until the dough resembles coarse crumbs. Stir in sesame seeds. Add the milk and vinegar. Shape dough into soft ball. (Or, place all ingredients in food processor and blend until mixture forms ball.)

Shape the dough into 20 balls, each 1-inch in diameter, and place on baking sheet at least 2 inches apart. Using the bottom of a drinking glass or a rolling pin, flatten the balls to approximately 1/8-inch thick. Use your fingers to smooth circle edges.

Bake for 12-15 minutes, or until crackers look firm and slightly toasted. Turn each cracker and bake another 5-7 minutes or until golden brown. (You may sprinkle with additional sesame seeds and salt, if desired.)

Preparation = 30 minutes. Makes about 20 crackers.
Calories Per Cracker: 45 (42% from fat); Fat 2 g; Prot. 1g; Carb 6g; Sod 93 mg; Chol. 4 mg.

*Bean flour is available from Authentic Foods. See Mail-Order Sources.

Pretzels

Pretzels make great snacks and travel very well. Store them in airtight containers.

1 tablespoon gf dry yeast
2/3 cup warm water (105°)
1/2 teaspoon sugar
1/2 cup brown rice flour
1/2 cup tapioca flour
1 tablespoon dry milk powder
   non-dairy milk powder
2 teaspoons xanthan gum
1/2 teaspoon salt

1 teaspoon gf onion powder
1 teaspoon unflavored gelatin
   powder
1 tablespoon olive oil
1 teaspoon cider vinegar
1 large egg white, beaten
   to a foam
1 tablespoon coarse salt
cooking spray

Combine yeast, warm water, and sugar in a small bowl. Set aside for 5 minutes or until yeast is foamy.

In medium mixer bowl, blend the flours, dry milk powder, xanthan gum, salt, onion powder, and gelatin powder on low speed. Add yeast mixture, olive oil and vinegar. Beat on high speed for 3 minutes.

Place dough in large, heavy-duty plastic resealable bag that has 1/4-inch opening cut on one corner (makes 1/2-inch circle). Squeeze dough through opening onto baking sheet that has been coated with cooking spray. It works best to hold the bag upright as you squeeze the dough out. You may make traditional pretzel shapes, but straight 3-inch sticks are easier. Brush lightly with beaten egg white, then sprinkle with coarse salt. Place pretzels in warm place to rise for 10-15 minutes.

Preheat oven to 400 degrees. Bake until pretzels are dry and golden brown. When cool, store in airtight container.

Preparation = 1 1/4 hours. Makes about 2 1/2 dozen pretzels.

Calories per pretzel: 25 (19% from fat); Fat .5g; Prot 7g; Carb 4g; Sod 227mg; Chol 0mg.

Scones

I had to resist these on my last trip to England. But, I can enjoy them at home. You can purchase scone cream (Devonshire Cream or clotted cream) at gourmet stores or make your own low-fat version (see below). The Scone Cream is dairy-based.

1 1/4 cups brown rice flour
1/2 cup tapioca flour
1 1/2 teaspoons cream of tartar
3/4 teaspoon baking soda
1 teaspoon xanthan gum
1/4 teaspoon salt
4 tablespoons sugar
4 tablespoons butter or oleo --
   (1/2 stick), in 1/2-inch slices
2/3 cup low-fat plain yogurt or
   1/2 cup non-dairy milk

1 large egg, lightly beaten
1/3 cup currants
2 tablespoons milk (cow, soy
   rice, or nut--for brushing top)
cooking spray

SCONE CREAM
1 cup Yogurt Cheese (See Index)
1/4 cup half and half
2 tablespoons powdered sugar

Preheat oven to 450 degrees. Coat baking sheet with cooking spray. Set aside.

In food processor, place flours, cream of tartar, baking soda, xanthan gum, salt, and sugar. Pulse on and off to combine the ingredients. Add cold butter and pulse about 15-20 times or until the mixture resembles coarse meal.

Combine the lightly beaten egg and yogurt. Pour over the flour mixture and process for about 10 seconds or until the dough forms large curds. Scrape the dough into a bowl. Quickly, but gently stir or fold in the currants with a spatula.

On baking sheet, pat dough to 8-inch circle, 3/4-inch thick. Brush top with 2 tablespoons milk. Bake for 12-15 minutes. Cut into 6 or 8 wedges. Top with Scone Cream.

Preparation = 20 minutes. Serves 6-8.

Calories (for 8 servings) 233 (27% from fat); Fat 7g; Prot 5g; Carb 39g; Sod 522mg; Chol 43mg.

Spoon Bread

There are many different versions of spoon bread. Try this one, but experiment on your own since the dough is very forgiving. Non-dairy substitutes are not appropriate for this recipe.

2 large eggs
1/2 cup finely chopped onion
 2 tablespoons canola oil
1 cup Yogurt Cheese (See Index)
4 ounces diced green chiles,
    (1 can) (optional)

1 teaspoon baking powder
1 teaspoon gf garlic salt
3/4 cup yellow cornmeal
1 cup corn kernels
1 cup shredded low-fat
    cheddar cheese
cooking spray

Spray a 9-inch cast iron skillet or 9-inch square nonstick baking pan with cooking spray. Preheat oven to 350 degrees.

In a large bowl, beat eggs. Add onion, canola oil, Yogurt Cheese, and chiles (if using).

In another bowl, combine baking powder, garlic salt, and cornmeal. Add to egg mixture. Stir in corn and 1/2 cup of the cheddar cheese.

Pour batter into prepared pans. Sprinkle remaining 1/2 cup of cheese over top.

Bake for 40-50 minutes, or until top is golden brown. Spoon out of pan to serve.

Preparation = 1 hour. Serves 8.

Calories 196 (44% from fat); Fat 9%; Prot 8g; Carb 18g; Sod 213mg; Chol 69mg.

BREAKFAST & BRUNCH

Breakfast is perhaps the most important meal of the day. For many of us, it's also our <u>favorite</u> meal. It helps wake us up and then prepares our bodies with the necessary nutrients and energy to start the day.

But, unfortunately, many of the foods we associate with breakfast or brunch are made with wheat. Therefore, foods such as toast, muffins, pancakes, doughnuts, biscuits, and even some breakfast cereals are off-limits to wheat or gluten-sensitive persons.

Using the recipes in this section, you can now eat all of these foods—and many more, as well. There are typical breakfast foods such as Biscuits and Pancakes, but also elegant brunch dishes such as Stuffed French Toast or Eggs Benedict. You'll even find a recipe for Baked Doughnuts. You would never guess they're wheat-free and they're baked—not fried—which eliminates a great deal of fat.

All baked goods feature the traditional combinations of rice flour, potato starch, and tapioca flour. However, if you wish to introduce more variety into your diet, several recipes suggest alternative flours such as amaranth, quinoa, or buckwheat—if these are permissible for your diet.

Many of us like to eat hot cereal for breakfast, so you'll find a section on cooked cereals using a variety of delicious, alternative grains such amaranth, quinoa, and buckwheat. Many wheat-sensitive persons can tolerate these grains, while gluten-intolerant persons are advised to avoid them. Check with your physician first—just to be sure.

Baked Doughnuts

Now you can have a very flavorful, low-fat doughnut because these are baked rather than fried. These doughnuts work best when baked in the mini-Bundt or mini-angel food baking pans. Look for these pans in your gourmet cooking store or in the cookware section of department stores. You can also use 6-muffin tins.

1 cup brown rice flour
1/2 cup potato starch
1/2 cup tapioca flour
2 teaspoons xanthan gum
1 teaspoon unflavored gelatin
   powder
1 1/2 teaspoons baking powder
1 1/2 teaspoons baking soda
1/2 teaspoon salt
2 teaspoons ground cinnamon
1/4 teaspoon ground cloves
1/4 teaspoon ground nutmeg
1/4 teaspoon ground allspice
1 large egg, lightly beaten

2/3 cup dark brown sugar,
   firmly packed
1/2 cup apple juice frozen
   concentrate, thawed
1/3 cup pure maple syrup
1/3 cup applesauce or prune
   baby food
1/3 cup low-fat yogurt (or 1/4
   cup milk-cow, rice, or soy)
3 tablespoons canola oil
cooking spray
FROSTING
1 1/4 cups powdered sugar
1 teaspoon vanilla extract
1/4 cup pure maple syrup

Preheat oven to 375 degrees. Coat molds of a mini-Bundt or mini-angel food cake pans with cooking spray. (Or use 6-muffin or cupcake tins.)

In a mixing bowl, stir together the flours, xanthan gum, gelatin powder, baking powder, baking soda, salt, cinnamon, cloves, nutmeg, and allspice. Set aside.

In another bowl, combine the egg, brown sugar, apple concentrate, maple syrup, applesauce (or prunes), yogurt, and oil. Add dry ingredients and stir just until moistened.

Divide the batter in half since you'll be baking the batter in two batches (unless you have two baking pans). Spoon half of the batter into prepared mini-molds—about 2 generous tablespoons per mold.

Bake for 20-25 minutes or until tops spring back when touched lightly. Loosen edges of doughnuts and turn out into a rack to cool. Clean pan, spray again with cooking spray, and fill molds with 2 tablespoonful of batter each. Bake for 20-25 minutes each.

To frost, combine powdered sugar, vanilla, and maple syrup, adding more maple syrup, if needed, to make frosting of spreading consistency. Dip the shaped (under) side of doughnut into frosting and set on waxed paper until frosting has "set". Makes 12 doughnuts or cupcakes.

Preparation = 45 minutes. Serves 12.

Calories 257 (15% from fat); Fat 4g; Prot 3g; Carb 52g; Sod 309mg; Chol 18mg. Brown Rice Substitute (not for celiacs): 1/2 cup amaranth flour and 1/2 cup quinoa flour.

Ever wonder why baked goods that use pureed fruits (for example, pureed prunes or applesauce) as fat substitutes also include some fats or oils? Fruit provides initial moisture, but a reduced amount of fat or oil is still necessary in baked goods to coat the flour, thereby preserving the desired texture. So, as a rule, never replace more than half of the fat with a fat substitute.

Blueberry-Lemon Muffins

For best results, bake these muffins in the 12-muffin size rather than 6-muffin tins. Freeze blueberries in the summer when they're plentiful, then toss them into the batter (frozen) just before spooning into muffin tins and increase baking time by 5 minutes. If you don't have applesauce, use a total of 1/3 cup oil instead.

1 cup white or brown rice flour
1/2 cup potato starch
1/2 cup tapioca flour
1 teaspoon unflavored gelatin
  powder
1 teaspoon xanthan gum
2 1/2 teaspoons baking powder
1/3 cup sugar + 1 tablespoon
3/4 teaspoon salt
3/4 cup milk (cow, rice, or soy)
2 tablespoons canola oil
1/4 cup applesauce

2 eggs, lightly beaten
1/2 teaspoon gf vanilla
1 teaspoon grated lemon peel
  or 1 teaspoon gf lemon extract
1 1/4 cups blueberries,
  fresh or frozen
cooking spray

GLAZE
2 tablespoons powdered sugar
2 tablespoons lemon juice

Preheat oven to 400 degrees. Coat a 12-cup muffin tin (2-inch diameter base, 1 1/4-inch deep) with cooking spray.

Stir together the flours, gelatin powder, xanthan gum, baking powder, sugar, and salt in large bowl. Make well in center.

In another bowl, combine milk, canola oil, applesauce, eggs, vanilla extract, and lemon peel (or extract). Pour into well of flour mixture. Stir just until ingredients are moistened. Add blueberries and gently stir in. Spoon dough into muffin tins.

Bake for approximately 25 minutes, or until tops of muffins are lightly browned. Remove from oven. Combine powdered sugar and lemon juice to form glaze. Drizzle over warm muffins. Makes 12.

Preparation = 40 minutes. Serves 6. (2 muffins each)

Calories 334 (19% from fat); Fat 7g; Prot 7g; Carb 60g; Sod 476mg; Chol 72mg.

Raspberry Muffins

If you can't find fresh raspberries, substitute the frozen kind. These muffins are full of flavor and make a wonderful addition to a special brunch. No applesauce? Use 1/3 cup oil instead.

3/4 cup brown rice flour
1/2 cup potato starch
1/4 cup tapioca flour
1/2 teaspoon xanthan gum
1/2 cup brown sugar, packed
2 teaspoons baking powder
1/4 teaspoon salt
1 teaspoon ground cinnamon
1 egg, lightly beaten
3 tablespoons canola oil
1/2 cup applesauce

1/2 cup skim milk (cow, rice, soy, or nut)
1 teaspoon grated lemon peel
1 1/4 cups raspberries
cooking spray
STREUSEL TOPPING
1/4 cup brown rice flour
1/2 cup brown sugar, packed
1 teaspoon ground cinnamon
1/4 cup chopped pecans
1 tablespoon canola oil

Preheat oven to 350 degrees. Coat a 12-muffin tin (2-inch diameter base, 1 1/4-inches deep) with cooking spray. (12-muffin tins produce a better textured muffin than 6-muffin tins.) BATTER: Combine first 8 ingredients in large mixing bowl. Make a well in center.

In another bowl, combine the egg, canola oil, applesauce, skim milk, and lemon peel. Beat well. Pour egg mixture into center of well in flour mixture. Stir just until ingredients are moistened. Gently stir in raspberries. Pour batter into prepared muffin tins.

TOPPING: Combine Streusel Topping ingredients. Sprinkle over batter in each muffin tin.

Bake for 20-25 minutes or until muffins are lightly browned. Preparation = 40 minutes. Serves 12. (1 muffin each)
Calories 202 (30% from fat); Fat 7g; Prot 3g; Carb 33g; Sod 60mg; Chol 18mg.

Bagels

Like many baked goods, these are best eaten warm from the oven.

1 cup white rice flour	2 tablespoons canola oil
3/4 cup brown rice flour	3 tablespoons honey
3/4 cup potato starch	1 large egg, lightly beaten
1/2 cup cornstarch	1 teaspoon cider vinegar
1 tablespoon gf dry yeast	cooking spray
1 tablespoon xanthan gum	**FOR CINNAMON BAGELS:**
1 teaspoon salt	2 teaspoons cinnamon
1 cup warm water (105°)	1/2 cup raisins

Combine flours, cornstarch, yeast, xanthan gum, and salt (and cinnamon, if using) in large mixer bowl. Add water, oil, honey, egg, and vinegar. Add to dry ingredients and beat with electric mixer until well blended. Mixture will be very thick and stiff. (Add raisins at this point, if using).

Place dough on flat, rice-floured surface. Divide into 8 equal portions. Dust each portion with rice flour, shape into ball, then flatten to 3-inch circle and punch hole in center—continuing to dust with flour, if necessary. Form into bagel shapes (turning rough edges of dough to underside). Place bagels on large baking sheet coated with cooking spray.

Place baking sheet in cold oven, then turn to 325 degrees. Bake for 15 minutes. Remove sheet from oven; leave oven on.

Meanwhile, bring 3 inches of water and 1 teaspoon sugar to boil in a deep skillet. Boil bagels on each side for 30 seconds. Return bagels to baking sheet that has been coated again with cooking spray. (Brush with optional beaten egg, if desired.)

Return baking sheet to oven and increase temperature to 400 degrees. Bake for 20-25 minutes, or until nicely browned. Remove bagels and cool on wire rack. Makes 8.

Preparation = 5 hours. Serves 8.

Calories 267 (17% from fat); Fat 5g; Prot 5g; Carb 51g; Sod 278mg; Chol 27mg. (Raisins add 30 calories and 8 grams of carb.)

Banana Bread

Don't throw away those extra-ripe bananas! The high sugar level and fuller flavor of these bananas makes them perfect for banana bread. Freeze the mashed pulp until you're ready to bake.

3 tablespoons canola oil
2/3 cup brown sugar, packed
2 large eggs
1 teaspoon gf vanilla extract
1 cup brown rice flour
1/2 cup tapioca flour
1/4 cup potato starch
2 teaspoons baking powder
1/2 teaspoon xanthan gum

1/2 teaspoon salt
1 teaspoon ground cinnamon
1/8 teaspoon ground cardamom
1/8 teaspoon ground mace
1 1/2 cups mashed ripe bananas
1/2 cup applesauce
1/2 cup chopped almonds or pecans
cooking spray

Preheat oven to 350 degrees. Coat a 9 x 5-inch loaf pan with cooking spray. (Or, for smaller loaves, use 3 small loaf pans, approximately 5 x 2 1/2 -inches each.)

Cream the canola oil and sugar together. Add eggs and vanilla and beat well. Mix together the flours, baking powder, xanthan gum, salt, cinnamon, cardamom, and mace. Mix bananas with applesauce. Add flour mixture to egg mixture, alternating with banana mixture. Stir in nuts.

Bake 9 x 5-inch loaf for 1 hour; 5 x 2 1/2-inch pans for 45 minutes. Cool on wire rack before cutting.

Preparation = 1 1/4 hours. Serves 8.

Calories 329 (31% from fat); Fat 1g; Prot 6g; Carb 52g; Sod 247mg; Chol 53mg. Brown Rice Substitute(not for celiacs): 1/2 cup amaranth flour and 1/2 cup quinoa flour.

Buttermilk Biscuits

Biscuits are one of the things I missed the most on a wheat-free diet. They are so versatile—top them with Creamed Chicken or try Biscuits and Gravy (See Index). Change the ingredients slightly and you have shortbread for fresh strawberries and whipped cream.

1/2 cup white or brown rice
  flour
1/4 cup potato starch
1/4 cup tapioca flour
1 teaspoon sugar
1 tablespoon baking powder
1/2 teaspoon xanthan gum

1/4 teaspoon salt
1/4 cup butter or shortening
1/2 cup buttermilk (or 1 teaspoon
  cider vinegar plus enough
  non-dairy milk to equal 1/2 cup)
cooking spray

Preheat oven to 450 degrees. Sift the dry ingredients together into medium bowl.

Cut butter or shortening into flour mixture until mixture resembles small peas. Stir in enough buttermilk to form soft dough that holds it shape (you may not need all of buttermilk).

Place the mixture on baking sheet that has been coated with cooking spray. Lay sheet of waxed paper over biscuit mixture and press to 1-inch thickness and about 6 x 6-inch square or circle. Remove sheet of waxed paper and cut into 8 or 9 round biscuit shapes using 2-inch biscuit cutter or open end of drinking glass. Remove uncut portions of biscuit dough and gently shape into 2-inch circles. Or, simply cut dough into 9 square pieces and spread pieces across baking sheet .

Bake for 10-12 minutes or until lightly browned. Makes about 9 biscuits, each 2-inches.

SHORTBREAD: Add 1/4 cup sugar. Proceed according to directions above. Increase buttermilk as needed to form soft dough.

Preparation = 30 minutes. Serves 4. (About 2 biscuits each).
Calories per biscuit: 138 (44% from fat); Fat 7g; Prot 2g; Carb 17g; Sod 191mg; Chol 4mg.

Pancakes

These pancakes are light, yet filling. You can freeze the extras.

2 large eggs
1/2 cup plain low-fat yogurt
   or 1/3 cup non-dairy liquid
1/4 cup brown rice flour
2 tablespoons potato starch
2 tablespoons tapioca flour
1 teaspoon baking powder

1/2 teaspoon baking soda
1 teaspoon sugar or honey
1/2 teaspoon salt
1 teaspoon gf vanilla extract
1 tablespoon canola oil
additional oil for frying

Blend eggs and yogurt (or milk) in blender or whisk vigorously in bowl. Add remaining ingredients and thoroughly blend.

Over medium heat, place large, non-stick skillet that's been lightly coated with canola oil. Pour batter into skillet and cook until tops are bubbly (3-5 minutes). Turn and cook until golden brown (2-3 minutes). Makes about 8 pancakes.

Preparation = 15 minutes. Serves 4 (2 per serving).

Calories 162 (23% from fat); Fat 4g; Prot 7g; Carb 23g; Sod 235mg; Chol 108mg.

German Pancakes

This dish is so easy, yet so impressive because it puffs up as it bakes, creating lots of little indentations for the toppings.

3 large eggs
3 tablespoons brown rice flour
1 tablespoon tapioca flour
1 tablespoon potato starch
1/4 teaspoon salt

1/3 cup skim milk (cow, rice, soy,
   or nut)
1 tablespoon soft butter or oleo
cooking spray

Preheat oven to 450 degrees. Coat a 9 or 10-inch cast-iron (or oven-proof) skillet with cooking spray. (Or, use small oven-proof dishes approximately 4 inches in diameter.)

In blender, beat eggs until thick and fluffy. Gradually add flours, salt, and milk until well blended. Beat in butter.

Pour into prepared pans. Bake for 10-15 minutes until puffed and lightly browned. After removing from the oven, the center will fall slightly, making an indentation for the filling. Immediately, spoon one of the following fillings into the pancake.

APPLES: Peel and slice 2 Granny Smith apples. Combine with 1 teaspoon cinnamon and 1/4 cup sugar. Microwave on high for 5-7 minutes or until apples are tender. Spoon apples on top of pancake and dust with powdered sugar. Serve warm.

EGGS AND BACON: Spoon scrambled eggs and crumbled bacon on top of pancake. Sprinkle with dried parsley. Serve immediately.

Preparation = 20 minutes. Serves 4.

Calories for pancake only: 167 (48% from fat); Fat 7g; Prot 6g; Carb 10g; Sod 220mg; Chol 167mg.

Waffles

Waffles are a special treat for breakfast. Make a whole batch, then freeze any leftovers for another morning.

1 cup brown rice flour
1/2 cup potato starch
1/4 cup tapioca flour
2 teaspoons baking powder
1 teaspoon salt
1 tablespoon sugar or honey
2 large eggs

1/4 cup canola oil
1 1/4 cups buttermilk (or 1 1/2 tablespoons cider vinegar plus enough non-dairy milk to equal 1 1/4 cup)
1 teaspoon gf vanilla extract
cooking spray

Heat waffle iron and coat with cooking spray. In a small bowl, sift together flours, baking powder, salt, and sugar. Beat eggs well in a large bowl. Add oil, buttermilk, vanilla extract, and the sifted dry ingredients. Beat just until blended.

Pour 1/4 of the batter onto the heated waffle iron. Follow manufacturer's directions. Close and bake until steaming stops, about 4-6 minutes. Repeat with remaining batter. Makes 4 waffles, 8 inches each.

Preparation = 30 minutes. Serves 4 (2 waffles per serving).

Calories 219 (52% from fat); Fat 16g; Prot 7g; Carb 28.4g; Sod 588; Chol 81mg.

Corn Waffles

These waffles are great for breakfast topped with pepper jelly. Or, serve them with a cream sauce containing fish, meat or chicken for a dinner entree.

1 cup yellow cornmeal
1/2 cup white or brown rice
   flour
1/4 cup potato starch
3 tablespoons tapioca flour
1 tablespoon baking powder
1 teaspoon xanthan gum

1/4 teaspoon salt
3 large eggs
8 ounces plain low-fat yogurt
   or 2/3 cup non-dairy liquid
1/2 cup milk (cow, rice, soy)
1/4 cup canola oil
cooking spray

In large mixing bowl, stir together the cornmeal, flours, baking powder, xanthan gum, and salt. In separate bowl, whisk together the eggs, yogurt, milk, and canola oil until well blended. Add egg mixture to flour mixture all at once. Stir just until combined, but mixture is still lumpy.

Preheat waffle iron. Pour approximately 1/4 of waffle batter onto grid of preheated waffle iron. Follow manufacturer's directions. Repeat with remaining batter.

Serve with maple syrup, pepper jelly, or honey. Makes 4 waffles, about 8 inches in size.

BLUE CORN WAFFLES: Substitute 1/2 cup blue corn meal for 1/2 cup of the yellow corn meal. Proceed as directed above. Preparation = 30 minutes. Serves 4.

Calories 228 (39% from fat); Fat 10g; Prot 7g; Carb 27.9g; Sod 256mg; Chol 82mg.

Biscuits & Gravy

Hot biscuits, fresh from the oven. . . topped with a creamy, flavorful gravy.

1 recipe Buttermilk Biscuits (See
   Index)
4 cups milk (cow, rice, or soy)
1/3 cup sweet rice flour
1/4 pound gf Sausage (See Index)

1 teaspoon salt
1/4 teaspoon dried thyme
1/2 teaspoon black pepper
1/4 cup fresh chopped parsley

   Mix sweet rice flour with 1/2 cup of the milk to form paste.
Set aside. Have Buttermilk Biscuits baked and ready.
   In heavy saucepan, brown sausage and break it into small
pieces as it cooks. Remove sausage to plate and keep warm.
   In same skillet and using sausage drippings, stir in sweet rice
flour paste, salt, dried thyme, pepper, and remainder of milk.
Stir over medium heat until mixture thickens.
Spoon over warmed Buttermilk Biscuits. Garnish with chopped
parsley.
Preparation = 20 minutes. (Assumes biscuits and sausage are
already baked or assembled). Serves 4.
Calories 336 (57% from fat); Fat 21g; Prot 13g; Carb 23g; Sod 928mg; Chol 60mg.

Quiche Lorraine

This Quiche Lorraine rests on crispy potatoes or use Pastry Crust for Pies. (See Index). Non-dairy cheeses do not work in this recipe.

3 cups peeled, grated potatoes
2 tablespoons canola oil
1 onion, diced
1 bacon slice (uncooked, chopped- omit for meatless)
4 large eggs
1 cup whole milk (cow, rice, or soy)

1/4 teaspoon salt
1/8 teaspoon white pepper
1/8 teaspoon nutmeg
1 1/2 cups Swiss cheese, diced
1 tablespoon tapioca flour
1/4 cup Parmesan cheese
cooking spray

Preheat oven to 425 degrees. Coat a 9-inch pie plate with cooking spray. Toss potatoes with canola oil and press evenly into pie plate on bottom and sides. Bake for 30 minutes or until lightly browned. Use foil on edges to avoid over-browning.

Meanwhile, in heavy skillet over medium heat, cook onion and bacon together until bacon is crisp and onions are lightly browned, stirring constantly. Set aside.

In separate bowl, combine eggs, milk, salt, pepper, and nutmeg. Stir in onion and bacon. Toss flour with cheese and add to mixture. Pour into baked shell. Sprinkle Parmesan cheese on top. Return to oven at a lowered temperature of 350 degrees and bake for 45 minutes or until center is set and a knife inserted comes out clean. Serve immediately.

Preparation = 1 hour. Serves 4.

In Potato Crust: Calories 333 (62% from fat); Fat 23g; Prot 19g; Carb 12g; Sod 468mg; Chol 184mg.

In Pastry Crust: Calories 288 (61% from fat); Fat 19g; Prot 19g; Carb 9g; Sod 476mg; Chol 187mg.

MEATLESS QUICHE LORRAINE: Omit bacon. Use cooking spray for sautéing onion.

Meatless Quiche Lorraine in Potato Crust: Calories 283 (60% from fat); Prot 16g; Carb 12g; Sod 311mg; Chol 176mg.

Ham & Egg Breakfast Casserole

This dish makes a wonderful Sunday brunch. And, because you make it the night before, you're free to do other things while it bakes. Use your leftover gf White Bread or French Bread (See Index). You may use your favorite non-dairy cheddar and jack cheeses, if you wish.

12 slices white gf bread
1 cup cheddar cheese
1 cup Monterey jack cheese
2 cups Canadian bacon, diced
1 tablespoon gf onion flakes
1/4 cup Parmesan cheese (cow,
      rice, or soy)

4 large eggs
2 cups lowfat milk (cow, rice, or soy)
1 teaspoon gf Worcestershire sauce
1 teaspoon dry mustard
2 tablespoons dried parsley
cooking spray

Grate Monterey Jack and cheddar cheeses. Set aside.
In 13 x 9-inch pan that has been coated with cooking spray, lay 6 slices of white bread. If using French bread, use enough 1-inch thick pieces to cover the bottom of the casserole dish.

Sprinkle 1/2 cup each of the cheddar cheese and Monterey jack cheese over bread. Sprinkle Canadian bacon, onion flakes, and Parmesan cheese on top. Lay another 6 slices (or however many slices it takes to cover casserole) of white bread on top. Sprinkle with remaining cheeses.

In a large bowl, beat together the eggs, milk, Worcestershire sauce, and mustard. Pour over the top of casserole. Refrigerate overnight.

Bake at 350 degrees for 45 minutes to 1 hour, or until top is browned. Sprinkle with chopped parsley before serving.
Preparation = 45 minutes. Serves 6.
Calories 385 (45% from fat); Fat 19g; Prot 29g; Carb 24g; Sod 1315mg; Chol 170mg.

Huevos Rancheros

The traditional Southwestern breakfast. Use homemade Corn Tortillas or purchased ones.

6 Corn Tortillas (See Index)
2 tablespoons canola oil
1/2 cup chopped onion
1 garlic clove, minced
4 large tomatoes (seeded, diced
4 ounces diced green chiles (1 can)
1/4 teaspoon dried oregano
1/4 teaspoon ground cumin

1/2 teaspoon salt
1/8 teaspoon white pepper
6 large eggs
1 cup shredded Monterey
   jack cheese (or non-dairy
   cheese of your choice)
1/2 cup fresh chopped cilantro
cooking spray

Preheat oven to 250 degrees. In small, heavy skillet heat 2 tablespoons of oil. Hold tortillas with tongs and dip into hot oil, one at a time for about 8-10 seconds or until limp. Line a 10 x 6-inch baking dish with the tortillas, letting edges of tortillas extend up sides of dish a bit. Cover with aluminum foil and keep warm in 250 degree oven.

In same skillet that has been sprayed with cooking spray, sauté the onion and garlic over low-medium heat until tender, about 5-8 minutes. Stir in tomatoes, green chiles, oregano, cumin, salt, and pepper. Simmer, uncovered, for 10 minutes. Spoon over tortillas.

Wipe skillet clean with paper towels and coat with cooking spray. Over medium heat, break eggs into skillet and sprinkle lightly with salt and pepper, to taste. When whites are set, and the edges cooked, add 1 tablespoon water. Cover skillet and cook eggs to desired degree of doneness.

Place oven rack in "broil" position and set temperature to "broil" setting. Carefully place cooked eggs over sauce in baking dish. Sprinkle with cheese. Place under broiler for 1 to 2 minutes or until cheese melts. Top with cilantro. Serve at once. NOTE: If you are fortunate enough to have fresh green New Mexico chiles, use 1 small green chile that has been roasted, peeled, seeded, and chopped finely. Remember, chiles can be hot; use them sparingly at first and wear gloves when handling. Preparation = 30 minutes. Serves 6.

Calories 273 (52% from fat); Fat 16g; Prot 14g; Carb 19.5g; Sod 44mg; Chol 229mg.

Mexican Tortilla Casserole

This dish makes a wonderful Sunday brunch dish, especially if your theme is Southwestern. You may use non-dairy cheeses for the cheddar and jack cheeses.

2 cans gf Mexican tomatoes
     (14.5 ounces each)
1/2 teaspoon dried oregano
1/2 teaspoon dried sage
1/2 cup chopped fresh cilantro
1 recipe Corn Tortillas
     (10 tortillas - See Index)
1/4 cup diced cooked pork

1 1/2 cups grated monterey jack
     cheese
1 1/2 cups grated cheddar cheese
1/2 cup sliced black olives
1/2 cup guacamole
1/4 cup sour cream (or sour
     cream alternative)
cooking spray

Puree tomatoes, oregano, sage, and cilantro in food processor. (You may substitute your favorite gf Mexican salsa). Mix the monterey jack and cheddar cheeses.

Preheat oven to 450 degrees.

Spray two 8-inch pie plates with cooking spray. In one pie plate, layer 1/4 cup of the tomato sauce. Top with 1 tortilla, 1/3 cup cheese, and 1/4 cup sauce. Repeat layers 3 more times. Top with fifth tortilla, pork, sauce and cheese. Repeat process for second pie plate.

Bake for 12-15 minutes or until cheese melts and sauce is bubbly. Cut each casserole in half to serve. Garnish with guacamole and sour cream.

MEATLESS MEXICAN TORTILLA CASSEROLE: Omit pork.

Preparation = 25 minutes. Serves 4.

Pork Version: Calories 629 (71% from fat); Fat 50g; Prot 36g; Carb 10g; Sod 863mg; Chol 139mg.

Meatless Version: Calories 449 (71% from fat); Fat 36g; Prot 23g; Carb 10g; Sod 697mg; Chol 88mg.

Mexican Breakfast Casserole

A mildly spicy breakfast dish that can be assembled the night before. See Index for Chorizo recipe. You may use non-dairy cheddar and jack cheeses, if you wish.

2 cups gf French Bread, cut in
   1/2-inch cubes (See Index)
1 small onion, chopped
4 ounces gf Chorizo sausage
4 large eggs
1 1/4 cups milk (cow, rice, soy)
1 teaspoon dry mustard
2 ounces green chiles
   (canned, drained)
1/2 cup minced fresh cilantro

1/4 teaspoon salt
1/8 teaspoon black pepper
1/2 cup shredded Monterey
   jack cheese
1/2 cup smoked cheddar cheese
1 1/2 cups Mexican salsa
1/2 cup guacamole (optional)
1/2 cup sour cream or sour
   cream alternative (optional)
cooking spray

Coat an 8 x 8-inch baking dish with cooking spray.

Place cut-up bread on cookie sheet and toast at 325 degrees for 10-15 minutes or until lightly toasted. (This is optional, but boosts the flavor).

Cook sausage and onion in heavy large skillet over medium heat until sausage is cooked and onion is lightly browned. Break up sausage with fork as it is browning. Drain.

Beat eggs, milk, dry mustard, green chiles, cilantro, salt, and pepper in large bowl to blend thoroughly.

Place bread cubes in bottom of prepared dish. Spoon sausage and onion over bread. Sprinkle cheese mixture over sausage. Pour egg mixture over all. Cover; refrigerate overnight.

Preheat oven to 350 degrees. Uncover dish and bake until casserole is set and bubbling, about 40-45 minutes.
Serve with Mexican salsa. Top with guacamole or sour cream, if desired.
Preparation = 45 minutes (Excludes chilling time) Serves 6.
Calories 567 (48% from fat); Fat 30g; Prot 24g; Carb 50g; Sod 1239mg; Chol 193mg.

Stuffed French Toast

This is a classic at our house for Sunday brunch and it always gets many compliments. You can vary the stuffing—perhaps a thin slice of prosciutto along with the cream cheese.

8 ounces cream cheese, softened (or firm silken tofu, creamed)	4 large eggs
1/2 teaspoon gf orange extract or orange peel	1 cup whole milk (cow, rice, soy)
1 teaspoon gf vanilla extract	1/2 teaspoon gf vanilla extract
1/2 cup walnuts, chopped	1/2 teaspoon ground nutmeg
1 gf French Bread loaf (See Index)	1 1/2 cups apricot preserves
	1/2 cup orange juice
	cooking spray

Beat together the cream cheese (or tofu), 1 teaspoon vanilla extract, and 1/2 teaspoon orange extract until fluffy. Stir in nuts.

Slice bread into 10 pieces, each 1 1/2 inches thick. Cut a pocket in top (crust) of each slice. Fill the pocket of each slice with 1 1/2 tablespoons of the creamed cheese mixture.

Beat together the eggs, milk, 1/2 teaspoon vanilla and nutmeg. Using tongs, dip each side of the bread slice into the egg mixture. Over low-medium heat, cook both sides of the bread slices on a griddle coated with cooking spray. Warm slices on a baking sheet in a warm oven.

Meanwhile, heat together the apricot preserves and orange juice in the microwave oven. To serve, drizzle the apricot mixture over French toast. For added flavor, drizzle some apricot mixture over bread slices while they warm in the oven. Pass extra apricot mixture at serving time.

VARIATION: Use Raisin Bread (See Index).

Preparation = 30 minutes. Serves 10. (1 slice each)

Calories 375 (37% from fat); Fat 16g; Prot 11g; Carb 50g; Sod 394mg; Chol 113mg.

Eggs Benedict

Use your own homemade English Muffins in this dish. It features Canadian bacon (lower fat than ham) and a low-fat Hollandaise.

4 **English Muffins (See Index)**
8 **slices Canadian bacon**
8 **large poached eggs**

1 1/3 **cups Hollandaise Sauce**
    (See Index)
1/4 **cup fresh chopped parsley**
    paprika (for garnish)

Make the Hollandaise Sauce. Keep warm in double boiler. Warm the sliced English Muffins (in microwave or wrapped in foil in a 250-degree oven.)

Meanwhile, warm the Canadian bacon in the microwave to desired serving temperature. Poach eggs.

Arrange 2 halves of an English Muffin on each of 4 plates. Top each half with a slice of Canadian Bacon, then a poached egg. Top with Hollandaise Sauce, parsley, and paprika.

Preparation = 30 minutes. Serves 4.

Calories 458 (43% from fat); Fat 22g; Prot 31g; Carb 34g; Sod 1742; Chol 471mg.

Cooking Grains

For many of us, hot cereal is an absolute necessity at breakfast —summer, winter, spring or fall. Just because you don't eat wheat doesn't mean you can't have cooked cereal. There are many other grains to cook for breakfast besides wheat.

The following table shows you how to cook these alternative grains. I like to stir in a teaspoon of gf vanilla to the cooked cereal—just to boost the flavor. Use salt as you wish. Serves 4.

Grain (1 cup)	Water	Cooking Time
Amaranth*	2 cups	15-20 minutes
Brown rice	2 1/2 cups	30-45 minutes
Buckwheat *	1 cup	15-20 minutes
Millet*	3 1/2 to 4 cups	35-45 minutes
Oats*	2 cups	10-15 minutes
Quinoa*	2 cups	15-20 minutes
Wild Rice	4 cups	40 minutes
White Rice	2 cups	15-20 minutes

Favorite toppings for hot cereal include sugar, cinnamon, honey, maple syrup, pancake syrup, brown sugar, fresh fruit, jam, jelly, or fruit sauces. For some cereals (for example, amaranth, buckwheat, and millet), combining them with small amounts of cooked brown or white rice is advisable.

*Amaranth, Buckwheat, Oats, and Quinoa are not always tolerated by wheat-sensitive persons. Check with your physician. Those with Celiac Sprue should definitely not consume these grains without first checking with your physician.

Granola

Commercially prepared granolas can be very high in fat and sugar, but you can control the amount of sugar and oil you add to this recipe. Gluten-sensitive persons should substitute puffed rice or puffed corn flakes for the oatmeal.

5 cups rolled oats, puffed rice,
   or puffed corn
1 teaspoon cinnamon
1/2 cup sunflower seeds
1/2 cup almond slivers

1/2 cup coconut flakes
2 teaspoons gf vanilla extract
2 teaspoons canola oil
1/2 cup light corn syrup
1/2 cup golden raisins
cooking spray

Combine all ingredients, except raisins. Spread on baking sheet that's been coated with cooking spray. Bake at 300 degrees for 30-40 minutes, or until lightly browned. Stir every 10 minutes to assure even browning. Add raisins.
Preparation = 45 minutes. Serves 12. (About 1/2 cup each).
Calories 401 (12% from fat); Fat 12g; Prot 14g; Carb 62g; Sod 27mg; Chol 0mg.

Granola Bars

Commercially prepared granola bars can be very high in sugar and fat. And they sometimes contain many ingredients we don't need in our bodies. These bars are great for quick, nutritious snacks and they travel well.

2 cups brown rice
4 cups water
1/2 teaspoon salt
1 teaspoon gf vanilla extract
1/2 cup dried apricot halves
1/2 cup sunflower seeds

1/4 cup brown sugar
2 tablespoons canola oil
2 cups canned peaches, drained
1/2 cup coconut flakes
1/2 cup golden raisins
cooking spray

Cook brown rice in water for 30-45 minutes. Cool.
In a food processor, blend cooked rice with remaining ingredients (except coconut and raisins) in two batches until smooth. Stir in coconut and raisins.

Spread in 13 x 9-inch pan coated with cooking spray. Bake at 300 degrees for one hour. Cut into 12 squares. Continue baking another 20 minutes or until mixture is lightly browned. Store in refrigerator. Wrap individual bars in plastic wrap or aluminum foil. You can freeze the bars for 1 month.

Preparation = 1 1/2 hours. Serves 12.

Calories 180 (31% from fat); Fat 7g; Prot 3g; Carb 30g; Sod 105mg; Chol 0mg.

Yogurt Breakfast Trifle

This dish looks pretty in individual, clear glass goblets—or, in a straight sided, glass serving dish which allows the layers of ingredients to be visible from the side. You can vary the fruits.

**1 recipe gf Yellow Cake, cut in
     1/2-inch cubes (See Index)
6 cups sliced strawberries
1/2 cup orange juice**

**1 tablespoon powdered sugar
3 cups yogurt (vanilla, lemon,
   or orange-may use soy
   yogurt)**

Combine the strawberries, orange juice, and sugar in a bowl. Layer the ingredients in the serving dish, starting and ending with the yogurt. For example, place a layer of yogurt, then cake, then the strawberries, then the yogurt, and so on. Garnish with a few remaining pieces of whole fruit. Cover and chill, a few hours or overnight. Serve chilled.

Preparation = 15 minutes. Serves 6.

Calories 240 (33% from fat); Fat 9g; Prot 8g; Carb 33g; Sod 171; Chol 43mg.

PASTA, GRAINS, BEANS & RICE

Pasta
Asian Soba Noodles 78
Basil-Garlic Pasta * 69
Chile Pasta* 70
Egg Noodles w/ Herbs* 72
Fettucine Alfredo* 71
Pasta* 69
Ravioli* 70
Lasagna* 251
Linguine w/ Pine Nuts* 72
Macaroni & Cheese 73
Pasta Primavera* 74
Pasta Salad w/ Feta Cheese* 76
Pasta Salad w/ Vegetables* 77
Pasta Salad* 75
Spaghetti & Meatballs* 249
Spinach Pasta* 69
Tomato Pasta* 70

Beans
Boston Baked Beans 89
Red Beans & Rice 91
Refried Beans 90
Southwestern Beans 90
White Bean Cassoulet
    w/ Sausage 252

Rice
Curried Rice Pilaf w/ Raisins 83
Herbed Brown Rice 82
Mexican Rice 82
Rice Pilaf w/ Dried Fruits &
    Nuts 84
Risotto w/ Mushrooms & Herbs 85
Saffron Rice Pilaf 86
Wild Rice Pancakes w/ Pecans 87
Wild Rice w/ Dried Fruits 88

Grains
Grilled Vegetables & Quinoa (or Brown Rice) 184
Lentil Tabbouleh 80
Polenta w/ Mushrooms 81
Quinoa, Wild Rice, & Cranberry Pilaf 83
Tabbouleh (Quinoa or Brown Rice) 79
Veggiburgers 92

* Pasta can be made using electric pasta machine.

Pasta is one of the foods we miss the most on a wheat-free diet. Now you can eat pasta as often as you're willing to make it. You'll find recipes for homemade egg Pasta that can be made into spaghetti, fettucine, linguine, ravioli, and a variety of pasta salads.

I heartily recommend that you invest in an electric pasta machine. It will save you countless hours. I once thought of pasta machines as extravagant. Now I think they're a necessity. Of course, you can purchase some excellent, ready-made wheat-free, gluten-free pasta—but homemade noodles taste fresh and are absolutely wonderful.

In addition to pasta, you'll also find other recipes for grains, beans and rice—featuring family favorites such as Macaroni & Cheese, but you'll find lighter, contemporary cuisine such as Risotto with Mushrooms & Herbs or Lentil Tabbouleh.

This section introduces you to a new grain called Quinoa (pronounced keen-wah). Originally grown by the Incas high in the Andes, Quinoa is now grown in the United States. Unlike other grains such as rice and corn that must be combined with other protein sources to be complete, Quinoa is a complete protein in itself. It is also low in fat, high in fiber, and has a unique, nutty flavor.

NOTE: Quinoa is not generally approved for persons with celiac sprue. So, if you suffer from celiac sprue or suspect that you do, consult your physician before consuming this grain.

Pasta

This pasta is absolutely wonderful, easy to make, and freezes well.

1/2 cup brown rice flour	2 large eggs
1/2 cup tapioca flour	1/4 cup water
1/4 cup potato starch	canola oil (1 *teaspoon* for
1/2 cup cornstarch	electric pasta machine;
4 teaspoons xanthan gum	1 *tablespoon* for hand
1 teaspoon gelatin powder	version)
1/2 teaspoon salt	

HAND-MADE PASTA: Combine eggs, water and *1 table-spoon* oil in food processor and process until eggs are light yellow in color. Add flours, cornstarch, xanthan gum, gelatin powder, and salt. Process until thoroughly blended and mixture forms ball. Remove lid of food processor and break up dough into smaller egg-sized pieces. Replace lid, process until ball forms again.

Transfer dough to pastry board or smooth surface. For easiest handling, roll dough between two sheets of waxed paper or plastic wrap that have been dusted with rice flour. Roll as thin as possible and cut into desired shapes with sharp knife or pastry cutter.

ELECTRIC PASTA MACHINE: Follow machine directions, since different machines require different processes. My machine calls for placing *1 teaspoon* oil in machine. Then thoroughly mix together dry ingredients and add to machine. Combine eggs and water; whisk together until light yellow and foamy. All egg membranes should be thoroughly broken up before slowly adding mixture to machine. It is a good idea to withhold the final two tablespoons of egg mixture until you're sure it's needed. Follow machine directions from this point.

BASIC-GARLIC PASTA: Add 1 teaspoon dried basil and 1/2 teaspoon garlic powder.

SPINACH PASTA: Cook 1 cup packed fresh spinach leaves in boiling water for 5 minutes. (Or use 1/2 cup frozen spinach, thawed). Drain all but 2 tablespoons of water from spinach. Using hand-held blender, puree spinach until smooth. Use pureed spinach mixture in place of 1/4 cup water in Pasta recipe.

TOMATO PASTA: Use 1/4 cup tomato juice in place of 1/4 cup water.

CHILE PASTA: Add 1 teaspoon New Mexico chile powder.
Preparation = 30 minutes. Serves 4.
Calories 291 (20% from fat); Fat 6g; Prot 8g; Carb 49g; Sod 303mg; Chol 106mg.

Homemade Ravioli

It is so wonderful to have pasta back in your diet! Although ravioli takes a little time to make, it is well worth the effort.

1 tablespoon each grated
  mozzarella and Romano
  cheese, (or non-dairy cheese
  of choice)
1 teaspoon gf Italian seasoning
1 large egg, separated
1 tablespoon water

1/2 cup Parmesan cheese,
  (cow, rice, or soy) for garnish
1 recipe gf Pasta (See Index)
1 1/2 cups Spaghetti Sauce
  (See Index)
1/2 cup ricotta cheese or
  firm silken tofu, creamed

In a small bowl, blend the cheeses, Italian seasoning, and egg yolk until smooth. Set aside.

Prepare the pasta, using directions for your machine if you have one. If using a ravioli tray, follow directions for using it. If shaping ravioli by hand, roll out the dough to about 12 inches square on a potato starch-floured surface. Brush one-half of the dough with a combination of egg white and water which has been whisked together until smooth. Place teaspoonfuls of cheese filling on the egg-painted side of the dough about

2 inches apart. Fold unpainted half of dough over the filled portion and seal edges with fingers. Press the dough together with fingers between mounds. Cut the ravioli into squares with a pastry cutter, following the lines where you've pressed the dough together. Or, use a special pastry tool that both cuts and crimps the dough at the same time.

When ravioli are made, boil in salted water for 5-10 minutes or until done. Freeze for later use. Makes about 30 ravioli, enough for 7-8 ravioli per person.
Preparation = 30 minutes. Serves 4.
Calories 305 (45% from fat); Fat 15g; Prot 14g; Carb 29g; Sod 795mg; Chol 107mg.

Fettucine Alfredo

This is fabulous—and has a lower fat content than usual. Unfortunately for those with dairy-sensitivities, it is dairy-based.

1 1/2 cups low-fat cottage cheese
3 tablespoons skim milk (cow, rice, soy, or nut)
1/4 cup grated Parmesan cheese
1 small garlic clove, minced
2 tablespoons butter (or Butter Buds)

1 teaspoon gf butter extract (optional)
4 cups homemade gf Pasta noodles, cooked (See Index)
1/4 cup fresh parsley, chopped
1 teaspoon gf lemon pepper

In food processor, combine cottage cheese, skim milk, Parmesan cheese, minced garlic, butter, and butter extract. Puree until mixture is very, very smooth. Transfer mixture to heavy, medium saucepan and whisk over medium heat until mixture reaches serving temperature. Serve over hot noodles. Garnish with chopped parsley and lemon pepper, if desired.
Preparation = 20 minutes. Serves 4.
Calories 867 (30% from fat); Fat 29g; Prot 30g; Carb 118g; Sod 1423mg; Chol 283mg.

Linguine with Pine Nuts

This is quick, easy and delicious. It makes a great dish for company.

2 cups gf Pasta, in linguine
   shape (See Index)
1/2 teaspoon salt
1/4 cup pine nuts, toasted
1/4 cup fresh parsley

1/4 cup Parmesan cheese, grated
   (cow, rice, or soy)
1 teaspoon gf lemon pepper
2 tablespoons olive oil

Add pasta to boiling water along with 1/2 teaspoon salt. While pasta boils, toast pine nuts in 350 degree oven for 5-10 minutes or in skillet over medium heat for 5-10 minutes. Drain linguine and toss with remaining ingredients. Serve immediately. Garnish with chopped fresh parsley.
Preparation = 15 minutes. Serves 4.
Calories 438 (35% from fat); Fat 17g; Prot 14g; Carb 57g; Sod 794mg; Chol 124mg.

Egg Noodles with Herbs

Combine homemade noodles with herbs and lemon for great taste.

4 cups hot cooked gf noodles
   using Pasta (See Index)
2 tablespoons olive oil
1 tablespoon dried chives
1 tablespoon dried parsley
1/4 teaspoon black pepper

2 tablespoons fresh lemon juice
1 teaspoon grated lemon peel
1/2 teaspoon herb seasoning
   (such as Fines Herbs)
1/4 cup Parmesan cheese (cow,
   rice, or soy)

Combine hot cooked noodles with remaining ingredients and toss gently. Serve warm. Garnish with Parmesan cheese.
Preparation = 10 minutes. Serves 4.
Calories: 744; (28% from fat); Fat 23g; Prot 20g; Carb 111g; Sod 779mg; Chol 244mg.

Macaroni & Cheese

This is the ultimate "comfort-food." But, it's usually off-limits for wheat-free diets because macaroni pasta is made with wheat flour. However, there are some very good wheat-free macaroni pastas on the market today. Check your local health food store or mail-order sources (see Mail-Order Sources in Index). This recipe is dairy-based.

1 teaspoon cornstarch
1 teaspoon salt
1/4 teaspoon cayenne pepper
2 1/2 cups skim milk
1 tablespoon Dijonnaise mustard
1/2 cup low-fat mozzarella cheese

1 cup cheddar cheese, shredded (extra-sharp)
1/2 cup Parmesan cheese — plus 1 tablespoon
10 ounces cooked elbow macaroni (wheat-free)
cooking spray

In heavy ovenproof skillet or pan, combine cornstarch (or arrowroot), salt, cayenne pepper, and milk. Mix well. Bring to boil and boil for 1 minute, stirring constantly. Stir in mustard, mozzarella, cheddar cheese, and Parmesan cheese, reserving 1 tablespoon of the Parmesan cheese for topping.

Stir elbow macaroni into cheese sauce. Transfer to oven-proof serving dish or leave in skillet. Sprinkle with remaining 1 tablespoon of Parmesan and broil until top is browned.
Preparation 30 minutes. Serves 6.
Calories 345 (25% from fat); Fat 9%; Prot 20g; Carb 44g; Sod 725mg; Chol 27mg.

Pasta Primavera

Primavera means spring in Italian and this combination of pasta and springtime vegetables is delightful. You can vary the vegetables as you wish.

1 cup diagonally sliced asparagus
1 cup diagonally halved snow peas
1 tablespoon olive oil
1/2 cup chopped red bell pepper
1/4 cup chopped onion
1 garlic clove, minced
1/2 cup Parmesan cheese (cow, rice, or soy)
1/4 cup chopped fresh parsley

2 tablespoons dry white wine
1 tablespoon balsamic vinegar
1 teaspoon olive oil
1/2 teaspoon salt
1/4 teaspoon white pepper
4 cups hot cooked gf noodles from Pasta (See Index)
additional Parmesan cheese, for garnish

Cook asparagus and snow peas in boiling water for 1-2 minutes. Drain and rinse immediately. Set aside.

In large Dutch oven, sauté onion in olive oil for 3-5 minutes over low-medium heat. Remove from heat. Add remaining ingredients, including vegetables, and stir to combine. Toss gently with hot cooked noodles.

Preparation = 20 minutes. Serves 4.

Calories 783 (26% from fat); Fat 22g; Prot 25g; Carb 117g; Sod 1272mg; Chol 248mg.

Pasta Salad

Pasta salads are so popular these days—so now you can enjoy them like everyone else. You can vary the vegetables as you wish.

1/4 cup chopped onion
1 tablespoon olive oil
1 garlic clove, minced
1/2 cup chopped red bell pepper
1 tablespoon Dijonnaise mustard
1 tablespoon balsamic vinegar
2 tablespoons cider vinegar
2 tablespoons lemon juice

4 cups uncooked wide noodles
    from Pasta (See Index) or
    use purchased gf pasta
1 cup broccoli flowerets
1/2 cup black olives
1/4 cup chopped fresh parsley
1/4 teaspoon black pepper
1/2 cup Parmesan cheese

In heavy skillet, sauté onion and minced garlic for 3-5 minutes, or until onion is tender. Add red bell pepper, mustard, vinegars, and lemon juice and set aside.

In boiling water, cook noodles until done—adding broccoli during last minute of cooking. Drain well. Combine onion mixture with noodle mixture and add olives, parsley, black pepper, and Parmesan cheese. Toss gently. Serve.

Preparation = 20 minutes. Serves 4.

Calories 778 (27% from fat); Fat 23g; Prot 24g; Carb 116g; Sod 1117mg; Chol 248mg.

Pasta Salad with Feta Cheese

This makes a wonderful summer salad. Add cooked chicken or salmon if you want to serve it as a main dish. Feta cheese is made from goat's milk, so if you have milk allergies you should avoid this dish.

4 cups uncooked rotini
noodles (purchased, or use
noodles from Pasta, See Index)
1/3 cup yellow bell pepper
1/3 cup red bell pepper
1/4 cup green onion tops
1/4 cup red wine vinegar
1/4 cup lemon juice
2 tablespoons gf dry white wine
1/4 teaspoon sugar or honey

1/4 teaspoon salt
1/4 teaspoon white pepper
1/4 cup olive oil
1/3 cup sun-dried tomatoes,
chopped (not oil-packed)
1/3 cup black olives, halved
1/2 cup feta cheese, crumbled
1/3 cup pine nuts, toasted
1 small garlic clove, minced

Cook noodles in boiling water to desired degree of doneness. Drain and chill.

Meanwhile, chop bell peppers into 1/2-inch cubes. Chop green onion tops into 1/4-inch pieces. Set peppers and onions aside.

In screw-top jar, combine red wine vinegar, lemon juice, white wine, sugar, salt, and pepper. Shake vigorously to blend. Add olive oil and shake again.

Combine remaining ingredients with pasta in large bowl. Toss with dressing. Chill. Let stand at room temperature for 20 minutes before serving.

Preparation = 45 minutes. Serves 4.

Calories 414 (55% from fat); Fat 26g; Prot 12g; Carb 37g; Sod 495mg; Chol 49mg.

Pasta Salad with Vegetables

This makes a very colorful salad and can be combined with cooked chicken or salmon for a heartier version.

2 cups uncooked wheat-free rotini noodles (purchased or use Pasta, See Index)
1/4 cup red wine vinegar
2 tablespoons lemon juice
1 teaspoon Dijonnaise mustard
1/4 teaspoon salt
1/4 teaspoon white pepper
1/4 cup olive oil

1 tablespoon dried basil
1 small garlic clove, minced
1 cup snow peas, blanched
1 cup broccoli flowerets, blanched
1 small red bell pepper, chopped
1/4 cup black olives, halved
1/4 cup pine nuts, toasted

Cook noodles in boiling water until desired degree of doneness. Drain and chill.

Meanwhile, in screw-top jar combine red wine vinegar, lemon juice, mustard, salt, pepper and olive oil. Shake vigorously to blend.

Combine remaining ingredients in large bowl. Toss with dressing to taste. Chill. Let stand at room temperature for 20 minutes before serving.

Preparation = 45 minutes. Serves 4.

Calories 551 (43.3% from fat); Fat 27; Prot 14.4g; Carb 65.6g; Sod 663mg; Chol 120mg.

Asian Soba Noodles

Soba noodles are made of buckwheat which is not actually wheat, but rather a member of the fruit family. You may substitute wheat-free, commercially-made spaghetti if pure buckwheat noodles are not available or you don't like buckwheat. This dish goes great with grilled fish.

1 pound soba noodles (pure buckwheat noodles or wheat-free spaghetti)
1/4 teaspoon salt
2 tablespoons sesame oil
2 tablespoons water
1/4 cup low sodium, wheat-free soy sauce
2 tablespoons sugar or honey
1 1/2 tablespoons red wine vinegar
1 cup fresh chopped cilantro
1/2 cup chopped green onions
1/2 jalapeno pepper, chopped
1/2 cup diced red bell pepper
1/2 cup pine nuts, toasted

Cook soba noodles in large pot of rapidly boiling water with 1/4 teaspoon salt until just tender, about 10 minutes. Drain and immerse noodles in ice water until cool. Drain well. Transfer to large bowl.

Combine sesame oil, water, soy sauce, sugar, and vinegar in screw-top jar. Shake vigorously until well-blended. Pour over noodles. Add chopped cilantro, green onions, and jalapeno pepper and mix well. Sprinkle toasted pine nuts over salad and serve.

Preparation = 30 minutes. Serves 6.

Calories 466 (33% from fat); Fat 18g; Prot 186g; Carb 68g; Sod 1017mg; Chol 0mg.

Tabbouleh

This dish is a delicious variation of the traditional tabbouleh made with bulgur wheat. You'll never miss the wheat. Go easy with the feta cheese—a little goes a long way.

1 cup uncooked quinoa, washed twice or 1 cup uncooked brown rice
1/2 teaspoon salt
2 cups water
1/4 cup shelled pumpkin seeds or pine nuts (toasted)
2 tablespoons fresh lemon juice
3 tablespoons olive oil
1 tablespoon white wine vinegar
1/4 teaspoon salt
1/8 teaspoon white pepper
1 cucumber, chopped
3 green onions, chopped
1 large tomato, chopped
1/2 cup chopped fresh parsley
1/2 cup chopped fresh cilantro
1/4 cup chopped fresh mint
1/4 cup crumbled feta cheese, (optional). Dairy-allergic people should avoid feta cheese.

Rinse quinoa in sieve, rubbing grains between fingers. Drain and repeat or until water runs clear. Transfer quinoa to large, heavy skillet and toast over moderate heat, until grain is light golden brown, about 4 minutes.

In heavy medium saucepan, combine toasted quinoa (or brown rice, untoasted), 1/2 teaspoon salt, and 2 cups water. Bring to boil. Cover and reduce heat, simmering for 12-15 minutes. Transfer to a strainer and drain well.

Meanwhile, toast pumpkin seeds in skillet over medium heat, stirring constantly until lightly browned, about 5 minutes. Combine lemon juice, olive oil, white wine vinegar, 1/4 teaspoon salt, and white pepper in screw-top jar. Shake vigorously to blend. Combine cooked quinoa or brown rice and all remaining ingredients in large bowl. Toss well. Refrigerate for 4 hours. Let stand for 20 minutes before serving.
Preparation = 30 minutes. Serves 4.
Calories 372 (36% from fat); Fat 16g; Prot 13g; Carb 50g; Sod 556mg; Chol 6mg.

Lentil Tabbouleh

Instead of bulgur wheat, try this variation of the traditional Tabbouleh.

4 cups water
1 cup brown or green lentils
1 garlic clove, peeled
1 bay leaf
1/2 teaspoon salt
1/2 teaspoon black pepper
1 cucumber (peeled, chopped)
1 small red bell pepper, diced

1/4 cup chopped red onion
1/2 cup chopped fresh mint
1/2 cup chopped fresh parsley
1 teaspoon fresh lemon juice
1 teaspoon fresh lime juice
2 teaspoons red wine vinegar
1 1/2 tablespoons olive oil

In large saucepan, combine 4 cups of water with lentils, garlic, bay leaf, salt, and pepper. Bring to boil, then reduce heat, cover, and simmer for 30 minutes. Drain lentils, discard bay leaf and garlic. Set aside to cool. Then toss with cucumber, red bell pepper, red onion, mint, and parsley.

In screw-top jar, combine lemon juice, lime juice, vinegar, and olive oil. Shake vigorously until well blended. Pour over lentil mixture. Refrigerate for 4 hours or overnight. Serve chilled or at room temperature.

Preparation = 1 hour. Serves 4.

Calories 238 (21% from fat); Fat 6g; Prot 15g; Carb 34g; Sod 293mg; Chol 0mg.

Polenta with Mushrooms

An old, traditional Italian dish—Polenta has been revived and holds "gourmet" status in many restaurants. This version is very easy and the mushrooms add an interesting texture. I use regular cornmeal, although there is a coarser version especially for Polenta.

1 small onion, chopped
1 tablespoon olive oil
3 tablespoons water
2 cups chopped fresh mushrooms (shitake or regular)
1 tablespoon butter or oleo
1/2 teaspoon dried oregano
3/4 teaspoon salt (See directions)
1/8 teaspoon black pepper

3/4 cup low sodium chicken
   broth (See directions)
1 cup low-fat milk (cow, rice, soy)
1/2 cup water
1/2 cup regular cornmeal
2 tablespoons Parmesan cheese
   (cow, rice, or soy)
cooking spray

In 12-inch skillet over medium heat, cook onion in olive oil and water until tender and lightly browned. Remove onions. To same skillet, add chopped mushrooms along with butter, oregano, 1/4 teaspoon of the salt, and pepper and cook for 3-5 minutes, stirring constantly. Add 1/4 cup of the chicken broth and boil for 1 minute to thicken slightly. Remove from heat and keep warm.

In large saucepan over high heat, combine milk, remaining 1/2 teaspoon salt, and remaining 1/2 cup chicken broth and heat to boiling. Reduce heat to low; gradually sprinkle in cornmeal, whisking constantly. Cook, stirring, for 5 minutes or until thick. Stir in Parmesan cheese. Serve Polenta topped with mushroom mixture. Makes 4 side-dish servings.

Preparation = 30 minutes. Serves 4.

Calories 150 (30% from fat); Fat 5g; Prot 8g; Carb 20g; Sod 713mg; Chol 4mg.

Mexican Rice

This rice dish is perfect with a Mexican or Southwestern meal.

1 teaspoon canola oil
1 cup chopped onion
1 garlic clove, minced
1 cup white rice, uncooked
1 cup low-sodium chicken broth

1/2 teaspoon dried oregano
10 ounces tomatoes with
    green chiles (undrained)
1/2 cup chopped fresh cilantro
1/4 cup black olives, sliced

Heat oil in large saucepan over medium heat. Sauté onion for 3-5 minutes. Add garlic, rice, broth, oregano, and tomatoes. Bring to a boil, cover, and simmer for 20-25 minutes or until liquid is absorbed. Add cilantro and olives.
Preparation = 30 minutes. Serves 4.
Calories 226 (10% from fat); Fat 3g; Prot 8g; Carb 46g; Sod 496mg; Chol 0mg.

Herbed Brown Rice

You can use chicken, beef, or vegetable broth in this dish.

1 cup chopped onion
1 tablespoon olive oil
1 package brown rice (12 ounces)
2 garlic cloves, minced
1 1/2 cups low sodium broth

1 teaspoon each dried basil,
    chives, and parsley
3/4 teaspoon black pepper
1/2 teaspoon salt

In 3-quart, oven-proof saucepan over medium heat, sauté onion in olive oil for 5 minutes, stirring frequently. Add rice to pan; stir for 2 minutes. Add remaining ingredients. Cook, covered, in a 350 degree oven for 40 minutes or until rice is tender.
Preparation = 45 minutes. Serves 6.
Calories 243 (14% from fat); Fat 4g; Prot 7g; Carb 47g; Sod 388mg; Chol 0mg.

Curried Rice Pilaf with Raisins

Basmati rice is a fragrant, aromatic rice originally grown in India and Pakistan. It is a favorite for pilafs because of its nutty flavor.

1 cup chopped onion
1 tablespoon peanut oil
1 1/2 teaspoons curry powder
1 teaspoon gf chili powder
1 cup basmati or long-grain rice

1/2 cup golden raisins
1/2 teaspoon salt
2 cups low sodium chicken broth
1/2 cup almond slivers, toasted

In large, heavy saucepan cook the onion, curry powder, and chili powder in peanut oil over medium heat until onions are tender, about 5 minutes. Add uncooked rice, raisins, and salt.

Add chicken broth, cover, and simmer for about 20 minutes or until the water is absorbed and the rice is tender. Sprinkle with toasted almonds just before serving.

Preparation = 30 minutes. Serves 4.

Calories 382 (29% from fat); Fat 14g; Prot 14g; Carb 59g; Sod 685mg. Chol 0mg.

Quinoa, Wild Rice, and Cranberry Pilaf

You can substitute dried cherries for the cranberries, if you like. Make sure quinoa is appropriate for your diet.

3/4 cup wild rice
3 cups low sodium chicken broth
1/2 cup quinoa
1/4 cup dried cranberries

1/4 cup golden raisins
1 teaspoon olive oil
1/3 cup toasted almonds

Rinse wild rice in water. In saucepan, combine wild rice and chicken broth and bring to boil. Reduce heat, cover, and simmer for 15 minutes. Rinse quinoa in sieve with cold water, at least 3 times or until water is no longer cloudy. Remove wild rice from heat. Stir in quinoa, cranberries, raisins, and olive oil. Spoon into 1 1/2 quart casserole. Bake, covered, in 325 degree oven for 1 hour or until wild rice and quinoa are tender and liquid is absorbed. Sprinkle with almonds.

Preparation = 1 1/4 hours. Serves 6.

Calories 236 (26% from fat); Fat 7g; Prot 12g; Carb 33g; Sod 789mg; Chol 1mg.

Rice Pilaf with Dried Fruits & Nuts

This is a very flavorful rice pilaf, packed with lots of texture from the dried fruits and nuts. It makes a wonderful dish for company.

1/4 teaspoon ground cloves	1 cup white long grain rice
1/8 teaspoon saffron	2 cups low sodium chicken broth
1/8 teaspoon allspice	1/2 cup chopped dried apricots
1/2 cup onion, chopped	1/2 cup golden raisins
1 garlic clove, minced	1/2 cup dried cherries
1 tablespoon butter	1/2 cup toasted almonds
1/2 teaspoon salt	1 tablespoon chopped fresh parsley

Combine spices and set aside.

In a large, heavy pan sauté the onion and garlic in butter until onion is limp. Add the spice mixture and salt and cook for 1 minute, stirring constantly to slightly toast the spices. Add rice and cook for another minute. Add broth, apricots, raisins, and cherries and cook, covered, for about 20 minutes or until rice is tender. Add almonds; sprinkle with parsley.

Preparation = 30 minutes. Serves 6.

Calories 330 (25% from fat); Fat 10g; Prot 10mg; Carb 55%; Sod 778mg; Chol 7mg.

Risotto with Mushrooms & Herbs

The creamy texture and delicate flavors of this risotto are very palate-pleasing. You don't have to use arborio rice, however, the end result will be more like the traditional risotto if you do. If fresh herbs are not available, use 1 teaspoon dried herbs per tablespoon of fresh.

1 1/2 tablespoons extra
   virgin olive oil
1 small onion, finely chopped
1 garlic clove, minced
1 1/2 cups arborio rice (or
   medium grain)
1/2 cup gf dry white wine
4 cups low sodium chicken
   broth (simmering)
1 tablespoon fresh basil

1 tablespoon fresh thyme
1 tablespoon fresh rosemary
1 tablespoon fresh chives
1/2 pound fresh wild
   mushrooms (sliced)
4 tablespoons Parmesan cheese
   (cow, rice, or soy)
1/2 teaspoon salt
1/4 teaspoon white pepper

Heat the olive oil in large heavy saucepan over medium heat. Sauté onion and garlic in olive oil until onion is soft but not brown, about 5 minutes. Stir in the rice and cook for about 1 minute, stirring constantly until all grains are shiny.

Add the wine and bring to boil, stirring steadily. When most of the wine is absorbed, add 1/2 cup of heated chicken broth. Cook the rice at a gentle boil, stirring constantly. When most of the liquid is absorbed, add another 1/2 cup chicken broth. Continue adding the broth, 1/2 cup at a time until the 4 cups are used up. Be sure to stir constantly. If rice seems hard, add another 1/2 cup of chicken broth (or water). Remove the pan from the heat and add herbs, mushrooms, Parmesan cheese, salt, and pepper. Serve hot.

Preparation = 30 minutes. Serves 4.

Calories 390 (17% from fat); Fat 8g; Prot 20g; Carb 64g; Sod 1024mg; Chol 4mg.

Saffron Rice Pilaf

Saffron lends a delicate flavor and color to this dish.

2 tablespoons almond slivers
1 teaspoon canola oil
1 onion, finely chopped
2 tablespoons pine nuts
1 cup long grain rice
2 1/4 cups low-sodium
  chicken broth
2 teaspoons lemon zest

1/4 teaspoon saffron
1/2 cup golden raisins
1/2 teaspoon salt
1/2 teaspoon thyme
1/8 teaspoon cardamom
1 tablespoon chopped fresh
  parsley

Toast almonds in pie plate in 400 degree oven for 5 minutes, or until golden brown. Set aside.

Heat canola oil in medium-sized heavy saucepan over medium heat. Sauté onions and pine nuts until the onions are soft and pine nuts lightly browned, 5-7 minutes, stirring frequently. Stir in rice and cook an additional 3-4 minutes, stirring frequently. This lightly toasts the rice and produces a fuller flavor. Add the chicken broth, lemon zest, saffron, raisins, salt, thyme, and cardamom. Stir well.

Reduce heat to low, cover, and simmer until all the liquid is absorbed, about 15-20 minutes. Remove from heat, fluff with fork. Stir in the almonds. Sprinkle with parsley. Serve hot. Preparation = 30 minutes. Serves 4.

Calories 208 (17% from fat); Fat 4; Prot 9g; Carb 38; Sod 468mg; Chol 0mg.

Wild Rice Pancakes with Pecans

Pancakes make an unusual, but very delectable side dish when served with an elegant dinner. You can serve them plain or with a topping such as applesauce or gravy. These pancakes can be the basis for a main dish when topped with a meat or fish sauce.

2/3 cup wild rice, rinsed
3 cups low-sodium chicken broth
1/2 cup brown rice flour
1/2 teaspoon baking powder
1/2 teaspoon baking soda
1/4 teaspoon black pepper
2 tablespoons dried chives
1/4 teaspoon dried thyme

1/2 teaspoon salt
1 large egg
1/2 cup buttermilk (or 1 teaspoon cider vinegar with enough non-dairy milk to equal 1/2 cup)
1/4 cup pecans, chopped
cooking spray

Combine wild rice and chicken broth in medium saucepan. Bring to boil, then reduce heat and simmer until wild rice is tender, about 40 minutes. Drain. Cool to room temperature.

Mix flour, baking powder, baking soda, black pepper, chives, thyme, and salt in medium bowl.

In a small bowl, whisk together the egg and buttermilk. Add to flour mixture and stir until well blended. Mix in cooked wild rice and chopped pecans.

Coat large nonstick skillet with cooking spray. On medium heat, drop batter onto skillet to form 3-inch pancakes.

Cook until golden brown, about two minutes per side. Repeat with remaining batter, using more cooking spray if necessary. Makes 12 pancakes.

Preparation = 1 hour. Serves 4. (3 pancakes per serving)

Calories 198 (8% from fat); Fat 2g; Prot 16g; Carb 35g; Sod 908mg; Chol 54mg.

Wild Rice with Dried Fruits

The combination of nutty, crunchy wild rice and the sweet, yet tart flavor of dried fruit makes an irresistible dish.

1 cup wild rice, rinsed
1/2 cup chopped green onion
3 cups water
1/2 cup chopped dried apricots
1/4 cup golden raisins
2 tablespoons fresh parsley
1/4 cup pine nuts, toasted

1 teaspoon olive oil
2 tablespoons balsamic vinegar
2 tablespoons orange juice
1/4 teaspoon orange zest
1 garlic clove, minced
1/4 teaspoon salt
1/8 teaspoon black pepper

Cook rice and green onions in 3 cups water for 45 minutes, or until tender. Drain.

Combine rice with apricots, raisins, parsley, and toasted pine nuts. Toss gently.

Combine oil, vinegar, orange juice, orange zest, minced garlic, salt, and pepper in screw-top jar. Shake vigorously to blend well. Pour over rice mixture and toss gently. Serve hot. Preparation = 45 minutes. Serves 4.

Calories 282 (20% from fat); Fat 7g; Prot 10g; Carb 52g; Sod 150mg; Chol 0mg.

Boston Baked Beans

No picnic is complete without this summer favorite. If you don't have time for this long-simmering version, substitute 2 cans (16 ounces each) of rinsed and drained pork'n'beans for the dried navy beans. Combine all remaining ingredients (except water) and heat to serving temperature in microwave.

2 cups dried navy beans, washed and picked over
water for soaking
4 cups water for cooking
1/2 cup dark molasses
1/4 cup brown sugar, packed
1 teaspoon dry mustard
1/4 teaspoon ground cloves
1/4 teaspoon chili powder
1/4 teaspoon black pepper
2 tablespoons dried minced onion
1/3 cup gf ketchup
1/2 teaspoon salt
cooking spray

Place beans in large Dutch oven and cover with water to 2 inches above beans. Bring to boil, then let stand 1 hour. Drain. Combine beans with 4 cups water plus remaining ingredients, except ketchup and salt. Cover and bake at 325 degrees for 3 1/2 to 4 hours. Stir occasionally. Add ketchup and salt, cover again, and bake another 30-45minutes or until beans are tender. Preparation = 5 hours. Serves 10.

Calories 215 (3% from fat); Fat .6g; Prot 10g; Carb 45g; Sod 213mg; Chol 0mg.

Southwestern Beans

Beans are almost a staple in the Southwest. Here, they're combined with interesting herbs and spices to produce a wonderful blend of flavors and aroma.

1 slice bacon, uncooked	1/8 teaspoon ground cloves
1 small onion, chopped	1 tablespoon gf instant coffee powder
1 garlic clove, minced	1 tablespoon brown sugar, packed
1 bay leaf	1 pound dried pinto beans
2 teaspoons dried oregano	(picked over, washed)
1 teaspoon ground cumin	6 cups water

In heavy Dutch oven, fry bacon until crisp and brown. Remove bacon from skillet and crumble when cool. Add chopped onion to same pan and sauté over medium heat in remaining bacon fat until golden brown. Return crumbled bacon slice to pan and add remaining ingredients. Bring to boil, then reduce heat and cook, covered, for 2-3 hours or until beans are tender.

CROCK POT: When ingredients are fully assembled, transfer mixture to crock pot and cook on medium-high heat for 2-3 hours, depending on crock pot temperature settings.

REFRIED BEANS: To fry beans, place 1 teaspoon canola oil in large, heavy skillet that has been sprayed with cooking spray. Add 2 cups cooked Southwestern Beans. Mash beans completely, using a potato masher or spatula. Cook, uncovered, over medium heat about 10 minutes or until thick, stirring often.

Preparation = 3 hours. Serves 6.

Calories 331 (15% from fat); Fat 6g; Prot 19g; Carb 52g; Sod 265mg; Chol 8mg.

Red Beans & Rice

This is a great dish—high in fiber and low in fat and calories.

1 small yellow onion, chopped
1 celery stalk, chopped
3 garlic cloves, minced
1 teaspoon olive oil
1 pound dried red beans
   (not kidney beans)
1 teaspoon dried basil
1 teaspoon dried tarragon
1 teaspoon dried rosemary
1 1/2 teaspoons salt

1 teaspoon black pepper
1/3 cup brown sugar, packed
2 dashes hot pepper sauce
2 bay leaves
1 smoked ham hock
   (trimmed, sliced)
water to cover beans
4 cups cooked white rice
1 tablespoon parsley

In large, heavy saucepan over medium heat, sauté onion, celery, and garlic in 1 teaspoon olive oil until translucent.

Rinse and pick over beans to remove stones or debris. Add to saucepan along with basil, tarragon, rosemary, salt, black pepper, brown sugar, hot pepper sauce, and bay leaves. Trim as much fat as possible from ham hock and add to beans. Add enough water to cover beans and simmer over medium heat for 2 hours. Serve over 4 cups cooked white rice. Garnish with parsley.

CROCK POT: Assemble the ingredients in the morning and cook all day.

Preparation = 2 hours. Serves 6.

Calories 398 (4% from fat); Fat 2g; Prot 17g; Carb 80g; Sod 557mg; Chol 0mg.

Veggiburgers

You'll never miss the meat in these burgers. Substitute 1 1/3 cups garbanzo beans for the quinoa, if you prefer. Make sure quinoa is appropriate for your diet.

2/3 cup quinoa, rinsed 3 times
2/3 cup brown lentils
2/3 cup brown rice
3 cups boiling water
1/4 cup canola or olive oil
2 cups grated carrots
1 cup chopped onion
1 cup chopped celery
1/4 cup shelled sunflower seeds
1 large minced garlic clove

1 teaspoon dried basil
1 teaspoon dried thyme
1 teaspoon dried oregano
1 teaspoon salt
1/2 teaspoon black pepper
2 tablespoons Dijonnaise mustard
4 large eggs
6 tablespoons brown rice flour
additional oil for frying
lettuce leaves and sliced tomatoes

Rinse quinoa in sieve at least 3 times or until water is clear, rubbing grains between fingers to dislodge coating. Drain.

Combine quinoa, lentils, and brown rice in 3 cups boiling water. Cover, and reduce heat to low. Cook until grains are tender, about 40 minutes. Drain and cool.

Sauté carrots, onion, celery, sunflower seeds, and garlic in oil in heavy skillet over low-medium heat about 8-10 minutes. Add to grains. Cool slightly. Stir in basil, thyme, oregano, salt, and pepper. Remove 1 cup of mixture and puree in food processor. Return to grain mixture.

Stir mustard, beaten eggs, and flour into grain mixture. Press 1/2 cup of the mixture between hands to form patties.
Cook patties in heavy skillet in canola oil until golden brown on each side, about 5 minutes per side.

Serve plain or on Hamburger Buns (See Index). Garnish with lettuce, tomatoes, and condiments of your choice.
Preparation = 1 hour. Serves 8. (2 burgers each)
Calories 338 (35% from fat); Fat 13g; Prot 13g; Carb 43g; Sod 330mg; Chol 106mg.

DESSERTS

Cakes
Carrot Cake 99
Cheesecake (New York) 107
Chocolate Pound Cake 100
Easy Chocolate Cheesecake 108
Flourless Chocolate Torte 109
Gingerbread w/ Lemon Sauce 106
Mexican Chocolate Cake 101
Spice Cake 103
Sponge Cake 105
Yellow Cake 102
Pineapple Upside-Down Cake 101

Bars & Cookies
Anise-Pine Nut Cookies 118
Apricot Rum Balls 115
Biscotti 114
Chocolate Brownies 110
Chocolate Chip Cookies 111
Chocolate Wafer Cookies 112
Coconut Macaroons 113
Gingersnaps 116
Lemon Bars 117
Mexican Wedding Cakes 115
Vanilla Wafers 118

Fruit Desserts
Bananas w/ Rum Sauce 97
Blackberry Cobbler 95
Cherry-Apricot Crisp 96
Clafouti 98

Puddings & Custards
Bread Pudding w/ Lemon Sauce 128
Butterscotch Pudding 123
Chocolate Pudding 124
Chocolate Soufflé 125
Lemon Pudding 129
Mexican Flan 126
Natillas 127
Vanilla Custard 130

Pies
Banana Cream Pie 119
Boston Cream Pie 119
Coconut Cream Pie 119
Crumb Crust for Pies 121
Pie Crust of Dried Fruit & Nuts 121
Pastry Crust for Pies 122
Rhubarb Meringue Dessert 120

Miscellaneous
Chocolate Glaze 133
Coffee 7-Minute Frosting 134
Cream Cheese Frosting 99
Cream Puffs 131
Crepes 132
Lemon Sauce 106, 128
Shortbread 51
White Chocolate Topping 164

All kinds of desserts—cakes, pies, cookies, and bars—are off-limits to wheat and gluten-sensitive persons because they're made with wheat. Of course, in today's weight-conscious society, desserts are also off-limits for other reasons, as well. But, it's no fun to avoid dessert, especially when those around you are enjoying it. In this section, you'll find a tempting array of sweets specially designed for you!

Some of these desserts are family favorites such as Gingerbread, Chocolate Chip Cookies, Chocolate Cake, and Banana Cream Pie. Others simply satisfy our need for indulgence, such as Cheesecake, Chocolate Soufflé, and Cream Puffs. But, there are also fruit desserts such as Blackberry Cobbler and Clafouti. And there are the traditional Southwestern favorites of Flan, Natillas, and Mexican Wedding Cakes.

While this is not a low-fat, low calorie cookbook, much of the fat and sugar have been removed from the recipes in this section. There's even a Chocolate Cheesecake that has fewer than 200 calories per serving and almost no fat!

So, enjoy these desserts. Think of them as your reward for committing to and sticking with a wheat-free, gluten-free diet.

Blackberry Cobbler

Fresh blackberries are such a treat. . . nestled under this rich, biscuit blanket. Top with frozen yogurt or ice cream, if you wish.

FRUIT FILLING
4 cups blackberries (washed and sorted)
1/2 cup sugar
1 tablespoon quick-cooking tapioca
1 teaspoon grated lemon peel
1 tablespoon fresh lemon juice
1 teaspoon gf vanilla
cooking spray

COBBLER TOPPING
1/2 cup white or brown rice flour
1/4 cup potato starch
1/4 cup tapioca flour
1/4 teaspoon xanthan gum
1 teaspoon grated lemon peel
1/2 teaspoon baking soda
1/2 teaspoon baking powder
1/4 teaspoon salt
1/2 cup non-fat plain yogurt or 1/3 cup milk (cow, rice, or soy)
2 tablespoons lemon juice
2 tablespoons oleo, melted
1 teaspoon gf vanilla
2 large egg whites

Preheat oven to 400 degrees. Spray 8 x 8-inch pan with cooking spray. Combine fruit filling ingredients in prepared pan and set aside.

In large bowl, combine flours, xanthan gum, lemon peel, baking soda, baking powder, and salt.

In another bowl, whisk together yogurt (or milk), lemon juice, margarine, vanilla, and egg whites. Add to dry ingredients, stirring just until dry ingredients are moistened. Drop by tablespoonfuls onto blackberry mixture.

Bake for 20-25 minutes or filling is bubbly and crust is golden. Serve warm.

Preparation = 45 minutes. Serves 6.

Calories 267 (15% from fat); Fat 5 g; Prot 5g; Carb 53g; Sod 302mg; Chol 0mg.

Cherry-Apricot Crisp

The combination of cherries, dried apricots, and a hint of almond is very pleasing to your palate.

1 pound red sour cherries (pitted and drained)
1 package dried apricots (6-ounce package, chopped)
3/4 cup sugar
2 tablespoons tapioca (quick-cooking)
1/2 teaspoon gf almond extract
2 tablespoons canola oil
1/2 cup brown rice flour
1/4 cup brown sugar, packed
1/4 teaspoon cinnamon
1/2 teaspoon grated lemon peel
1/4 cup sliced almonds
cooking spray

Spray 8 x 8-inch square pan with cooking spray. Combine first five ingredients (cherries through almond extract) in prepared pan. Let stand for 30 minutes.

Preheat oven to 375 degrees.

Cut oil, flour, brown sugar, cinnamon, and lemon peel together with pastry blender until mixture resembles coarse meal. Mix in almonds. Sprinkle topping over fruit, leaving a 1-inch border on all sides.

Bake until topping is browned, about 30 minutes. Let cool for 20 minutes before serving. Top with frozen vanilla yogurt (optional).

Preparation = 1 1/4 hours. Serves 6.

Calories 383 (18% from fat); Fat 8g; Prot 4g; Carb 77g; Sod 10 mg; Chol 0mg.

Bananas with Rum Sauce

This is so simple and a refreshing change from cakes, pies or cookies for dessert. And, this dessert provides another serving of fruit to your daily intake.

2 teaspoons canola oil
2 tablespoons brown sugar
2 teaspoons gf vanilla extract
1/4 cup thawed orange juice
  concentrate

1/2 teaspoon cinnamon
1 teaspoon gf rum extract
4 bananas
additional cinnamon for garnish

Combine oil, brown sugar, vanilla extract, orange juice concentrate, cinnamon, and rum flavoring in large, non-stick skillet and cook for one minute over low heat.

Peel bananas. Cut each banana in half, then lengthwise so there are a total of 4 pieces per banana. Add to pan and cook for 30 seconds.

Arrange four banana pieces on each of 4 plates. Spoon sauce over bananas and garnish with a sprinkle of cinnamon.
Preparation = 10 minutes. Serves 4.
Calories 175 (14% from fat); Fat 3g; Prot 2g; Carb 38g; Sod 4mg; Chol 0mg.

Clafouti

This is one of the easiest dishes to make. A variety of different fruits will work—try apricots, cherries, or apples next time instead of peaches.

3 tablespoons white rice flour
1 tablespoon potato starch
1/2 teaspoon salt
2 large eggs
1/3 cup milk (cow, rice, or soy)

1 teaspoon gf vanilla extract
1/2 teaspoon grated lemon peel
2 tablespoons canola oil
3 cups chopped peaches
2 tablespoons powdered sugar
cooking spray

Preheat oven to 375 degrees.

Combine the flours, salt, eggs, milk, vanilla, lemon peel, and oil in a blender and whirl for one full minute on high speed. (I use a hand-held, immersion blender).

Spray one 9-inch, oven-proof skillet or 2 small, oven-proof skillets with cooking spray. Place skillet(s) over medium heat and pour in 1/4 of the batter, spreading it over the bottom of the pan. Cook until the batter resembles a cooked pancake, about 2-3 minutes. Remove from heat.

Put the fruit on top of the cooked batter. Top with remaining batter. Bake small skillets for 20-25 minutes; large skillet for 35-40 minutes, or until top is puffy and golden brown. Remove from oven and dust with powdered sugar. Serve immediately. Preparation = 45 minutes. Serves 4.

Calories 219 (40% from fat); Fat 10g; Prot 5g; Carb 27g; Sod 311 mg; Chol 110mg.

Carrot Cake

This version of the popular carrot cake derives extra flavor and texture from pineapple, coconut, and nuts. My family loved this one. Omit the frosting if you have dairy sensitivities.

1 1/2 cups brown rice flour
1/2 cup potato starch
1/2 cup soy flour
1 teaspoon xanthan gum
2 teaspoons baking soda
2 teaspoons cinnamon
1 teaspoon salt
1/2 teaspoon ground ginger
4 large eggs
1 cup brown sugar, packed
1 cup sugar
1/3 cup canola oil
1 cup non-fat plain yogurt or (3/4 cup non-dairy liquid)

1 teaspoon gf vanilla extract
3 cups shredded carrots
1 1/2 cups crushed pineapple, drained
1 cup shredded coconut
1 cup walnuts, chopped
cooking spray
FROSTING:
3 ounces cream cheese, softened
2 cups powdered sugar
2 tablespoons skim milk
1 teaspoon gf vanilla extract

Preheat oven to 350 degrees. Spray 10-cup nonstick bundt pan with cooking spray. Combine flours, xanthan gum, baking soda, cinnamon, salt, and ginger together in a bowl. Set aside.

In large mixer bowl, beat together eggs, sugars, oil, yogurt, and vanilla extract. Add flour mixture slowly until just blended. Stir in carrots, pineapple, coconut, and nuts.

Pour batter into prepared pan. Bake 45-50 minutes or until toothpick inserted in center of cake comes out clean. Cool on wire rack. Frost with Cream Cheese Frosting.

CREAM CHEESE FROSTING: Combine softened cream cheese, powdered sugar, and vanilla. Beat until smooth.

Preparation = 1 1/4 hours. Serves 12.

Calories 513 (29% from fat); Fat 17g; Prot 10g; Carb 83g; Sod 463mg; Chol 71mg. Brown Rice Substitute (not for celiacs): 1 cup quinoa flour and 1/2 cup amaranth flour.

Chocolate Pound Cake

This is a very versatile dessert. Serve it plain, with a dusting of powdered sugar, or with a glaze of 1/2 cup powdered sugar and 2 tablespoons strongly brewed coffee. Save the leftovers and crumble them into crusts for pies or cheesecakes.

1/2 cup brown rice flour
1/4 cup potato starch
1/4 cup tapioca flour
1/2 cup unsweetened
  Dutch cocoa powder
1/2 teaspoon xanthan gum
1/2 teaspoon baking soda
1/4 teaspoon baking powder
1/4 teaspoon salt
2 tablespoons strongly
  brewed coffee

2 1/2 ounces prune baby food
  (1 jar)
1 teaspoon gf vanilla extract
1/2 cup nonfat coffee yogurt
  (or plain yogurt or 1/3 cup
  milk -cow, rice, or soy)
1/4 stick unsalted butter or oleo
2 large eggs
1 cup sugar
1 teaspoon grated orange
  peel (optional)
cooking spray

Preheat oven to 350 degrees. Spray 6 or 8-cup tube or bundt cake pan with cooking spray. Sift flours, cocoa, xanthan gum, baking soda, baking powder, and salt in a bowl. In another small bowl, combine coffee, prunes, vanilla, and yogurt.

In large bowl, use electric mixer to beat butter, eggs, sugar, and orange peel for four minutes at high speed. At low speed, add flour mixture alternately with yogurt mixture in three separate additions. Continually scrape edges of bowl.

Place batter in prepared pan and bake for 40 minutes, or until toothpick inserted into center comes out clean. Remove from oven and cool on rack for 10 minutes. Turn cake onto serving plate. Cool completely.

Preparation = 1 1/4 hours. Serves 12.

Calories 150 (7% from fat); Fat 1g; Prot 4g; Carb 33g; Sod 127mg; Chol 18mg.
Brown Rice Substitute (not for celiacs): 1/2 cup amaranth flour.

Mexican Chocolate Cake

For a Southwestern adaptation of the Chocolate Pound Cake on the previous page, try this version.

Add 1 1/2 tablespoons gf almond extract and 1 tablespoon ground cinnamon to Chocolate Pound Cake on previous page. Bake as instructed. Frost with Chocolate Glaze (See Index).

Preparation = 1 1/4 hours. Serves 12.
Calories 150 (7% from fat); Fat 1g; Prot 4g; Carb 33g; Sod 127mg; Chol 18mg.

Pineapple Upside-Down Cake

Using the Yellow Cake recipe (See Index), this family favorite is so easy.

1 gf Yellow Cake (See Index)
1/2 cup brown sugar, packed
16 ounces pineapple rings in
   juice, drained (about 7 rings)

7 maraschino cherries,
   drained (or raspberries)
cooking spray
whipping cream for garnish
   (optional)

Preheat oven to 350 degrees.

In 10-inch pie plate or skillet (or special pan designed for upside-down cake), spray with cooking spray. Evenly sprinkle brown sugar over bottom of pan. Arrange 7 pineapple slices with maraschino cherry in center of each circle. Pour Yellow Cake batter evenly on top.

Bake 35-40 minutes or until top springs back when touched. Cool 5 minutes, then invert onto serving plate. Garnish with whipping cream, if desired.

Preparation = 45 minutes. Serves 8.
Calories 354 (4% from fat); Fat 2g; Prot 1g; Carb 87g; Sod 128mg; Chol 8mg.

Yellow Cake

A good yellow cake is an absolute essential for so many recipes. Freeze portions of this cake for later use, such as the Yogurt Breakfast Trifle (See Index). Or, bake as cupcakes.

6 tablespoons unsalted butter or oleo
1 cup sugar
2 large eggs, beaten
1 3/4 teaspoons grated lemon peel
1 cup white rice flour
6 tablespoons potato starch
2 tablespoons tapioca flour

1 teaspoon xanthan gum
1/4 teaspoon baking powder
1/4 teaspoon baking soda
1/3 teaspoon salt
3/4 cup buttermilk (or 1 tablespoon lemon juice plus enough non-dairy milk to equal 3/4 cup)
1 teaspoon gf vanilla extract
cooking spray

Preheat oven to 325 degrees. Coat an 8 x 4-inch nonstick loaf pan with cooking spray. Set aside.

Using an electric mixer and a large mixer bowl, cream together the butter and sugar on medium speed until light and fluffy. Mix in the eggs on low speed until blended. Add the grated lemon peel.

In a medium bowl, sift together the flours, xanthan gum, baking powder, baking soda, and salt. In another medium bowl, combine the buttermilk and vanilla. On low speed, beat the dry ingredients into the butter mixture, alternating with the buttermilk—beginning and ending with the dry ingredients. Mix just until combined. Spoon the batter into the prepared pan and smooth the top.

Bake the cake for about 50 minutes or until top is golden brown and a cake tester inserted into center comes out clean. Cool cake in pan for 5 minutes, then remove from pan and cool on rack. Cake can be frozen (wrapped in foil) for one month. Preparation = 1 hour. Serves 10.

Calories 238 (30% from fat); Fat 8g; Prot 4g; Carb 38g; Sod 148mg; Chol 61mg.

Spice Cake

The spicy flavors of this delicious cake combine very well with the coffee-flavored frosting. You'd never know this cake is wheat-free.

1 cup brown rice flour
2/3 cup potato starch
1/3 cup tapioca flour
1 teaspoon xanthan gum
1 3/4 teaspoons baking soda
3/4 teaspoon salt
1 tablespoon ground ginger
2 teaspoons ground cinnamon
1/2 teaspoon ground nutmeg
1/4 teaspoon ground cloves

1 1/2 cups milk (cow, soy, rice, or nut)
1 1/2 cups brown sugar, packed
1/4 cup butter or oleo
1/4 cup canola oil
1/3 cup molasses
1 teaspoon gf vanilla extract
2 large eggs, beaten
cooking spray
Coffee 7-Minute Frosting (See below)

Preheat oven to 325 degrees. Coat a 9-inch round nonstick pan with cooking spray. Line bottom with waxed paper, then spray again.

Sift together the flours, xanthan gum, baking soda, salt, ginger, cinnamon, nutmeg, and cloves in a large mixing bowl.

Combine milk and brown sugar in heavy saucepan and bring just to a boil over medium heat. Remove from heat and add butter, canola oil, molasses, and vanilla.

When butter is melted, add butter and sugar mixture to flour mixture in mixing bowl and mix until thoroughly blended. Add eggs and mix until blended.

Pour batter into prepared pan. Bake for 50 minutes, or until toothpick inserted in center of cake comes out clean.
Cool cake on pan for 5 minutes. Invert the cake onto a plate to finish cooling and remove waxed paper.
COFFEE 7-MINUTE FROSTING: Dissolve 1 teaspoon instant coffee crystals in 1 teaspoon very hot tap water or hot coffee. Set aside.

In double boiler over boiling water, combine 3 large egg whites, 1 1/4 cups granulated sugar, 1/4 teaspoon cream of tartar, and 3 tablespoons cold water. Beat with portable electric mixer for 7 minutes. Remove from heat and stir in 1 teaspoon vanilla extract and coffee liquid and beat with a spatula until glossy and desired spreading consistency is reached. Use immediately.

Cut cooled cake in half, horizontally, and remove top half. Spread about 3/4 cup of the frosting on the bottom half. Place top half of cake on bottom half and frost sides and top. Top with garnishes of your choice including shaved chocolate, cocoa powder, or chopped nuts.

Preparation = 1 1/4 hours. Serves 10.

Calories 329 (32% from fat); Fat 112g; Prot 4g; Carb 53g; Sod 459mg; Chol 17mg. Brown Rice Substitute (not for celiacs): 3/4 cup amaranth flour and 1/4 cup quinoa flour.

Sponge Cake

This cake, similar to angel food cake, is wonderful to serve with fresh fruit, such as strawberries. . . and a dollop of whipped cream.

1/4 cup fresh lemon juice	1/4 cup granulated sugar
1 teaspoon grated lemon peel	1 cup potato starch
9 extra large eggs	1/4 teaspoon cream of tartar
1 cup powdered sugar	1 teaspoon gf vanilla extract

Preheat oven to 375 degrees. Mix lemon juice and lemon peel.

Separate 7 of the eggs, being careful not to get any egg yolk in the egg whites. To the 7 egg yolks, add 2 whole eggs. Beat until foamy and lemon-colored. Gradually add powdered sugar and granulated sugar. Mix again. Add vanilla extract.

Put potato starch into sifter. Sift potato starch into yolk mixture, alternating with lemon juice and peel. Use low speed of mixer.

Beat egg whites until stiff peaks form. Add cream of tartar. Pour yolk mixture over egg whites. Use wire whisk or perforated spoon to carefully and slowly fold egg whites into egg mixture. It's important not to disturb the egg whites too much or the cake will fall.

Pour batter into ungreased, 10-inch tube pan with removable bottom. Bake on center shelf of preheated oven for 30-35 minutes. Remove from oven. Invert cake pan (cake remains in pan) on a rack to cool for an hour. Remove cake from pan using sharp knife to loosen edges. Carefully remove bottom of pan from cake with a thin, sharp knife.

Preparation = 1 1/2 hours. Serves 12.

Calories 138 (24% from fat); Fat 34g; Prot 5g; Carb 22g; Sod 48mg; Chol 159mg.

Gingerbread with Lemon Sauce

Dense, moist and flavorful—this gingerbread is further enhanced by Lemon Sauce. Or, top with whipped cream or powdered sugar.

1/2 cup brown sugar, packed
1/4 cup canola oil
1 large egg
1/2 cup molasses
3/4 cup brown rice flour
1/2 cup potato starch
1/4 cup tapioca flour
1 teaspoon baking soda
1 1/2 teaspoons ground ginger
3/4 teaspoon cinnamon
1/2 teaspoon cloves
1/2 teaspoon salt

1/2 cup buttermilk (or 1 teaspoon cider vinegar plus enough non-dairy milk to equal 1/2 cup)
LEMON SAUCE
1/4 cup sugar
1 tablespoon cornstarch
1/8 teaspoon salt
1/2 cup hot water
2 teaspoons grated lemon peel
1 tablespoon lemon juice
2 teaspoons butter or oleo
cooking spray

Preheat oven to 350 degrees. In large bowl, cream brown sugar and canola oil with electric mixer. Add egg, then molasses and beat well. Mix flours with baking soda, ginger, cinnamon, cloves, and salt. Add flour mixture alternately with buttermilk to creamed mixture.

Pour into 8 or 9-inch square nonstick pan coated with cooking spray. Bake for 30 minutes, or until a toothpick inserted into center of gingerbread comes out clean. Cool pan on wire rack.
LEMON SAUCE: In small saucepan, combine sugar, cornstarch, and salt until blended. Gradually stir in hot water. Cook and stir over medium heat until mixture boils and thickens. Stir in lemon peel, lemon juice, and butter. Serve warm over Gingerbread.

Preparation = 45 minutes. Serves 6.

Calories 396 (27% from fat); Fat 12g; Prot 5g; Carb 69g; Sod 491mg; Chol 39mg. Brown Rice Substitute (not for celiacs): 1/2 cup amaranth flour and 1/4 cup quinoa flour.

Cheesecake (New York Style)

This tastes just like the authentic New York cheesecake. For variation, top with fresh fruit such as strawberries or blueberries. This recipe is dairy-based.

1 cup crushed Vanilla Wafers, (See Index)
1 cup low-fat dry curd cottage cheese
3 large eggs
2 8-ounce packages of no-fat cream cheese, softened

1 teaspoon grated lemon peel
2 tablespoons fresh lemon juice
1 tablespoon tapioca flour
1 cup sugar
1 1/2 teaspoons gf vanilla extract
1/4 teaspoon salt
cooking spray

CRUST: Spray bottom and sides of 7-inch springform pan with cooking spray. Press crushed Vanilla Wafers onto bottom of pan and slightly up the sides. Chill while preparing filling. FILLING: Preheat oven to 300 degrees. In food processor, puree cottage cheese and eggs for 3 minutes until cottage cheese is very, very smooth. Add remaining ingredients and puree until very smooth. Slowly pour into chilled crust. Bake for 1 hour or until cheesecake is set. Let cool in pan on wire rack. Cover and chill up to 8 hours or overnight. Remove sides of pan and transfer cheesecake to serving plate. Garnish with fresh strawberries or raspberries.

Preparation = 1 1/4 hours. Serves 10.

Calories 253 (22% from fat); Fat 6g; Prot 8g; Carb 42g; Sod 181mg; Chol 66mg.

Easy Chocolate Cheesecake

One of my tasters called this dessert "rich and yummy" even though it uses no-fat cream cheese and low-fat cottage cheese. Be sure to keep a few Chocolate Wafer Cookies on hand for the crust. This dessert is so quick and easy to make in your food processor. This recipe is dairy-based.

1/4 cup crushed Chocolate Wafer Cookies (See Index)
2 8-ounce packages no-fat cream cheese
1 cup cottage cheese (1%-fat)
1 cup brown sugar, packed
1/3 cup unsweetened cocoa + 1 tablespoon (not Dutch)
1/2 cup tapioca flour

1/4 cup skim milk
1 teaspoon gf vanilla extract
1 teaspoon gf chocolate extract (optional)
1/4 teaspoon salt
1 large egg
2 tablespoons gf chocolate chips
cooking spray

Preheat oven to 300 degrees.

Sprinkle Chocolate Wafer Cookie crumbs in bottom of 7-inch springform pan that has been coated with cooking spray. Set aside.

In food processor, cream together the cream cheese and cottage cheese until very, very smooth. Add brown sugar, cocoa, flour, milk, vanilla extract, chocolate extract, and salt. Process until smooth. Add egg and blend just until blended. Stir in chocolate chips.

Slowly pour mixture over crumbs in pan. Bake for 1 hour, or until cheesecake is set. Let cool in pan on wire rack. Cover and chill for at least 8 hours or overnight. Remove sides of pan and transfer cake to a serving plate. Garnish with fresh fruit. Makes 12 servings.

Preparation = 1 1/4 hours. Serves 10.

Calories 166 (14% from fat); Fat 3g; Prot 7g; Carb 30g; Sod 223mg; Chol 23mg.

Flourless Chocolate Torte

This torte avoids flour altogether! If only all restaurants had at least one dessert like this for their wheat-sensitive customers!

2/3 cup brown sugar, packed
3 ounces bittersweet chocolate
1/2 cup unsweetened cocoa (not Dutch)
1/3 cup boiling water
2 large egg yolks at room temperature
3/4 cup whole almonds
1 teaspoon xanthan gum
4 large egg whites at room temperature
1/4 teaspoon cream of tartar
1 tablespoon brown sugar
1 teaspoon gf vanilla extract
1/2 teaspoon gf almond extract
cooking spray

Preheat oven to 375 degrees. Line bottom of 8-inch spring-form pan with parchment paper. Spray parchment paper and sides of pan with spray.

Combine brown sugar, bittersweet chocolate, cocoa, and boiling water in small bowl. Stir until chocolate is melted. Whisk in egg yolks.

Finely grind almonds in food processor. Add xanthan gum. Using electric mixer, beat egg whites and cream of tartar until soft peaks form. Add tablespoon of brown sugar, vanilla extract, and almond extract and beat until stiff, but not dry. Carefully whisk ground almond mixture into chocolate mixture. Fold in egg whites, in two additions.

Transfer batter to prepared pan. Place pan in larger pan of boiling water so that water comes up one inch on outer sides of springform pan. Bake for 35 minutes or until toothpick inserted into center comes out clean. Cool torte in pan on rack. Cut around edge of torte to loosen from pan edges. Release pan sides. Slice into 10 pieces.

Preparation = 10 minutes. Serves 8.

Calories 217 (46% from fat); Fat 12g; Prot 7g; Carb 26g; Sod 38mg; Chol 53mg.

Chocolate Brownies

These brownies are very dense, more like fudge than cake. Serve them plain or with a dusting of powdered sugar. Or, for a really decadent brownie, top with melted bittersweet chocolate.

1/2 cup brown rice flour
2 tablespoons tapioca flour
1/2 cup cocoa (not Dutch)
1/2 teaspoon baking powder
1/2 teaspoon salt
6 tablespoons canola oil

1 1/2 cups brown sugar, packed
2 large eggs
1 teaspoon gf vanilla extract
1/2 cup chopped walnuts
cooking spray

Preheat oven to 350 degrees. Spray 8-inch square pan with cooking spray. Stir together the flours, cocoa, baking powder and salt.

In large mixing bowl, beat the oil and brown sugar with electric mixer on medium speed until well combined. Blend in eggs and vanilla. With mixer on low speed, add dry ingredients. Mix until just blended (a few lumps may remain). Stir in nuts.

Spread batter in prepared pan and bake for 35 minutes or until a toothpick inserted in center comes out almost clean. Cool brownies before cutting.

Preparation 45 minutes. Serves 16. (very small pieces)
Calories 135 (39% from fat); Fat 6g; Prot 3g; Carb 19g; Sod 92mg; Chol 27mg.
Brown Rice Substitute (not for celiacs): 1/2 cup amaranth flour

Chocolate Chip Cookies

Everybody's favorite. Now you can enjoy these treats along with everyone else. For chocolate chip bars, bake the dough in an 8 x 8-inch pan for 25-30 minutes or until golden brown.

3/4 cup white rice flour
1/2 cup potato starch
1/4 cup tapioca flour
1/2 teaspoon baking soda
1/2 teaspoon xanthan gum
1/4 teaspoon salt
1/4 cup vegetable shortening
   or oleo (room temperature,
   not melted)

5 tablespoons granulated sugar
3/4 cup brown sugar, packed
1/2 teaspoon gf vanilla extract
1 extra large egg
1 cup semisweet chocolate chips
1/4 cup chopped walnuts
cooking spray

Preheat oven to 350 degrees. Sift together flours, baking soda, xanthan gum, and salt. Set aside.

In large bowl, use electric mixer to beat vegetable shortening with granulated sugar and brown sugar until blended. Beat in vanilla extract and egg, scraping sides of bowl frequently. Beat in flour mixture on low speed, mixing thoroughly. Stir in chocolate chips and nuts.

Drop by tablespoonfuls on cookie sheet that has been coated with cooking spray. Bake on center rack of oven for 10 minutes. Cool for 2-3 minutes before removing from cookie sheet.

Preparation = 25 minutes. Makes 24 cookies.

Calories per cookie: 124 (37% from fat); Fat 5g; Prot 2g; Carb 18g; Sod 55mg; Chol 9mg.

Chocolate Wafer Cookies

Use these cookies just as you would use the purchased kind—either as a treat in themselves, or crush them into Crumb Crusts (See Index) for pies and cheesecakes. I keep a batch in the freezer, then make them into crumbs with my food processor.

1/4 cup butter or oleo at
   room temperature
2 tablespoons honey
1/2 cup brown sugar, firmly
   packed
1 large egg
1 teaspoon gf vanilla extract
1 cup brown rice flour

3 tablespoons potato starch
2 tablespoons tapioca flour
1/4 cup unsweetened cocoa
   (not Dutch)
1/2 teaspoon xanthan gum
1/2 teaspoon salt
1 1/2 teaspoons baking powder
cooking spray

In a large mixing bowl, beat together the butter, honey, brown sugar, egg, and vanilla.

In another bowl, combine the flours, cocoa, xanthan gum, salt, and baking powder. Stir this mixture into the creamed mixture. Shape the dough into a soft ball. Cover and refrigerate for 1 hour.

Preheat oven to 325 degrees. Coat cookie sheet with cooking spray.

Dust hands with cocoa powder (or cooking spray) and shape dough into 1-inch balls. Place on cookie sheet. Flatten slightly with bottom of glass dipped into cocoa powder or sprayed with cooking spray.

Bake for about 25-30 minutes or until cookies appear dry on top. Makes about 2 dozen cookies.

Preparation = 45 minutes. Serves 12 (2 cookies per serving)
Calories 137 (31% from fat); Fat 5g; Prot 2g; Carb 23g; Sod 182mg; Chol 28mg.
Brown Rice Substitute (not for celiacs): 7/8 cup amaranth flour

Coconut Macaroons

This is a very moist, chewy macaroon! Topping the macaroons with chocolate makes them even more delectable.

14 ounces sweetened coconut
   flakes (two 7- ounce packages)
2/3 cup powdered sugar
1/4 cup cream of coconut,
   (such as Coco Lopez)
1 ounce cream cheese or firm
   silken tofu

2 tablespoons rice flour
1 large egg white
1 teaspoon gf vanilla extract
dash salt
1 pound bittersweet chocolate

Preheat oven to 325 degrees. Line large cookie sheet with heavy-duty aluminum foil. Coat with cooking spray and dust with rice flour.

In food processor, chop one 7-ounce package of coconut and 2/3 cup powdered sugar until mixture feels moist. Add cream of coconut, cream cheese, rice flour, egg white, vanilla, and salt. Process until well blended, scraping down sides of bowl. Transfer dough to large bowl.

Place remaining 7-ounce package of flaked coconut in pie plate. Drop rounded tablespoonful of dough onto coconut and roll to coat completely. Use palms of hands to roll dough into balls, each about 1 1/2 inches in diameter. Arrange macaroons on cookie sheet. Bake macaroons until golden brown and just firm to touch, about 35 minutes. Cool.

Line another cookie sheet with waxed paper. Melt bittersweet chocolate in top of double boiler set over simmering water. Partially dip each macaroon into chocolate or drizzle chocolate on top. Place on wax paper and refrigerate until chocolate gets firm, about 30 minutes. Store in sealed container in refrigerator up to 3 days or freeze for 2 weeks. Best at room temperature. Preparation 1 hour. Makes 12 macaroons.

Calories per macaroon: 407 (52% from fat); Fat 25g; Prot 4g; Carb 49g; Sod 97mg; Chol 0mg.

Biscotti

These biscotti store well in a covered tin and are especially great to keep on hand for a quick snack with your coffee (or tea).

1 1/2 cups almond slivers	3/4 cup sugar
1 1/4 cups white rice flour	1 stick unsalted butter or oleo
1/2 cup potato starch	2 large eggs
1/4 cup tapioca flour	1/4 cup corn syrup
1 teaspoon baking powder	1/2 teaspoon gf vanilla extract
1 teaspoon xanthan gum	1/2 teaspoon gf almond extract
1/4 teaspoon salt	cooking spray

Preheat oven to 350 degrees. Lightly coat a nonstick cookie sheet with cooking spray.

Process almonds in food processor until finely ground. Add flours, baking powder, xanthan gum, salt, and sugar and pulse on and off until mixture resembles coarse meal.

Lightly beat the butter, eggs, corn syrup, vanilla extract, and almond extract together in a small bowl. Pour the egg mixture evenly over dough in food processor and pulse the machine on and off about 20 times to moisten dough.

Form dough into ball. Divide dough in half and shape each half into a 12-inch long log, about 2 inches wide and about 1/2-inch thick.

Bake about 20 minutes, or until dough is browned at edges. Remove from oven and cool for 5 minutes. Leave oven on. With a sharp knife or electric knife, cut each log on the diagonal into about 3/4-inch thick slices. Arrange slices on their sides (cut sides down) on the cookie sheet and return to the oven.

Bake for another 5-7 minutes, or until biscotti starts to brown. Transfer to wire rack. Makes about 2 1/2 dozen biscotti. Preparation = 45 minutes. Serves 30. (1 biscotti each)
Calories 105 (35% from fat); Fat 4g; Prot 3g; Carb 15g; Sod 36mg; Chol 14 mg.

Apricot Rum Balls

Keep these on hand for unexpected holiday company.

2 cups dried apricots	1/2 teaspoon gf vanilla extract
2/3 cup almonds	2 teaspoons orange zest
2/3 cup powdered sugar	3 ounces bittersweet
1/4 cup gf light or dark rum	chocolate, crushed

In a food processor, combine apricots and almonds. Pulse just until finely chopped. Transfer to medium bowl. Stir in sugar, rum, vanilla, orange zest and crushed bittersweet chocolate. (Chocolate should be in pieces no larger than 1/4 inch). Roll mixture into 1-inch balls. Store in refrigerator, tightly covered. Preparation = 15 minutes. Serves 24. (1 cookie each)

Calories per cookie: 96 (29% from fat); Fat 3g; Prot 2g; Carb 16g; Sod 2mg; Chol 0mg.

Mexican Wedding Cakes

Store these Southwestern treats in a cool place.

1 cup butter or oleo, softened	1/2 cup tapioca flour
1 cup powdered sugar	1/3 cup finely chopped pecans
1 1/2 cups white rice flour	1 teaspoon gf vanilla extract
1/2 cup potato starch	1/2 teaspoon salt
1 teaspoon xanthan gum	cooking spray

Preheat oven to 350 degrees. Combine all ingredients in food processor until mixture forms ball. Shape into ball and refrigerate, covered. Form into 1 1/2-inch balls. Bake balls on cookie sheet (sprayed with cooking spray) for 10-15 minutes or until set. Roll in powdered sugar while warm. Makes 36. Preparation = 30 minutes. (1 cookie per serving.)

Calories per cookie: 100 (50% from fat); Fat 6g; Prot 1g; Carb 12g; Sod 81mg; Chol 14mg.

Gingersnaps

These cookies are great for snacking at home, but they also travel very, very well. Keep some in your freezer to make crumb crusts for pies. You may also mix the dough in a food processor, if you wish.

1/4 cup butter or oleo
3 tablespoons molasses
1/2 cup brown sugar, packed
1 teaspoon gf vanilla extract
3/4 cup brown rice flour
1/2 cup tapioca flour
1/4 cup soy flour
1 teaspoon xanthan gum
1/2 teaspoon salt

1 teaspoon baking powder
1 1/2 teaspoons ground ginger
1 1/2 teaspoons ground cinnamon
1/4 teaspoon ground nutmeg
1/4 teaspoon ground cloves
2 tablespoons water (if needed)
1 tablespoon granulated sugar
    (for rolling)
cooking spray

In large mixing bowl, beat together the butter, molasses, brown sugar, and vanilla.

In another bowl, combine the flours, xanthan gum, salt, baking powder, and spices. Stir this mixture into the flour mixture, alternating with the water (using only enough water to hold the dough together in a soft ball). Refrigerate for one hour.

Preheat oven to 325 degrees.

Dust hands with rice flour and shape into 1-inch balls. Roll each ball in the granulated sugar and place on cookie sheet that has been sprayed with cooking spray. Flatten slightly with bottom of drinking glass or with your palm.

Bake for 20-25 minutes, or until cookies start to brown on the bottom. Cool cookies on the cookie sheet for about 5 minutes, then transfer to wire rack to cool. Store in airtight containers. Preparation = 45 minutes. Makes 16 cookies.

Calories per cookie: 104 (27% from fat); Fat 3g; Prot 3g; Carb 2g; Sod 122mg; Chol 8mg.

Lemon Bars

This is one of my favorite desserts. I avoided it for years until I developed this wheat-free version.

1/2 cup white rice flour
1/4 cup potato starch
1/4 cup tapioca flour
1/2 cup cold unsalted
   butter or oleo
1/3 cup powdered sugar
1 cup granulated sugar

1/2 teaspoon baking powder
2 large eggs
1/4 cup fresh lemon juice
2 teaspoons grated lemon peel
cooking spray
powdered sugar for dusting

Preheat oven to 350 degrees. Coat 8-inch square pan with cooking spray.

CRUST: In small bowl, mix together the flours. In food processor, mix together the butter, 2/3 cup of the mixed flours, and 1/3 cup powdered sugar until crumbly. Press into pan. Bake 20 minutes or until set. Cool.

FILLING: In bowl, whisk together the remaining flours, 1 cup granulated sugar, baking powder, eggs, lemon juice, and grated lemon peel. Pour over crust. Bake 20-30 minutes or until set. Cool.

Cut into 8 pieces. Dust with additional powdered sugar.
Preparation = 45 minutes. Serves 8.

Calories 302 (37% from fat); Fat 12g; Prot 3g; Carb 44g; Sod 41mg; Chol 84mg.

Vanilla Wafers

These little cookies taste great and they're indispensable—they travel well, they make great Crumb Crusts for Pies (See Index) and they can be crumbled over puddings and fruit desserts.

1/4 cup butter or oleo at room temperature
2 tablespoons honey
1/2 cup brown sugar, packed
3 teaspoons gf vanilla extract
3/4 cup brown rice flour
1/2 cup sweet rice flour
1/4 cup potato starch
1/2 teaspoon xanthan gum
1/2 teaspoon salt
3/4 teaspoon baking soda
1 teaspoon cider vinegar
2 tablespoons water (if needed)
cooking spray

In a food processor, combine all ingredients—adding water only if necessary. Shape into ball. Cover tightly and refrigerate for 1 hour.

Preheat oven to 325 degrees.

With rice floured hands, shape dough into 1-inch balls. Place on cookie sheet that has been sprayed with cooking spray. Bake for about 20-25 minutes, or until cookies are lightly browned. Remove from cookie sheet and cool. Makes 16-20.

ANISE-PINE NUT COOKIES: Add 1-2 teaspoons gf anise flavoring and 1/4 cup toasted pine nuts. Bake as usual. Makes 16 cookies.

Preparation = 45 minutes. (Excludes chill time)

Calories per cookie: 105 (27% from fat); Fat 3g; Prot 1g; Carb 18g; Sod 132mg; Chol 8mg.

Cream Pies

Cream pies are so delicious and rich-tasting, yet they're often made with wheat. Now, you can enjoy them using these recipes.

1 recipe Vanilla Custard (See Index)   **1 recipe Crumb Crust for Pies (See Index)**

BANANA CREAM PIE: Slice 2 bananas into prepared Crumb Crust for Pies. Top with Vanilla Custard. Chill. To serve, top each slice with 1 tablespoon whipped cream (optional).
Preparation = 10 minutes. (Excludes chill time). Serves 6.
Calories 263 (45% from fat); Fat 13g; Prot 4g; Carb 33g; Sod 82mg; Chol 161mg.

COCONUT CREAM MERINGUE PIE: Add 1 cup sweetened coconut flakes to Vanilla Custard. Fill Crumb Crust for Pies with Vanilla Custard. Top with meringue made from 2 egg whites beaten stiff with 2 tablespoons sugar. Sprinkle with 2 tablespoons of sweetened coconut flakes. Bake in preheated 425-degree oven until meringue browns. Chill before cutting.
Preparation = 15 minutes. (Excludes chill time). Serves 6.
Calories 281 (44% from fat); Fat 14g; Prot 5g; Carb 35g; Sod 132mg; Chol 148mg.

BOSTON CREAM PIE: Bake Yellow Cake (See Index) in 8-inch round cake pan. Slice horizontally into two layers (or bake in two 8-inch pans). Top bottom layer with Vanilla Custard (See Index); place top layer on custard. Top with Chocolate Glaze (See Index).
Preparation = 15 minutes. Serves 10.
Calories 237 (54% from fat); Fat 15g; Prot 3g; Carb 26g; Sod 45mg; Chol 71mg.

Rhubarb Meringue Dessert

Similar to a meringue pie, this dessert is great in the summertime when fresh rhubarb is plentiful.

CRUST
3/4 cup brown rice flour
1/4 cup finely chopped pecans
2 tablespoons sugar
1/4 cup canola oil
cooking spray

MERINGUE
3 large egg whites
1/4 teaspoon cream of tartar
4 tablespoons sugar

FILLING
3 large egg yolks
3 tablespoons sweet rice flour
1 cup sugar
3 cups rhubarb, finely diced
1 drop red food coloring (optional)
1 teaspoon gf vanilla extract

CRUST: Preheat oven to 325 degrees. Mix brown rice flour, chopped pecans, sugar, and canola oil together. Pat into 11 x 7-inch pan that has been sprayed with cooking spray. Bake for 8 minutes or until lightly browned.

RHUBARB FILLING: In heavy, nonreactive saucepan, combine egg yolks, sweet rice flour, sugar, and rhubarb. Cook over medium heat until mixture thickens, about 5 minutes. Add red food coloring and vanilla. Pour over crust.

MERINGUE: Increase oven temperature to 425 degrees. Beat egg whites with cream of tartar until soft peaks form. Continue beating, gradually adding sugar until stiff peaks form.

Spread meringue over rhubarb mixture in pan. Brown meringue until light golden brown. Watch carefully so it doesn't burn. Cool. Cut into squares.

Preparation = 45 minutes. Serves 8.

Calories 310 (32% from fat); Fat 11; Prot 4g; Carb 49g; Sod 2mg; Chol 80mg.
Brown Rice Substitute (not for celiacs): 3/4 cup quinoa flour.

Crumb Crust for Pies

This crust is great for cheesecakes and no-bake pie fillings such as puddings and custards.

1 cup crushed cookie crumbs
  (Vanilla Wafers or Chocolate Wafer Cookies - See Index)
4 tablespoons soft butter or oleo

1/4 cup finely chopped nuts
  (if you prefer to avoid nuts,
  use 1 1/4 cups cookie crumbs)
2 tablespoons sugar

Combine all ingredients and press into 9-inch microwave-safe pie plate. Cook 2-3 minutes on High until firm. Fill crust with no-bake filling of your choice.
Preparation = 10 minutes. Serves 6.
Calories 186 (64% from fat); Fat 14g; Prot 2g; Carb 16g; Sod 132mg; Chol 0mg.

Pie Crust of Dried Fruit & Nuts

Use this crust for puddings or fresh fruit pie fillings. It's crunchy and slightly tart and adds a very interesting note to smooth-textured fillings. You may vary the nuts as you wish.

1 cup finely chopped dried
  apricots

1 cup finely ground pecans
1 tablespoon canola oil
  cooking spray

Combine apricots, ground nuts and canola oil in food processor until well mixed. Press into bottom of 9-inch pie plate coated with cooking spray. Bake in preheated 325 degree oven for 5 minutes. Fill crust with filling of your choice.
Preparation = 15 minutes. Serves 6.
Calories 203 (60% from fat); Fat 15g; Prot 2g; Carb 20g; Sod 3mg; Chol 0mg.

Pastry Crust for Pies

Smaller pie crusts work better with this dough, so I use an 8-inch pie plate. For easier handling and no cutting, you can also press this dough into small tart pans for individual servings. For a richer crust, omit the Yogurt Cheese or tofu and use 1/2 cup shortening, instead.

1/2 cup white rice flour	1/4 cup vegetable shortening,
1/2 cup tapioca flour	melted
1/2 teaspoon baking powder	1/4 cup Yogurt Cheese (See Index)
1/2 teaspoon xanthan gum	or silken tofu, creamed
1/2 teaspoon unflavored	GLAZE: (optional)
gelatin powder	2 tablespoons milk (cow or rice)
1/4 teaspoon salt	1 teaspoon granulated sugar

In a medium mixing bowl, sift together the flours, baking powder, xanthan gum, gelatin powder, and salt. Stir in melted shortening and Yogurt Cheese. Shape into ball and cover. Chill until dough is firm enough to handle easily, about 1 hour.

Roll out the dough between two rice-floured pieces of plastic wrap or waxed paper. To place in 8-inch pie plate, remove one piece of paper and invert onto plate. Remove remaining paper and press into place. If dough is difficult to handle, press entire bottom crust in place with your fingers.

For a pie that is to be filled before baking, follow instructions for that recipe. Brush top crust with milk. (Or, combine 1 egg white and 1 tablespoon water and brush top with egg mixture.) Sprinkle with granulated sugar. Bake as directed.

For a baked crust (to fill later, e.g., puddings), bake in preheated 400 degree oven for 25 minutes or until crust is flaky and lightly browned.

Makes enough pastry for a double crust, 8-inch pie. For a larger double-crust pie (9 or 10-inch), double the recipe. Preparation = 30 minutes (excluding chilling time). Serves 6.

Calories 173 (47% from fat); Fat 9g; Prot 3g; Carb 20g; Sod 130mg; Chol 6mg.

Butterscotch Pudding

Extremely rich and satisfying. This is a great dessert for company because you can make it ahead of time and there's no last minute preparation.

1/2 cup dark brown sugar,
  firmly packed
2 tablespoons cornstarch
1/4 teaspoon salt
1 1/2 cups evaporated skim milk or
  1 1/3 cups non-dairy milk

1 large egg yolk
1 tablespoon butter or oleo
1 teaspoon gf vanilla extract
1/2 teaspoon gf butter-
  flavored extract (optional)

In a large, heavy saucepan over medium heat, whisk together the sugar, cornstarch, and salt. Add the milk gradually, whisking constantly. Whisk in egg yolk and bring the mixture to a boil, whisking constantly. Immediately reduce heat to low and continue to boil for another full minute. (This boiling time is critical because it develops the caramel, butterscotch flavor —but be careful, the mixture may splatter as it boils).

Remove from heat and stir in butter, vanilla extract, and butter extract. Divide among 4 dessert cups and chill for 2 hours. Serve with a dollop of whipped cream or shaved chocolate, if desired.

Preparation = 30 minutes. Serves 4.

Calories 238 (66% from fat); Fat 18g; Prot 4g; Carb 23g; Sod 273; Chol 64mg.

Chocolate Pudding

This is a favorite "stand-by" dessert at our house. It can be prepared ahead of time and has a rich chocolate taste.

1/3 cup white or brown sugar
2 tablespoons cornstarch
2 tablespoons cocoa powder
1 teaspoon instant expresso granules (optional)

1/8 teaspoon salt
1 3/4 cups skim milk (cow, soy, rice, or nut)
1 ounce bittersweet chocolate
1 teaspoon gf vanilla extract

Combine first five ingredients in sauce pan; stir well. Gradually whisk in milk. Bring to a boil over medium heat, whisking constantly. Add bittersweet chocolate and cook for one minute, stirring constantly. Remove from heat and add vanilla. Pour into a bowl or four individual serving bowls. Chill two hours.

Preparation = 15 minutes. Serves 4.

Calories 165 (15% from fat); Fat 3g; Prot 5g; Carb 33g; Sod 134mg; Chol 2mg.

Chocolate Soufflé

This is a very elegant, very special dessert. Put the prepared soufflés in the oven when you sit down to dinner. They'll be ready to eat when you're ready for dessert. Serve plain or with White Chocolate Topping (See Index).

1/4 cup whipping cream
4 ounces bittersweet chocolate
2 large egg yolks
1 teaspoon gf orange-flavored extract (optional)

1 teaspoon grated orange peel
3 tablespoons granulated sugar
3 large egg whites
1/8 teaspoon cream of tartar

Cook cream and chocolate in heavy saucepan over low heat, until chocolate melts. Remove from heat and beat in egg yolks, one yolk at a time. Mix in orange extract and orange peel. Place in refrigerator to cool for five minutes.

Preheat oven to 375 degrees. Grease one 4-cup or two 1 3/4-cup soufflé dishes and dust with 1 tablespoon of the granulated sugar.

Beat egg whites and cream of tartar in medium bowl until soft peaks form. Beat in remaining two tablespoons sugar. Remove chocolate from refrigerator. Fold 1/4 cup of egg whites into chocolate, then gently fold in remaining egg whites. Spoon into prepared dishes.

Bake large soufflé for 30 minutes or smaller soufflés for 20 minutes—or until soufflé rises, but center remains slightly soft. Serve immediately—plain—or with White Chocolate Topping (See Index).

Preparation = 40 minutes. Serves 2.

Calories 529 (54% from fat); Fat 33g; Prot 11g; Carb 52g; Sod 107mg; Chol 253mg.

Mexican Flan

This is an easy, almost fool-proof version to make in the microwave oven. It is a creamy, tongue-soothing finale to a Southwestern meal. And the caramel sauce is exquisite. This recipe is dairy-based.

1/2 cup granulated sugar
2 tablespoons water
4 large eggs
14 ounces sweetened
  condensed milk (1 can)

12 ounces evaporated skim
  milk (1 can)
1/2 cup half and half
2 teaspoons gf vanilla extract
cooking spray

Coat six 6-ounce custard cups with cooking spray. Set aside. In a 2 cup glass (not plastic) measuring cup, microwave sugar and water on high for 5-7 minutes until mixture boils and turns a walnut-brown color. (Watch carefully after 5 minutes of the cooking period, since mixture can easily burn.) Quickly, pour mixture evenly into bottom of prepared custard cups.

In large bowl, whisk together the eggs until well blended, then add remaining ingredients. Pour an equal amount into each custard cup. Arrange custard cups in circle in microwave oven. Microwave on medium for 12-18 minutes, rotating them a quarter turn every 4 minutes. Custard is done when a knife inserted into edges comes out clean, but when inserted into center of custard comes out thickly coated with custard. (Center will firm up after chilling).

Cool custard cups on wire rack for 30 minutes. Refrigerate for at least 4-6 hours before unmolding.

To unmold, run a thin knife around edges of custard and unmold onto serving dish or bowl.

Preparation = 35 minutes. Serves 6.

Calories 409 (25% from fat); Fat 12g; Prot 14g; Carb 60g; Sod 200mg; Chol 174mg.

Natillas

This is a Mexican vanilla pudding that is light and refreshing.
If—like me—you prefer to avoid raw eggs, substitute meringue mix
(available in the baking section of your grocery store).

2 large egg yolks
2 tablespoons tapioca flour
   (heaping)
1/2 cup whole milk (cow, soy,
   rice, or nut)
1/4 cup granulated sugar
1 1/2 cups whole milk (cow
   rice, soy, or nut)

1/8 teaspoon salt
2 large egg whites, beaten to
   soft peaks*
1/2 teaspoon vanilla extract
1/2 teaspoon ground
   cinnamon

In a medium bowl, beat together the egg yolks and flour with
an electric mixer for 1 minute or until mixture is a smooth paste.
Add the 1/2 cup milk and mix in thoroughly.

In a medium, heavy saucepan place the sugar, the 1 1/2 cups
milk, and salt. Heat the ingredients on medium until the milk
scalds, about 1-3 minutes.

Lower the heat to medium low and, stirring constantly, slowly
pour in the egg yolk mixture in a steady stream. Continue to stir
the mixture until it is thickened (it should coat the back of a
spoon), about 5-8 minutes. Stir in vanilla. Remove pan from
heat and chill custard in refrigerator for 1 hour (or in freezer for
15 minutes, then place in refrigerator).

Remove chilled custard from refrigerator. Fold in beaten egg
whites or meringue mix, see * below). Sprinkle with cinnamon.
*Instead of raw egg whites, use 1 tablespoon of instant
meringue mix mixed with 1 tablespoon water and 2 tablespoons
granulated sugar. Beat with electric mixer until soft peaks form.
Instant meringue mix is in the baking section of grocery stores.
Preparation = 45 minutes. Serves 4.
Calories 177 (34% from fat); Fat 7g; Prot 8g; Carb 22g; Sod 158mg; Chol 123mg.

Bread Pudding with Lemon Sauce

This is a great way to use up leftover Popovers and French bread. To reduce calories, use your favorite milk in place of the half and half.

6 cups gf bread
2 cups whole milk (cow, soy, rice, or nut)
1/2 cup sugar
4 large eggs
1 teaspoon grated lemon peel
1 teaspoon gf vanilla extract
1 teaspoon gf lemon extract
1 cup blueberries
cooking spray

SAUCE
1 cup half and half (or 3/4 cup non-dairy liquid)
3 large egg yolks
2 tablespoons sugar
1 teaspoon cornstarch
1/4 cup honey
1 teaspoon gf lemon extract
1 teaspoon gf rum extract (optional)

Preheat oven to 325 degrees. Spray an 8-inch baking dish with cooking spray.

Cut bread into 1-inch cubes. Whisk together milk, sugar, 4 eggs, lemon peel, and vanilla and lemon extracts.

Place half of the cubed bread on the bottom of the dish. Top with the blueberries and half of the egg mixture. Top with remaining bread, then remaining egg mixture. Let stand 15 minutes, occasionally pressing down on bread.

Bake until top begins to brown, about 45 minutes to 1 hour. SAUCE: Bring half and half to a simmer in a heavy pan. Whisk together the egg yolks, sugar, and cornstarch in a medium-sized bowl. Gradually whisk in hot half-and-half. Return mixture to heavy pan and stir over low-medium heat until mixture thickens and leaves path on back of spoon when finger is drawn across, about 3 minutes. Do not boil. Mix in remaining ingredients. Serve on pudding.

Preparation = 1 hour. Serves 6.

Calories 967 (20% from fat); Fat 22 g; Prot 29g; Carb 162g; Sod 1376mg; Chol 276mg.

Lemon Pudding

This smooth lemon pudding is great by itself. It also makes a great lemon meringue pie filling.

3/4 cup sugar
1 tablespoon cornstarch
1/2 teaspoon grated lemon peel
1/3 cup water

1/3 cup fresh lemon juice
1 large egg, slightly beaten
1 large egg yolk
1 tablespoon butter or oleo

Combine sugar, cornstarch, and lemon peel in a heavy saucepan. Stir together, then whisk in water and lemon juice until blended. Bring to boil over medium heat and cook for one minute, stirring constantly. Remove from heat.

Slightly beat egg and egg yolk together in small bowl. Whisk 3 tablespoons of hot lemon mixture into egg mixture. Then add egg mixture to lemon mixture, stirring constantly. Cook over medium heat for 1 minute or until thickened, stirring constantly. Remove from heat. Stir in butter. Pour into bowl and chill.

Preparation = 20 minutes (excluding chill time). Serves 6.

Calories 144 (22% from fat); Fat 4g; Prot 2g; Carb 28g; Sod 32mg; Chol 76mg.

Vanilla Custard

This makes a rich, thick custard appropriate for Cream Puffs or Cream Pies (See Index). Or, just eat it as vanilla pudding with a dollop of whipped cream.

1/2 cup granulated sugar	1 cup hot milk (cow, rice, soy, or
1/4 cup cornstarch	nut)
4 large egg yolks at room	2 teaspoons gf vanilla extract
temperature	1 tablespoon butter or oleo

In small bowl, mix together the sugar and cornstarch. In another bowl, beat the egg yolks with an electric mixer until thick and lemon-colored. Slowly add cornstarch mixture, mixing thoroughly until smooth.

Continuing with electric mixer, gradually beat the hot milk into the yolk mixture.

Return mixture to pan and cook for 2 minutes, whisking constantly, over low heat until custard thickens.

Remove from heat. Stir in butter and vanilla extract. Transfer to bowl, cover with plastic wrap touching surface of custard to prevent skin forming. Refrigerate until chilled. Stir before serving. Makes about 1 1/4 cups custard.

Preparation = 15 minutes. (Excludes chill time) Serves 4.

Calories 249 (36% from fat); Fat 10g; Prot 6g; Carb 34g; Sod 66mg; Chol 229mg.

Cream Puffs

Cream Puffs are one of the easiest and most fool-proof desserts you can make with wheat-free flours. Or, instead of dessert, fill them will tuna or chicken salad for lunch. They will certainly impress your guests!

1/2 cup white rice flour
1/4 cup potato starch
3/4 cup water
5 tablespoons butter or oleo, sliced
2 teaspoons sugar

1/4 teaspoon salt
3 large eggs at room temperature
cooking spray
1/2 cup whipping cream, whipped to stiff peaks
powdered sugar for garnish

Coat a cookie sheet with cooking spray. Set aside. Preheat oven to 450 degrees. Mix flours together and set aside.

Combine water, butter, sugar, and salt in medium saucepan over medium-high heat. Immediately after mixture comes to boil, remove from heat and stir in flour, all at once. Return to heat and continue stirring and pressing mixture against sides of the pan until it pulls away from edges of pan.

Remove from heat. Beat in eggs, one at a time, beating with electric mixer after each addition until smooth before adding the next egg.

Drop mounds of dough onto cookie sheet. Each mound should measure approximately 2 inches in diameter and 1 1/2 to 2 inches in height. With wet finger, smooth any points of dough that stick up, since these points will brown faster and may burn.

Bake at 450 degrees for 20 minutes, then reduce oven temperature to 350 and continue baking for another 15 minutes, or until cream puffs are deep golden brown. Remove from oven and immediately cut small horizontal 1-inch slit in side of cream puff, right where you'll eventually cut them completely in half. Cool on wire racks. When cool, cut completely in half horizontally along 1-inch slit and fill with whipped cream or desired filling (see Vanilla Custard in Index). Dust with powdered sugar. Makes 10-12.

To store before filling, place in plastic bag and store at room temperature for a day or freeze for up to 1 month. Thaw pastry at room temperature, then reheat in 350 oven to recrisp. Preparation = 40 minutes. Serves 12. (2 Cream Puffs each)
Calories 193 (57% from fat); Fat 12g; Prot 5g; Carb 16g; Sod 218mg; Chol 132mg.
CREAM PUFFS WITH VANILLA CUSTARD FILLING: Use Vanilla Custard (See Index) as filling instead of whipped cream.
Calories 275 (52% from fat); Fat 16; Prot 6g; Carb 27g; Sod 242mg; Chol 216mg.

Crepes

Crepes have unlimited uses as "containers" for desserts or entrees. Try filling these with cream cheese and top with strawberries or blueberries. Or, fold them in quarters, and simmer in a sauce of orange marmalade melted in orange juice for a variation of Crepe Suzette.

1/3 cup white rice flour	2 large eggs
1/3 cup brown rice flour	2 teaspoons canola oil
1/2 teaspoon xanthan gum	1 teaspoon gf vanilla extract
1/2 teaspoon gelatin powder, unflavored	1/8 teaspoon salt
3/4 cup lowfat milk (cow, soy, or rice)	cooking spray

Combine all ingredients in a blender and process until smooth. If possible, refrigerate (in blender) for about 30 minutes. If not, proceed to heat an 8-inch skillet or seasoned crepe pan. Heat crepe pan over medium-high heat until a drop of water dances on the surface. Pour a scant 2 tablespoons of batter into the pan and immediately tilt pan to coat the bottom evenly. Cook until

underside of crepe is brown and cook the other side for about 20-30 seconds. (Often the first crepe will not turn out as well as succeeding ones, due to the temperature of the pan.) Repeat with remaining batter. Makes about 12 crepes.
Preparation = 20 minutes. Serves 6. (2 crepes each)
Calories 117 (30% from fat); Fat 4g; Prot 5g; Carb 16%g; Sod 82mg; Chol 72mg.

Chocolate Glaze

Use this glaze on top of the Mexican Chocolate Pound Cake (See Index) or on fresh fruit or puddings. Whole milk (or non-dairy liquid) can be substituted for the half and half.

1/4 cup half and half
3 ounces Mexican chocolate
   (Ibarra)
1 ounce bittersweet chocolate

2 tablespoons canola oil
1 tablespoon honey
1 tablespoon pure maple syrup

In a small, heavy saucepan place half and half over medium heat for 5 minutes, until lightly scalded. Set aside.

In the top of a double boiler over simmering water (or in a microwave oven on low setting) heat chocolates, oil, honey, and maple syrup. Heat for 5 minutes or until chocolate is melted.

Remove from heat. Stir half and half and melted chocolate mixture together. Cool. Makes about 1 1/2 cups.
Preparation = 20 minutes. Serves 10. (2 tablespoons each)
Calories 100 (60% from fat); Fat 7g; Prot .6g; Carb 10g; Sod 4mg; Chol 2mg.

Coffee 7-Minute Frosting

This is a delicious, low-fat way to frost a cake, especially a Spice Cake (See Index). You can vary the flavor—omit the coffee for a vanilla frosting or substitute lemon or orange extract. Whatever you like!

1 teaspoon gf instant coffee powder
1 teaspoon very hot water or hot brewed coffee
3 large egg whites
1 1/4 cups granulated sugar
1/4 teaspoon cream of tartar
3 tablespoons cold water
1 teaspoon gf vanilla extract

Dissolve 1 teaspoon instant coffee crystals in 1 teaspoon very hot tap water or brewed coffee. Set aside.

In double boiler over boiling water, combine egg whites, granulated sugar, cream of tartar, and cold water. Beat with portable electric mixer for 7 minutes. Remove from heat and stir in vanilla extract and coffee liquid with a spatula until glossy and desired spreading consistency. Use immediately.

Preparation = 10 minutes. Frosts one 8-inch layer cake. Serves 10.

Calories 105 (.7% from fat); Fat .1g; Prot 1g; Carb 27g; Sod 21mg; Chol 0mg.

SOUPS

Soups

Soup Components

Soups can be a low-fat, low calorie component of a tasty, highly nutritious diet.

Persons on a wheat-free diet, however, sometimes avoid soups because wheat is often used as the thickener, especially in cream soups. Or, the bouillon base used in the soup may contain gluten. Or, a small amount of wheat-based pasta is included in the recipe, making the entire soup off-limits.

Of course, there are many soups that are safe for wheat-sensitive persons. You'll find them in any cookbook. So, the recipes in this section are those that usually contain wheat—but I've converted them to wheat-free versions so you and I can enjoy them.

These delicious homemade soups—which are often better than the canned variety—include cream soups such as New England Clam Chowder or Cream of Mushroom Soup. Even soups with noodles are no longer forbidden because Chicken Noodle Soup can be made with noodles from the Pasta recipe (See Index).

If there are other vegetables you'd like to use in cream soups (such as asparagus or corn), you can convert the Cream of Broccoli or Cream of Mushroom Soup recipes to suit your taste.

Cheese Soup

Hearty and flavorful, all you need with this soup is a crusty French bread and you have a robust meal. This recipe is dairy-based and works better with dairy cheddar cheese.

1/4 cup finely chopped onions
2 tablespoons canola oil
1/3 cup sweet rice flour
3 cups low-sodium chicken broth
1/2 teaspoon dry mustard
1/2 teaspoon paprika

1/8 teaspoon cayenne pepper
1/2 teaspoon salt
1 cup skim milk
1 1/2 cups Cheddar cheese, extra-sharp
2 tablespoons dried chives

In large Dutch oven, sauté onion in oil until soft. In screw-top jar, combine flour and 1 cup of the chicken broth. Shake vigorously to blend well.

Add flour mixture to Dutch oven, along with remaining chicken broth and remaining ingredients, except cheese.

Cook over moderate heat, stirring constantly, until mixture comes to a boil and thickens. Lower heat to low, add cheddar cheese and continue stirring, until cheese is melted and mixture is smooth. Makes about 5-6 cups.

Ladle into 4 soup bowls. Garnish with chopped chives. Preparation = 20 minutes. Serves 4.

Calories 303 (59% from fat); Fat 21g; Prot 20 g; Carb 13g; Sod 860mg; Chol 46mg.

Cream of Broccoli Soup

This soup has a delightful taste from the combination of basil and broccoli. You can substitute other vegetables, if you wish.

1 cup low-sodium chicken broth
3 cups broccoli flowerets
1 teaspoon olive oil
1 cup chopped onions
1 garlic clove, minced
1 1/2 tablespoons cornstarch or
  2 tablespoons sweet rice flour

2 cups evaporated skim milk
  (or 1 3/4 cups soy or rice
  milk)
1/2 teaspoon salt
1/4 teaspoon white pepper
3 tablespoons fresh basil or
  1 1/2 teaspoons dried basil
1/8 teaspoon ground nutmeg

Coarsely chop broccoli flowerets and boil in chicken broth for about 5 minutes or until fork tender. Set aside. Cool, but don't drain.

In heavy skillet, sauté onions and garlic in olive oil until tender, about 8-10 minutes. Add chicken broth used to boil broccoli.

Combine cornstarch (or sweet rice flour) with 1/4 cup of the cooled chicken broth to form smooth paste. Stir into skillet mixture over low-medium heat, whisking constantly until mixture thickens.

Add cooked broccoli, milk, salt, pepper, basil and nutmeg. Bring to serving temperature, but do not boil.

Preparation = 20 minutes. Serves 4.

Calories 179 (9% from fat); Fat 2g; Prot 16g; Carb 28g; Sod 296mg; Chol 5mg.

Cream of Mushroom Soup

The rich flavor of mushrooms (use any kind you wish) is tantalizing.

1 teaspoon olive oil
1 cup chopped onions
1 garlic clove, minced
3 cups evaporated skim milk
  (or soy or rice milk)
1 1/2 tablespoons cornstarch
  or 2 tablespoons sweet rice
  flour

1/4 cup water
3 cups mushrooms, chopped
1/2 teaspoon salt
1/4 teaspoon white pepper
3 tablespoons fresh parsley
  or 1 1/2 teaspoon dried
1/8 teaspoon ground nutmeg
1/2 teaspoon dried thyme

In heavy large saucepan over medium heat, sauté onions and garlic in olive oil until onions are tender, about 8-10 minutes.

Stir in milk and heat until bubbles form around edges. Combine cornstarch (or sweet rice flour) with water to form smooth paste. Whisk into milk and continue whisking until mixture thickens slightly. Do not boil.

Stir in mushrooms and remaining ingredients. Bring to serving temperature, but do not boil.

Preparation = 20 minutes. Serves 4.

Calories 161 (9% from fat); Fat 2g; Prot 14g; Carb 25g; Sod 283mg; Chol 5mg.

French Onion Soup

This soup derives it's deep flavor from the caramelized onions that take nearly an hour to cook. But, it's worth the effort! There is really no effective non-dairy substitute for Gruyere cheese.

3 tablespoons olive oil
1 tablespoon butter or oleo
2 pounds onions, sliced
1/2 teaspoon salt
1/2 teaspoon black pepper
1/2 teaspoon sugar
2 garlic cloves, minced
4 cups low-sodium beef broth
1 cup water

2 teaspoons gf brandy extract
1/4 teaspoon dried marjoram
1 bay leaf
1 tablespoon sweet rice flour
1/2 loaf gf bread
2 cups grated Gruyere cheese
2 tablespoons Parmesan
  cheese, for garnish (may
  use rice or soy Parmesan)

In a heavy Dutch oven, heat butter and oil over medium heat. Add onions, salt and pepper. Cook, stirring occasionally, until onions begin to soften, about 10 minutes. Reduce heat to low and cook slowly, stirring occasionally, until onions are caramelized, about 1 hour and 15 minutes. (After 30 minutes of cooking, the onions should be a light golden brown. By 45 minutes, onions will be deep brown—the secret for onion soup.)

When onions have cooked for 1 1/4 hours, slowly stir in sugar, garlic, beef broth, water, brandy extract, marjoram, and bay leaf. Simmer, partially covered, for 15 minutes. Mix flour with 1 tablespoon water, add to soup, and stir until thickened.

Heat oven to 325 degrees. Slice French bread into 3/4-inch slices, bake on baking sheet until dry, 5 minutes per side.

Heat broiler. Grate Gruyere cheese. Ladle soup into heat-proof soup bowls. Place a slice of toasted French bread on top of each bowl. Divide cheese equally among 4 bowls. Broil until golden brown, about 2-3 minutes. Garnish with Parmesan cheese.

Preparation = 2 1/4 hours. Serves 4.

Calories 607 (49% from fat); Fat 33g; Prot 35g; Carb 42mg; Sod 2238mg; Chol 71mg

Southwestern French Onion Soup

Use the French Onion Soup recipe on previous page. Instead of the thyme, add 1/2 teaspoon toasted ground cumin, 1/4 teaspoon ground coriander, 1/4 teaspoon dried oregano, and 1 tablespoon New Mexico ground red chile powder. Instead of the Gruyere or Swiss cheese, substitute Monterey Jack cheese with jalapeno chiles. At serving time, garnish with 2 tablespoons fresh cilantro.

Preparation = 2 1/4 hours. Serves 4.

Calories 584 (49% from fat); Fat 32g; Prot 33g; Carb 42g; Sod 2350mg; Chol 59mg.

Minestrone

Use your own homemade Pasta or purchased wheat-free pasta.

1 cup each carrots and cabbage
4 cups low-sodium beef broth
1/2 cup dried white navy beans
2 garlic cloves, minced
1/2 cup chopped onion
1 cup diced potatoes
1 cup canned tomatoes
1/4 cup green beans
1/4 teaspoon red pepper flakes

1/2 teaspoon each dried basil, thyme, sage, and oregano
1/4 teaspoon salt
1 cup fresh spinach
1/4 cup purchased wheat-free macaroni or 1/2 cup chopped noodles from Pasta (See Index)
1/4 cup Parmesan cheese (may use rice or soy version)

Coarsely chop carrots and cabbage. In large heavy Dutch oven, combine all ingredients except spinach, pasta, and Parmesan cheese. Bring to boil, cover and simmer for at least 3 hours or until beans are tender. Stir in spinach and pasta. Cook just until tender (time needed to cook pasta depends on pasta used).

Preparation = 3 hours. Serves 4.

Calories 212 (8% from fat); Fat 2g; Prot 22g; Carb 36g; Sod 873mg; Chol 4mg.

Chicken Noodle Soup

Everyone loves Chicken Noodle Soup. This version is full of flavor, due to several herbs and spices. If you prefer a milder version, reduce the seasonings. Keep noodles made from homemade egg Pasta (See Index) in your freezer, so you can just toss them into the simmering broth at the last minute. Dumplings are optional.

3 cups low-sodium chicken broth
1/2 cup celery, thinly sliced
1 cup diced chicken, cooked
1/4 cup minced instant onions
1 small carrots, thinly sliced
1/2 teaspoon poultry seasoning
6 peppercorns

1/4 teaspoon white pepper
1/8 teaspoon ground nutmeg
1 bay leaf
1/2 cup Pasta (See Index) made
    into noodles
1 recipe Dumplings (See Index)
1/4 cup fresh parsley, chopped

Combine chicken broth, celery, chicken, onions, carrots, poultry seasoning, peppercorns, white pepper, nutmeg, and bay leaf in a large Dutch oven and bring to boil. Reduce heat and simmer, covered, for 10 minutes.

Meanwhile, assemble ingredients for Dumplings (if using). Add Dumplings and simmer, covered, for 20 minutes without lifting the lid. Add noodles and cook another 5 minutes or until done.

To serve, divide among 4 serving bowls and garnish with chopped parsley.

Preparation = 30 minutes. Serves 4.

Calories 442 (24% from fat); Fat 12g; Prot 34g; Carb 55g; Sod 844mg; Chol 127mg.

Dumplings

This version lends itself to the big, hearty dumplings in noodle soups or to tiny German spaetzle that are sometimes served with green beans.

1 1/4 cups brown rice flour
2/3 cup potato starch
2 teaspoons baking powder
1/2 teaspoon baking soda
1/2 teaspoon salt
1 teaspoon unflavored gelatin
   powder
1 large egg

3 tablespoons butter or oleo
1/2 cup buttermilk (or 1 teaspoon cider vinegar plus
   enough milk–cow, rice, or
   soy–to equal 1/2 cup)
2 tablespoons fresh parsley,
   chopped

Combine dry ingredients in large mixer bowl. Make well in center.

In another bowl, whisk together the egg and butter. Add to flour mixture alternately with buttermilk. Stir in parsley. Mix only until moistened. This will be a stiff dough.

Drop dough by a tablespoonfuls into boiling soup. Cover, reduce heat to simmer, and cook without lifting cover for 20 minutes.

SPAETZLE: To make dough into spaetzle, add 1/4 cup buttermilk and press dough through colander holes into boiling water or soup.

Preparation = 25 minutes. Serves 4.

Calories 380 (29% from fat); Fat 12g; Prot 9g; Carb 58g; Sod 659mg; Chol 54mg.

New England Clam Chowder

Chowders make wonderful lunch dishes. However, teamed up with a hearty bread and a dinner salad, this soup could be served for supper.

1 bacon slice, uncooked
1 cup onion, chopped
1/2 cup celery, chopped
2 garlic cloves, minced
8 ounces clam broth (1 bottle)
1 1/2 cups chopped potatoes
1/4 teaspoon salt
1/8 teaspoon black pepper

1/2 teaspoon Beau Monde seasoning or gf seasoning salt
2 tablespoons potato starch
2 cups whole milk (may use soy or rice milk)
1 cup clams with liquid
2 tablespoons chopped fresh parsley chopped

In large Dutch oven, sauté bacon until crisp. Remove bacon from Dutch oven; set aside. In remaining fat from bacon, sauté onion, celery, and garlic until vegetables are soft. Crumble bacon and return to Dutch oven.

Add clam broth, potatoes, salt, pepper, and Beau Monde seasoning. Bring to boil, then reduce heat. Simmer, covered, for 20 minutes or until potatoes are tender. Mix potato starch with 1/4 cup of the milk until mixture is smooth. Add to Dutch oven along with remaining milk and cook, stirring constantly, until mixture thickens. Stir in clams (and their liquid). Bring to serving temperature.

Ladle into 4 serving bowls. Garnish with chopped parsley. Preparation = 30 minutes. Serves 4.

Calories 239 (45% from fat); Fat 12g; Prot 16g; Carb 16g; Sod 618mg; Chol 43mg.

Potato Soup

Potato soup is so comforting!! This version makes a great lunch dish or a light Sunday night supper.

1/2 cup low-sodium chicken broth
2 potatoes, thinly sliced
1/4 cup gf onion flakes
1/2 cup celery, thinly sliced
1 small carrot, grated

1/2 teaspoon celery salt
3 cups milk (cow, rice, or soy)
1/2 teaspoon dried marjoram
1/4 teaspoon dried thyme
1/4 cup chopped fresh parsley

Combine sliced potatoes, minced onions, celery, carrots and celery salt in chicken broth in large saucepan with cover. Bring to boil, reduce heat and simmer, covered, for 10 minutes or until potatoes are tender. (Add water if vegetables look dry during cooking.)

Remove 1/2 cup of potato mixture and puree in blender or with hand-held, immersion blender. Be careful, mixture will be hot. Return mixture to pan.

Add milk, marjoram, and thyme to pan and heat to serving temperature. Do not boil.

To serve, pour soup into 4 serving bowls. Garnish with fresh parsley.

Preparation = 20 minutes. Serves 4.

Calories 176 (31% from fat); Fat 6g; Prot 9g; Carb 22g; Sod 418mg; Chol 25mg.

Wild Rice Soup

This is a rich-tasting, very satisfying soup with lots of interesting texture.

2 tablespoons butter or oleo
1 tablespoon gf onion flakes or grated fresh onion
1/3 cup sweet rice flour
3 cups low-sodium chicken broth
2 cups cooked wild rice
1/2 teaspoon salt
1/3 cup shredded carrots
1/3 cup diced ham or Canadian Bacon
3 tablespoons almond slivers, toasted
1 cup evaporated skim milk (or use rice, soy, or nut milk)
1/4 cup fresh chopped chives or 2 tablespoons dried chives

In large Dutch oven, sauté onion flakes in butter until golden brown. Place flour in a screw-top jar and add 1 cup of the chicken broth. Shake vigorously to blend well. Add to Dutch oven, along with remaining chicken broth. Bring to boil and stir 1 minute. Add the cooked wild rice, salt, carrots, ham, and almonds and simmer for 5 minutes. Blend in evaporated skim milk. Heat to serving temperature and garnish with chives. Preparation = 30 minutes. Serves 6.

Calories 342 (19% from fat); Fat 7g; Port 19g; Carb 53g; Sod 633mg; Chol 16mg.

SAUCES & SALAD DRESSINGS

Salad Dressings
Asian Vinaigrette 167
Avocado Dressing 167
Buttermilk Dressing 168
Citrus Dressing 168
Hazelnut Vinaigrette 169
Herb Vinaigrette 169
Lime Cilantro Dressing 170
Peanut Dressing 170
Pine Nut Dressing 171
Raspberry Vinaigrette 172
Red Chile Dressing 173
Southwestern Dressing 173
Thousand Island Dressing 174
Walnut Oil Vinaigrette 174

Chutney and Salsa
Apple Chutney 163
Papaya Chutney 161
Pineapple Salsa 162
Tomatillo Apple Salsa 158

Miscellaneous
Spicy Yogurt Cheese 166
Yogurt Cheese 165

**Sauces for Entrees
  or Vegetables**
Alfredo Sauce 71
Apricot Sauce 149
Avocado Chile Sauce 149
Barbecue Sauce 156
Cream Sauce for
  Vegetables 160
Enchilada Sauce 150
Green Chile Sauce 155
Hollandaise Sauce 151
Honey Mustard Sauce 150
Lemon-Tomato Barbecue
  Sauce 154
Pizza Sauce 157
Red Chile Sauce 153
Red Wine Sauce 154
Spaghetti Sauce 157
Tandoori Sauce 152
Tomatillo Sauce 158
White Dill Sauce w/
  Mushrooms 159

Dessert Sauces
Hot Fudge Sauce 164
Raspberry Sauce 165
White Chocolate Topping 164

All too often, wheat and gluten-sensitive persons avoid sauces (and maybe salad dressings) because the contents are unknown. This can leave food bland, boring and unappealing. But it doesn't have to be that way.

The recipes for sauces and salad dressings in this chapter serve an important role in diets devoid of wheat and gluten. Put them on your food to provide variety in the form of pleasing tastes, interesting textures, and tempting aromas. And we all know that when food tastes good and smells good, it is far more satisfying.

Sauces not only add variety to our diets in terms of taste, texture and color—they often define the dish itself. Imagine Spaghetti & Meatballs without spaghetti sauce or Pizza without pizza sauce!

As for the salad dressings—there are many excellent bottled salad dressings on the market. However, some compensate for a low fat content by adding extra sugar—making them more like a syrup than a dressing. And, many contain far more ingredients than you want or need for a healthy diet.

Using recipes in this section, you can safely enjoy a wide variety of flavors and textures because you make your own sauces and salad dressings. You'll find the traditional entree sauces such as Barbecue Sauce, Spaghetti Sauce, or Pizza Sauce. For your Southwestern taste buds, you'll find Enchilada Sauce, Green Chile Sauce, and Red Chile Sauce. And, to add zest to main dishes you'll find Chutney and Salsas. And cream sauces for vegetables.

But the best part is you can enjoy all of these tastes and flavors knowing that they are wheat-free and gluten-free. And, they're so delicious that your family and friends will never know!

Apricot Sauce

This sauce is versatile. Baste Cornish game hens as they bake. Drizzle over pork chops. Toss with fresh fruit or put on French toast—just omit the thyme and salt if you use the sauce on fruit.

1/2 cup apricot preserves
1/4 cup water
1/2 teaspoon dried thyme

2 tablespoons fresh orange juice
1/2 teaspoon salt

In small saucepan, heat all ingredients over medium heat. Stir constantly until preserves melt and mixture is blended. Cool.
Preparation = 20 minutes. Serves 4. Makes 3/4 cup.
Calories 124 (.6% from fat); Fat .1g; Prot .3g; Carb 29g; Sod 16mg; Chol 0mg.

Avocado Chile Sauce

This sauce is great with the Southwestern Crab Cakes (See Index).

1 mashed avocado
1 teaspoon chipotle pepper
   sauce
1 tablespoon fresh lime juice
1/4 cup low-fat plain yogurt
   or 3 tablespoons non-dairy
   milk

2 teaspoons cider vinegar
1/2 teaspoon salt
1 teaspoon ground cumin, toasted
1 tablespoon olive oil
1/2 cup chopped fresh cilantro
1/4 cup chopped fresh parsley

Put all ingredients, except cilantro and parsley, in blender or food processor. Pulse the motor until mixture is not quite smooth. Add cilantro and parsley and pulse just until they are chopped. Serve sauce at room temperature.
Preparation = 20 minutes. Serves 4. Makes about 1 1/2 cups.
Calories 132 (72% from fat); Fat 11g; Prot 3g; Carb 7g; Sod 294mg; Chol 0mg.

Enchilada Sauce

Use this tasty sauce in your next Enchilada recipe.

1 tablespoon canola oil
1 small onion, finely chopped
1 small garlic clove, minced
16 ounces canned tomatoes,
    cut in small pieces
6 ounces gf tomato paste

1 teaspoon chili powder
1/2 teaspoon dried oregano
2 tablespoons chopped fresh
    cilantro
1/2 teaspoon salt
1 teaspoon sugar or honey

In heavy, medium saucepan sauté the onion and garlic in canola oil until transparent, about 3-5 minutes. Add tomatoes (including the liquid), tomato paste, chili powder, oregano, cilantro, salt, and sugar. Bring to boil. Reduce heat, cover, and simmer for five minutes. Makes about 2 1/2 cups.
Preparation = 20 minutes. Serves 4.
Calories 105 (32% from fat); Fat 4g; Prot 3g; Carb 16g; Sod 624mg; Chol 0mg.

Honey Mustard Sauce

This sauce is great on fish, especially thick fillets and steaks such as halibut or yellow-fin tuna. It's also great on chicken.

1/4 cup Dijonnaise mustard
2 tablespoons honey
1/4 cup white grape juice
1/4 teaspoon dried thyme

3 tablespoons low-sodium,
    wheat-free soy sauce
1/2 teaspoon ground ginger
1/4 teaspoon white pepper

Combine all ingredients in small, heavy saucepan. Over low heat, cook, uncovered, for about 5 minutes, stirring occasionally. Makes about 1/2 cup.
Preparation = 15 minutes. Serves 4.
Calories 60 (9% from fat); Fat .7g; Prot 1g; Carb 13g; Sod 551mg; Chol 0mg.

Hollandaise Sauce

I love Eggs Benedict, but the traditional Hollandaise Sauce is loaded with fat and calories. I've developed this alternate version which lowers the fat and calories dramatically. I think you'll agree—this is a winner!

2 large egg yolks	2 tablespoons butter or oleo
1 cup Yogurt Cheese (See Index) or soft silken tofu	1/4 teaspoon salt
	1/8 teaspoon cayenne pepper
2 tablespoons fresh lemon juice	1/8 teaspoon white pepper
1/2 teaspoon xanthan gum	1/4 teaspoon dry mustard

Blend egg yolks, Yogurt Cheese (or tofu), lemon juice, and xanthan gum in blender until light and fluffy. Place the egg yolk mixture in the top of a double boiler set over simmering, not boiling, water. (Don't let bottom of double boiler touch the water). Add butter, whisking constantly until butter melts and mixture thickens.

Remove from heat and stir in salt, cayenne pepper, white pepper, and dry mustard. (Mixture can be kept warm over simmering water for about 30 minutes. If it starts to separate, add a teaspoon of boiling water and whisk briskly until smooth.) Preparation = 15 minutes. Serves 4. Makes about 1 cup.

Calories 116 (64% from fat); Fat 8g; Prot 5g; Carb 6g; Sod 240mg; Chol 123mg.

Tandoori Sauce

This sauce is used in Tandoori recipes, resulting in meat that looks reddish when fully cooked. It's great on chicken. If you prefer to work with ground spices, use one-half teaspoon dried spices for each teaspoon of seeds.

2 teaspoons cumin seeds
1 teaspoon coriander seeds
1 teaspoon mustard seeds
1 tablespoon paprika
1/2 teaspoon cayenne pepper
1/2 teaspoon salt

1/2 teaspoon turmeric
1/2 cup low-fat plain yogurt
2 tablespoons fresh lime juice
1 small onion, chopped
4 garlic cloves, minced
1 tablespoon fresh grated ginger root

In a heavy skillet, toast the cumin, coriander, and mustard seeds over medium heat, shaking pan frequently until fragrant —about 5 minutes.

Transfer spices to clean coffee grinder (or, use mortar and pestle) and grind spices to a powder. Add paprika, cayenne pepper, salt, and turmeric.

In a blender or food processor, combine yogurt, lime juice, onions, garlic, and ginger root. Blend until smooth. Add spices and pulse to combine. Use immediately to marinate chicken or fish. Makes about 1 1/3 cups, enough to marinate 2 pounds of meat.

Preparation = 15 minutes. Serves 6.

Calories 24 (9% from fat); Fat .3g; Prot 2g; Carb 4g; Sod 285mg; Chol 0mg.

Red Chile Sauce

This sauce is practically a staple in Southwestern cooking. Be sure to use the New Mexico chile powder, not chili powder (which is actually a mix of different spices). You can order the New Mexico chile powder (See Mail Order Sources in Index) if your local stores don't carry it.

3 tablespoons red New
  Mexico chile powder*
1/4 teaspoon salt
1 teaspoon white pepper
1/2 teaspoon ground cumin
1/2 teaspoon dried oregano
1/2 teaspoon dried coriander
dash of ground cinnamon

dash of ground cloves
3 cups low-sodium chicken broth
1/4 teaspoon gf Worcestershire sauce
1 garlic clove, minced
1 tablespoon canola oil
2 tablespoons sweet rice flour
  or white rice flour

In a heavy saucepan, heat chile powder, salt, white pepper, cumin, oregano, coriander, cinnamon, and cloves over medium heat for 3-5 minutes, stirring constantly. This lightly toasts the spices, bringing out their flavor. The mixture should darken slightly.

Stir in the chicken broth (reserving 1/4 cup), Worcestershire sauce, garlic, and canola oil. Simmer, covered for 5-10 minutes. Stir sweet rice flour into reserved chicken broth to form paste. Add to chile sauce and cook until mixture comes to a boil and thickens, stirring constantly. Remove from heat.

* I use the Dixon-medium hot version. You may want to start with only 2 tablespoons of this chile powder or use choose a milder version of chile powder. If you like a hotter sauce, you can always add more chile powder.

Preparation = 30 minutes. Serves 4.

Calories 65 (38% from fat); Fat 4g; Prot 6g; Carb 6g; Sod 397mg; Chol 0mg.

Red Wine Sauce

Serve this sauce over beef or pork. It provides lots of flavor.

1 onion, finely chopped
1 garlic clove, minced
1 teaspoon canola oil
1 1/2 cups gf red wine
1/2 teaspoon Dijonnaise mustard
1/4 teaspoon granulated sugar

1/4 teaspoon dried thyme
1/4 teaspoon dried rosemary
1/4 teaspoon dried marjoram
1/4 teaspoon black pepper
1/4 teaspoon salt

In a medium, heavy saucepan sauté onion and garlic in teaspoon of canola oil for about 5 minutes. Add remaining ingredients; stir well. Turn heat to medium-high and cook, uncovered, until liquid is reduced by half—about 15 minutes. NON-ALCOHOLIC VARIATION: Substitute pure white grape juice for red wine. Add 2 tablespoons red wine vinegar and 1 teaspoon lemon juice. Omit granulated sugar.
Preparation = 20 minutes. Serves 4. Makes about 3/4 cup.
Calories 74 (5% from fat); Fat .1g; Prot .6g; Carb 4g; Sod 283mg; Chol 0mg.

Lemon-Tomato Barbecue Sauce

A very light sauce that is especially good on grilled chicken.

1 can tomato juice (6-oz can)
1 small garlic clove, minced
1/2 teaspoon gf onion powder
1 teaspoon grated lemon peel
1/2 teaspoon black pepper

1 teaspoon gf Worcestershire
    sauce
1/4 cup fresh lemon juice
1 tablespoon butter or oleo
dash of cayenne pepper

Place all ingredients in a small, heavy saucepan. Bring to boil over medium heat, reduce heat to low, and simmer for 5

minutes. Baste chicken as it cooks on the grill. Makes about 1 cup.
Preparation = 10 minutes. Serves 6.
Calories 31 (50% from fat); Fat 2g; Prot .5g; Carb 4g; Sod 230mg; Chol 5mg.

Green Chile Sauce

For many of us living in the Southwest, this is a dish we eat frequently to satisfy our craving for green chiles.

1 teaspoon canola oil	1/2 teaspoon ground oregano
1/2 cup onions, finely diced	2 tablespoons fresh chopped
1 garlic clove, minced	cilantro
2 cups low-sodium chicken broth	1/4 teaspoon salt
2 medium green chiles	2 teaspoons cornstarch
2 large diced Roma tomatoes	1 tablespoon water
1/2 teaspoon ground coriander	

Heat canola oil over medium heat in heavy skillet and sauté onions until just tender, about 3-5 minutes. Add all remaining ingredients (except cornstarch and water) and simmer, covered, for 15-20 minutes. Stir cornstarch into water to form paste. Add to green chile sauce and bring to boil, stirring constantly. Stir until mixture thickens slightly. Makes about 2 cups.
Preparation = 30 minutes. Serves 4.
Calories 73 (35% from fat); Fat 4g; Prot 7g; Carb 8g; Sod 475mg; Chol 0mg.

Barbecue Sauce

A rich, thick, barbecue sauce. I've been making this one for over 20 years and it remains a family favorite. It's wonderful on beef or pork.

1 cup gf ketchup
1/2 cup molasses
2 tablespoons gf onion flakes
2 tablespoons brown sugar
1 tablespoon mustard seed
1 teaspoon crushed red pepper
1 teaspoon dried oregano
1/2 teaspoon black pepper
2 teaspoons paprika
1 teaspoon chili powder
1/2 teaspoon salt
1 bay leaf
1 garlic clove, minced
1 teaspoon orange zest
1/2 cup fresh orange juice
1/4 cup olive oil
1/4 cup red wine vinegar
2 tablespoons gf Worcestershire sauce

Combine all ingredients in small saucepan. Bring to boil over medium heat. Reduce heat and simmer gently for 20 minutes. Remove bay leaf.

Preparation = 20 minutes. Serves 8. Makes 2 cups of sauce.
Calories 179 (35% from fat); Fat 8g; Prot 1g; Carb 29g; Sod 54mg; Chol 0mg.

Spaghetti Sauce

I've been making this sauce for nearly 25 years and, even though we've tried several others, it remains our favorite. The crock pot works best; however, you can simmer it on the stove if you wish.

1 large can tomato juice
  (48 ounces)
3 small cans gf tomato paste
  (6 ounces each)
3 tablespoons dried parsley
2 tablespoons dried basil
1 tablespoon dried rosemary

2 bay leaves
2 teaspoons dried oregano
1 teaspoon black pepper
3 tablespoons sugar
2 teaspoons salt (or to taste)
1/4 cup Romano cheese
  (optional)

In large crock pot, combine all ingredients. Mix well. Cook all day on low-medium heat. Stir occasionally.
Preparation = 6-8 hours. Serves 12.
Calories 84 (11% from fat); Fat 1g; Prot 4g; Carb 17g; Sod 825mg; Chol 2mg.

Pizza Sauce

Prepare this no-fat sauce while the Pizza Crust (See Index) bakes.

8 ounces gf tomato sauce
1/2 teaspoon dried oregano
1/2 teaspoon dried basil
1/2 teaspoon dried rosemary
1/2 teaspoon fennel seeds

1/4 teaspoon gf garlic powder
  or 1 minced garlic clove
2 teaspoons sugar or honey
1/2 teaspoon salt

Combine all ingredients in small saucepan and bring to boil over medium heat. Reduce heat to low and simmer for 15 minutes, while Pizza Crust is being assembled. Top Pizza Crust with sauce and your preferred toppings. Makes about 1 cup.
Preparation = 15 minutes. Serves 4.
Calories 28 (0% from fat); Fat 0g; Prot 1g; Carb 7g; Sod 610mg; Chol 0mg.

Tomatillo Apple Salsa

A great, slightly unusual salsa for grilled chicken or fish.

5 tomatillos (husked, washed and chopped)
1 yellow bell pepper (seeded, chopped)
1 small red delicious apple (unpeeled, chopped)
1/2 cup red onion, chopped

1/4 cup chopped fresh cilantro
1 tablespoon fresh lemon juice
1 small jalapeno (seeded, minced)
1/4 teaspoon ground cumin
1/2 teaspoon salt
1/4 teaspoon white pepper

Mix the ingredients together in a medium bowl and refrigerate. (Can be prepared 3 hours ahead). Serve at room temperature.

Preparation = 20 minutes. Serves 4.
Calories 63 (10% from fat); Fat .8g; Prot 2g; Carb 14g; Sod 272mg; Chol 0mg.

Tomatillo Sauce

You can use this sauce in the same way you'd use a Red or Green Chile Sauce—on burritos, eggs, and so on.

1 pound tomatillos (husked, washed)
1 cup chopped onion
1 teaspoon olive oil
1 cup low-sodium chicken broth
1 garlic clove, minced

1 serrano chile, minced
4 teaspoons cider vinegar
1/4 teaspoon dried oregano
1/4 teaspoon ground cumin
1/4 teaspoon sugar or honey
1/2 cup fresh chopped cilantro

Preheat oven to 350 degrees. Place washed and husked tomatillos in a pie plate that has been coated with cooking spray. Bake for 30 minutes or until tomatillos are soft, but not split. Cool. Chop into quarters.

Meanwhile, heat olive oil in a heavy skillet and sauté onion until golden brown. Add tomatillos, chicken broth, garlic, chile, vinegar, oregano, cumin, and sugar. Bring to a boil, cover, and simmer for 15 minutes. Cool slightly.

Transfer mixture to food processor or blender (or use hand held blender) to puree mixture, adding all but two teaspoons of cilantro. When mixture is pureed, stir in remaining cilantro. Makes about 1 cup.

Preparation = 1 hour. Serves 4.

Calories 77 (30% from fat); Fat 3g; Prot 3g; Carb 12g; Sod 349mg; Chol 0mg.

White Dill Sauce with Mushrooms

This is a perfect topping for thick-fleshed fish such as halibut or yellow-fin tuna. It's also great on chicken, such as Chicken Kiev.

2 cups fresh mushrooms
  (cleaned, sliced)
1/2 cup finely chopped onion
1 teaspoon canola oil
1/3 cup low-sodium chicken broth
1 cup milk (cow, rice, or soy)
1/4 teaspoon sugar or honey

1/2 teaspoon dry mustard
1/2 teaspoon salt
1/4 teaspoon white pepper
2 teaspoons dried dill weed
1 tablespoon cornstarch (or
  enough to thicken sauce)
1 tablespoon water

In heavy non-stick saucepan, sauté onion and mushrooms in canola oil over medium heat for about 5 minutes. Add remaining ingredients, except for dill, flour, and water. Bring mixture to a boil, reduce heat to medium and cook, uncovered, until mixture is reduced by half, about 15 minutes. Add dill.

Combine flour and water into paste. Stir into sauce and continue stirring until mixture thickens slightly. Best if served immediately. Makes about 2/3 cup.

NON-ALCOHOLIC VARIATION: Substitute white grape juice for wine. Add 2 tablespoons white wine vinegar and 1 teaspoon lemon juice.

Preparation = 20 minutes. Serves 4.

Calories 72 (39% from fat); Fat 3g; Prot 4g; Carb 8g; Sod 416mg; Chol 8mg.

Cream Sauce for Vegetables

Creamed vegetables remind us of home-style cooking. Use this sauce on creamed peas, asparagus, or carrots.

1 cup milk (cow, rice, soy, or nut)	1/8 teaspoon white pepper
1 tablespoon canola oil	2 tablespoons white rice flour
1/4 teaspoon salt	or sweet rice flour

Heat milk (all but 1/4 cup), oil, salt and pepper in medium saucepan over medium heat.

Stir flour into remaining milk until mixture is smooth. Gradually whisk flour mixture into milk, continuing to whisk until mixture thickens.

Preparation = 20 minutes. Serves 4. Makes about 1 cup.

Calories 82 (60% from fat); Fat 5g; Prot 24g; Carb 6g; Sod 163mg; Chol 8mg.

Papaya Chutney

This is an unusual, yet very tasty version of chutney. Try it with roast chicken, grilled fish, or pork.

1 teaspoon olive oil
1/2 cup red onion, diced
1 tablespoon grated fresh
  ginger root
1 small garlic clove, minced
1 teaspoon ground cumin
1/2 teaspoon crushed red
  pepper

1/2 cup fresh lime juice
1/4 cup brown sugar
1 cup diced papaya
2/3 cup diced Roma tomatoes
1/4 teaspoon salt
1/8 teaspoon white pepper
1 cup chopped fresh cilantro

In heavy skillet over low-medium, sauté onion in olive oil until slightly tender. Add ginger root, garlic, cumin, and crushed red pepper and cook for two minutes. Add lime juice and brown sugar and cook until sauce is thick enough to coat the back of a spoon. Add the papaya and tomatoes and cook just until tender. Add salt, pepper, and cilantro. Serve at room temperature. Preparation = 25 minutes. Serves 4. Makes about 1 1/2 cups.
Calories 95 (14% from fat); Fat 2g; Prot 2g; Carb 21g; Sod 151mg; Chol 0mg.

Pineapple Salsa

At first, I was skeptical about this salsa—pineapple on fish? However, the flavors are absolutely divine. Just goes to show that you can't always tell by reading a recipe whether you'll really like it or not.

2 cups chopped fresh pineapple, with juice*
2 tablespoons red onion, finely chopped
1 small jalapeno chile pepper (top 1/8-inch cut off)

1 tablespoon sugar or honey
2 tablespoons white wine vinegar
dash of salt
1/2 cup chopped fresh cilantro

Combine all ingredients, except cilantro, in heavy saucepan and simmer gently for 10 minutes, or until mixture thickens slightly. Remove from heat. Discard jalapeno chile pepper. Stir in fresh cilantro. Serve on grilled fish. Makes about 2 cups.
* Canned pineapple may be used instead of fresh pineapple.
Preparation = 20 minutes. Serves 6.
Calories 42 (6% from fat); Fat .3g; Prot .7g; Carb 10g; Sod .4g; Chol 0mg.

Apple Chutney

This chutney goes especially well with the Pork Tenderloin (See Index). Even though it has a lot of ingredients, it's well worth the effort. My guests raved about it! And your house will smell heavenly from the aroma!

3 cups Granny Smith apples (about 4 - peeled, chopped)
1 cup chopped onions
3/4 cup brown sugar, packed
1/2 cup cider vinegar
1 cup water
1/4 cup chopped red bell pepper
1/4 cup chopped yellow bell pepper
1/2 cup golden raisins

1 tablespoon fresh ginger root, chopped
1 garlic clove, minced
1/4 teaspoon crushed red pepper
1 teaspoon salt
1/4 teaspoon ground nutmeg
1/4 teaspoon ground allspice
1/8 teaspoon ground cloves
1/4 teaspoon salt
1/8 teaspoon white pepper

In heavy large saucepan, combine apples, onions, brown sugar, cider vinegar, water, bell peppers, raisins, ginger root, minced garlic, crushed red pepper, salt, nutmeg, allspice, and cloves. Bring to boil over medium heat, stirring until sugar dissolves.

Reduce heat and simmer for one hour. Add 1/4 teaspoon salt and 1/8 teaspoon white pepper. Cool. Keeps in refrigerator for up to 1 week. Serve warm or at room temperature.

Preparation = 1 1/4 hours. Serves 14. Makes 3 1/2 cups.

Calories 66 (2% from fat); Fat .2g; Prot .4g; Carb 17g; Sod 16mg;Chol 0mg.

White Chocolate Topping

This topping can be used on top of the Chocolate Brownie or Chocolate Soufflé (See Index). It's also good over fresh fruits.

1 ounce white chocolate
1 cup Yogurt Cheese (See Index)
   or soft silken tofu
1 tablespoon sugar or honey

1/4 cup milk (cow, rice, soy, nut)
1/2 teaspoon grated orange peel
1 tablespoon fresh orange juice

Dice chocolate into very small pieces. Combine remaining ingredients in blender until very smooth. Add chocolate pieces. Makes about 1 1/4 cups. Serve immediately.
Preparation = 10 minutes. Serves 4.
Calories 90 (44% from fat); Fat 5g; Prot 3g; Carb 11g; Sod 34mg; Chol 9mg.

Hot Fudge Sauce

This delectable, rich sauce keeps in the refrigerator for up to 1 month. Just warm in the microwave before serving.

2 cups brown sugar
2/3 cup cocoa (not Dutch)
1 cup evaporated skim milk
   (or soy, rice, or nut milk)

2 tablespoons butter or oleo
1 teaspoon gf vanilla extract
1/2 teaspoon salt

In heavy saucepan, combine brown sugar and cocoa. Add milk. Heat to rolling boil, stirring constantly for 1 minute. Reduce heat to low and beat with spoon until smooth. Remove from heat and stir in butter, vanilla, and salt.
Preparation = 20 minutes. Serves 12. Makes 3 cups.
Calories 147 (23% from fat); Fat 4g; Prot 2g; Carb 28g; Sod 141mg; Chol 11mg.

Raspberry Sauce

*This sauce is great on ice cream, as a coulis (pronounced coulee')
under desserts such as cakes or cheesecakes, or I sometimes use it as
a filling for layer cakes. You can also baste Cornish game hens with
it.*

3 **tablespoons raspberry jam**   1 **teaspoon gf orange extract**
   (use all fruit seedless type)   1 **tablespoon orange juice**

Combine all ingredients in small saucepan. Over medium
heat, stir constantly until jam is melted. Cool. Makes 1/4 cup.
For a larger amount, double or triple the ingredients.
Preparation = 20 minutes. Serves 4.
Calories 48 (0 % from fat); Fat 0g; Prot .1g; Carb 10g; Sod 6mg; Chol 0mg.

Yogurt Cheese

*This is one of the best innovations in low-fat cooking!! It is so simple,
yet produces the smooth, creamy texture we all crave—without all
the fat or calories. For a spicier version, see next recipe.*

8 ounces low-fat yogurt

Place coffee filter inside strainer and place strainer over bowl
or measuring cup. Place yogurt in coffee filter. Place plastic bag
around strainer and bowl so that it's sealed from air. Place in
refrigerator overnight or all day. Discard the liquids that collect
in bottom of bowl. Store in refrigerator.
This method can be used with flavored yogurts as well, but
yogurts with gelatin will not drain as thoroughly. I prefer to use
a brand that has a high acidophilus content.

Spicy Yogurt Cheese

1/2 teaspoon chili powder	1/4 teaspoon salt
1/2 teaspoon ground coriander	1 cup Yogurt Cheese (See
1 teaspoon pure maple syrup	previous page)

Toast chili and coriander in heavy skillet over medium-high heat for about 40 seconds or until spices become fragrant. Cool slightly. Combine with other ingredients. Chill. Serve at room temperature.

Preparation = 15 minutes. Serves 4. Makes about 1 cup.

Calories 38 (4% from fat); Fat .2g; Prot 3g;Carb 6g; Sod 182mg; Chol 1mg.

Asian Vinaigrette

A great dressing to serve over rice vermicelli or a combination of butter lettuce and mandarin oranges.

1 tablespoon low sodium gf soy sauce
2 tablespoons gf teriyaki sauce
4 teaspoons fresh lime juice

1 tablespoon honey
2 tablespoons olive oil
2 tablespoons sesame oil
2 tablespoons gf Worcestershire sauce

In screw-top jar, combine all ingredients. Cover and shake vigorously until blended. Refrigerate, covered, up to 1 week. Preparation = 5 minutes. Makes 1/2 to 3/4 cup. Serves 6.
Calories 62 (65% from fat); Fat 5g; Prot .3g; Carb 5g; Sod 262mg; Chol 0mg.

Avocado Dressing

This is a very tasty dressing for plain old lettuce.

1 large ripe avocado
1/4 cup water
1 teaspoon fresh lime juice
1/8 teaspoon grated lime peel

1/2 teaspoon grated fresh onion
1/8 teaspoon ground cumin
1 small garlic clove, minced
1/8 teaspoon white pepper

Peel and mash the avocado in a small bowl. Combine mashed avocado with water and remaining ingredients in food processor or blender. Puree mixture until desired consistency. This dressing is best if served immediately. Makes about 1 cup. Preparation = 5 minutes. Serves 8.
Calories 40 (77% from fat); Fat 4g; Prot .5g; Carb 2g; Sod 4mg; Chol 0mg.

Buttermilk Dressing

This is great on any lettuce salad, but it's especially good on the first tender lettuce from your garden.

1 cup buttermilk or 2 tablespoons cider vinegar and
   enough milk (cow, rice, or soy)
   to equal 1 cup
2 tablespoons red wine vinegar

2 teaspoons Dijonnaise mustard
1 small garlic clove, minced
1/4 teaspoon black pepper
1/2 teaspoon onion salt
1 teaspoon dried chives

Combine all ingredients in screw-top jar and shake vigorously to blend. Store in refrigerator for one week, covered.
Preparation = 10 minutes. Makes about 1 1/2 cups. Serves 12.
Calories 10 (19% from fat); Fat .2g; Prot .7g; Carb 1g; Sod 100mg; Chol 1mg.

Citrus Dressing

The citrus base of this dressing, accented by fennel and basil, is refreshing.

2 tablespoons rice vinegar
2 tablespoons olive oil
1/4 cup fresh orange juice
2 teaspoons fresh lime juice
1 tablespoon grated orange peel
1/4 teaspoon crushed red pepper
2 teaspoons grated lime peel

2 teaspoons fennel seed,
   toasted
2 tablespoons fresh basil,
   finely chopped
1/8 teaspoon salt
dash white pepper

Combine all ingredients in screw-top jar and shake vigorously to blend. Refrigerate for up to 1 week.
Preparation = 10 minutes. Makes about 1/2 cup. Serves 4.
Calories 48 (80% from fat); Fat 5g; Prot .2g; Carb 2g; Sod 45mg; Chol 0mg.

Hazelnut Vinaigrette

Flavored oils, though somewhat expensive, are great to have on hand for salad dressings such as this one.

1/4 cup hazelnut oil	1 tablespoon fresh snipped chives
1/4 cup water	or 1 teaspoon dried chives
1/4 cup white wine vinegar	1 tablespoon Dijonnaise mustard
2 tablespoons fresh lemon juice	1/4 teaspoon black pepper
1 teaspoon sugar or honey	

In screw-top jar, combine all ingredients. Cover and shake well. Store in refrigerator for up to 2 weeks.
Preparation = 10 minutes. Makes about 1 cup. Serves 8.
Calories 70 (85% from fat); Fat 7g; Prot .1g; Carb 3g; Sod 24mg; Chol 0mg.

Herb Vinaigrette

The nice thing about making your own vinaigrettes is that you can control what goes into them. This one also doubles as a marinade for meats.

1/4 cup olive oil	1/2 teaspoon dry mustard
1/4 cup water	1/2 teaspoon dried chives
1/4 cup red wine vinegar	1/4 teaspoon dried chervil
1 tablespoon dried parsley	1/4 teaspoon powdered sugar

Combine all ingredients in screw-top jar. Cover and shake vigorously until well blended. Store, covered, in refrigerator for up to 1 week. Makes about 1 cup
Preparation = 10 minutes. Serves 8.
Calories 64 (92% from fat); Fat 7g; Prot .1g; Carb 1g; Sod 1mg; Chol 0mg.

Lime Cilantro Dressing

This is a perfect dressing for a salad in a Southwestern meal.

1 teaspoon lime zest
1/4 cup fresh lime juice
1/4 cup chopped fresh cilantro
1/2 teaspoon salt
1 small garlic clove, minced

1/2 teaspoon powdered sugar
1/2 cup olive oil
1/4 cup water
1/4 cup rice vinegar
1/8 teaspoon ground cumin

Combine all ingredients in screw-top jar. Cover and shake vigorously until well-blended. Store, covered, in refrigerator for up to 1 week. Makes about 1 cup.
Preparation = 10 minutes. Serves 8.
Calories 66 (88% from fat); Fat 7g; Prot .2g; Carb 2g; Sod 135mg; Chol 0mg.

Peanut Dressing

This is the perfect dressing for buckwheat noodles.

2 tablespoons olive oil
1 tablespoon gf peanut butter
   (commercial, not freshly
   ground)
1 tablespoon gf soy sauce

3 tablespoons rice vinegar
1 tablespoon water
1 teaspoon brown sugar
1/8 teaspoon crushed red
   pepper

In medium bowl, combine all ingredients. Heat on high in microwave for 1 minute or until mixture is hot. Stir mixture until peanut butter melts. Serve warm or at room temperature.
Preparation = 10 minutes. Makes 1/2 cup. Serves 4.
Calories 102 (78% from fat); Fat 9g; Prot 1g; Carb 4g; Sod 332mg; Chol 1mg.

Pine Nut Dressing

This is a unique way to use pine nuts, which are almost a staple in the Southwest. I like to leave some of the pine nuts in chopped form to add some texture.

1/4 cup pine nuts, lightly
   toasted
1/4 cup grapefruit juice
   (red or pink)
2 teaspoons white wine vinegar

2 tablespoons fresh orange juice
1/4 teaspoon powdered sugar
1/8 teaspoon salt
dash of white pepper
2 tablespoons olive oil

In a blender, blend together all ingredients (except olive oil) until smooth. With blender running, add olive oil in thin stream and blend until the dressing is emulsified. Store dressing in refrigerator, covered, for about 1 week. Makes about 1/2 cup Preparation = 10 minutes. Serves 4.

Calories 122 (80% from fat); Fat 12g; Prot 3g; Carb 4g; Sod 67mg; Chol 0mg.

Raspberry Vinaigrette

Salad dressings with raspberry vinegar are very popular these days. When you taste this one, you'll see why. It's great!

1/4 cup fresh raspberries (pressed through sieve)	1/4 cup water
	1/4 teaspoon salt
1/4 cup raspberry vinegar*	1/2 teaspoon gf onion powder
1/4 cup white grape or apple juice	1 teaspoon sugar
	1 teaspoon Dijonnaise mustard
1/4 cup fresh lemon juice	1/4 cup olive oil

Combine all ingredients except olive oil and whisk vigorously until well blended. Continue whisking while adding olive oil in a thin stream.

(Using a regular blender or a hand-held, immersion blender works very well, also. Blend all ingredients except olive oil. With blender on, add oil in thin stream).

Strain dressing through a fine sieve. Makes 1 1/4 cups.
Preparation = 10 minutes. Serves 10.
Calories 58 (86% from fat); Fat 5g; Prot .1g; Carb 2g; Sod 60mg; Chol 0mg.

*To make raspberry vinegar, place 2 raspberry-flavored herbal tea bags in 1/4 cup rice vinegar (or cider vinegar). Let steep at room temperature for 2-3 hours.

Red Chile Dressing

This is perfect for salads served with a Southwestern meal. Be sure to use red chile powder—preferably from New Mexico—not chili powder (which is actually a mix of several spices).

1 minced garlic clove
1 teaspoon red chile powder
1/2 teaspoon paprika
1 tablespoon cider vinegar
1 tablespoon fresh lemon juice
1/4 cup water

1 tablespoon gf Worchester-
   shire sauce
2 teaspoons Dijonnaise mustard
1/2 teaspoon Reese anchovy paste
1/4 cup olive oil

In a food processor or blender, puree all ingredients together except for the olive oil. With the processor still running, slowly add olive oil and continue processing until the mixture is emulsified. Store in refrigerator, covered, for about 1 week. Preparation = 10 minutes. Makes about 1 cup. Serves 8.
Calories 66 (91% from fat); Fat 7g; Prot .3g; Carb 1g; Sod 48mg; Chol 0mg.

Southwestern Dressing

A very simple, yet tasty Southwestern way to dress salad greens.

1/4 cup red wine vinegar
2 tablespoons olive oil
1/4 teaspoon black pepper
1 teaspoon chili powder

1 teaspoon dried oregano
1 teaspoon ground cumin,
   toasted lightly

Combine all ingredients in screw-top jar. Shake vigorously to blend well.
Preparation = 15 minutes. Makes about 1/4 cup. Serves 4.
Calories 67 (88.7% from fat); Fat 7g; Prot .2g; Carb 1.8g; Sod 7mg; Chol 0mg.

Thousand Island Dressing

This dressing is a critical component of Reuben sandwiches. It's the preferred dressing for those who like creamy salad dressings.

1 cup low-fat gf mayonnaise
3 tablespoons gf cocktail sauce
1 tablespoon green bell pepper, finely chopped

1 tablespoon red bell pepper, finely chopped
1 teaspoon dried chives

Blend ingredients thoroughly with a wire whisk. Store in refrigerator, covered, for up to 1 week.
Preparation = 10 minutes. Makes about 2 cups. Serves 16.
Calories 198 (97% from fat); Fat 22g; Prot .3g; Carb .8g; Sod 157mg; Chol 16mg.

Walnut Oil Vinaigrette

Walnut oil makes this vinaigrette a special way to dress salad greens, but it also tastes great on cooked Brussels sprouts.

2 teaspoons balsamic vinegar
1/4 cup fresh orange juice
1/2 cup walnut oil

1/4 teaspoon salt
1/8 teaspoon black pepper
1/2 teaspoon dried thyme

Combine all ingredients in screw-top jar. Cover and shake vigorously until well blended. Store, covered, in refrigerator for up to 1 week. Best served with orange or citrus-based salads.
Preparation = 10 minutes. Makes about 1/2 cup. Serves 4.
Calories 128 (93% from fat); Fat 14g; Prot .1g Carb 2g; Sod 134mg; Chol 0mg.

VEGETABLES

Potatoes
Hash Brown Casserole 179
Hot German Potato Salad 180
Oven-Fried Potatoes 181
Potato Pancakes 182
Scalloped Potatoes 183
Scalloped Potatoes w/ Ham 183

Miscellaneous
Creamed Corn 177
Eggplant Parmesan 178
Grilled Vegetables & Quinoa or
    Brown Rice 184
Cream Sauce for Vegetables 160

Many of us should include more vegetables in our diets because they are important sources of nutrients and fiber. The USDA recommends 3-5 servings daily, but it's often hard to achieve that goal.

One of the concerns for wheat and gluten-sensitive persons is not knowing the source of sauces, thickeners, or seasonings often found on prepared vegetables—either in restaurants, other people's homes, or in pre-packaged vegetables at the grocery store.

You'll notice that there aren't many recipes in this section. That's because there are many ways to eat vegetables without any need for flour. You can eat them raw, of course, or cooked and topped with Parmesan cheese or herbs, or glazed with a little sugar, maple syrup, or flavored oil. But this excludes some of our favorite vegetable dishes.

So, this section concentrates on recipes that would typically include wheat. Family favorites are featured such as Scalloped Potatoes, Hash Brown Casserole, and Creamed Corn. There is even a Cream Sauce for vegetables so you can enjoy creamed peas, asparagus, or even potatoes.

Creamed Corn

Creamed corn is a perfect accompaniment to a meal of roast chicken or roast beef.

1 cup water
1 teaspoon cornstarch
1/2 teaspoon salt
2 teaspoons sugar or honey

1/8 teaspoon white pepper
1 cup corn kernels—fresh or frozen

Combine cornstarch with 2 tablespoons of the water. In medium saucepan over medium heat, add cornstarch mixture to remaining water and heat, stirring constantly until mixture thickens. Remove from heat. Add salt, sugar, and pepper.

Add corn kernels. You can use two different ways to puree the corn. Using a hand-held, immersion blender, hold blender in saucepan and blend until about 1/2 of the corn is pureed, leaving some whole kernels. An alternate method is to put 1/2 of the corn and cornstarch mixture into a blender and pulse on/off to desired consistency. Return mixture to saucepan. Add remaining corn kernels. Heat creamed corn to serving temperature.

Preparation = 15 minutes. Serves 4.

Calories 47 (5% from fat); Fat .3g; Prot 1g; Carb 11g; Sod 270mg; Chol 0mg.

Eggplant Parmesan

Imagine my dismay to learn that the Eggplant Parmesan I thought was safe in restaurants actually contained wheat bread crumbs. But you can enjoy it at home using this recipe.

3 tablespoons balsamic vinegar
1 tablespoon olive oil
1/2 teaspoon salt
1/2 teaspoon sugar or honey
1/4 teaspoon dried oregano
1/4 teaspoon basil
1/2 teaspoon black pepper
1 1/2 pounds eggplant,
   sliced 1/2-inch thick

4 ounces low-fat mozzarella
   cheese, shredded - or use
   non-dairy cheese
1 tablespoon Parmesan
   cheese (cow, rice, or soy)
2 1/2 cups Spaghetti Sauce
   (See Index)
cooking spray
fresh basil leaves (optional)
Parmesan cheese (optional)

Preheat oven to 400 degrees. Combine vinegar, olive oil, salt, sugar, oregano, basil, and pepper in bowl. Dip each eggplant slice in mixture and lay on baking sheet that has been coated with cooking spray. Bake 15 minutes per side or until tender.

Coat shallow 2-quart baking dish with cooking spray. Spoon 3/4 cup of the spaghetti sauce into dish. Arrange half of the eggplant over sauce. Spoon 3/4 cup of the spaghetti sauce over eggplant. Sprinkle with half of the mozzarella cheese. Arrange half of the remaining eggplant over sauce. Top with remaining eggplant and sauce, ending with remaining mozzarella and the Parmesan cheese.

Cover with foil and bake at 400 degrees for 20 minutes. Uncover and bake for another 15 minutes, until bubbly. Let stand 15 minutes for easier cutting.

Preparation = 50 minutes. Serves 4.

Calories 222 (42% from fat); Fat 10g; Prot 8g; Carb 25g; Sod 811mg; Chol 11mg.

Hash Brown Casserole

This dish falls into the "comfort food" category. It tastes good, the texture is pleasing and it reminds me of old-fashioned, home-cooked meals. This recipe is dairy-based.

3/4 cup onions, chopped
1 1/2 tablespoons tapioca flour
1/4 teaspoon dry mustard
1/4 teaspoon salt
1/4 cup low-sodium chicken
  broth
1/2 cup skim milk (cow, rice, soy, or nut)
1/2 cup low-fat, sharp cheddar cheese, shredded
1/4 cup low-fat Swiss cheese, shredded
1/4 teaspoon white pepper
1/2 cup Yogurt Cheese (See Index)
1 pound gf hash brown potatoes, thawed (or grate your own fresh potatoes)
paprika (for garnish)
cooking spray

Coat a medium saucepan with cooking spray. Cook onions, covered, for 3 minutes or until tender. Combine flour, mustard, salt, chicken broth, and milk in screw top jar and shake until well blended (or blend in blender). Add to saucepan and cook for 5 minutes or until mixture thickens.

Remove from heat. Add cheddar cheese, Swiss cheese, and pepper, stirring until cheeses are melted. Stir in Yogurt Cheese. Combine cheese mixture and potatoes. Spread into 8 x 8-inch pan that has been coated with cooking spray. Sprinkle with paprika. Cover and bake at 350 degrees for 30 minutes. Uncover and bake an additional 20 minutes.

Preparation = 1 1/4 hours. Serves 6.

Calories 225 (44% from fat); Fat 11g; Prot 8g; Carb 22g; Sod 628mg; Chol 14mg.

Hot German Potato Salad

A great side dish for Smoked Pork Chops or Pork Roast. The combination of sweet and tart flavors is very tantalizing.

3 1/2 cups new potatoes,
   (peeled, cooked and diced)
1 strip lean bacon, uncooked
1/2 cup brown sugar
1/2 cup cider vinegar
1 teaspoon Dijonnaise mustard
3/4 teaspoon celery seed
1 tablespoon onion, grated

1/2 teaspoon salt
1/4 teaspoon black pepper
1/4 cup green bell pepper,
   chopped
1/4 cup minced red bell pepper
1 tablespoon chopped fresh
   parsley,

Slice cooked, hot new potatoes into large serving dish. Meanwhile, fry the bacon in a skillet until crisp. Remove bacon. Into skillet, add sugar, vinegar, mustard, celery seed, onion, salt, black pepper, and bell peppers. Stir over medium heat until mixture comes to a boil.

Reduce heat and simmer for one minute. Stir in crumbled bacon. Pour mixture over potatoes and toss with spatula until well coated. Sprinkle with chopped parsley. Serve warm. Preparation = 30 minutes. Serves 4.

Calories 172 (5% from fat); Fat 1g; Prot 2g; Carb 40g; Sod 61mg; Chol 1mg.

Oven-Fried Potatoes

These potatoes have a crisp exterior, yet a soft inside.

2 large baking potatoes, cut
   lengthwise into 8 wedges
1/2 tablespoon olive oil
1/2 teaspoon paprika

1/2 teaspoon rosemary leaves,
   crushed
1/2 teaspoon salt
cooking spray

Preheat oven to 400 degrees. Place potato wedges in plastic bag or bowl. Add olive oil. Toss or shake to coat with oil. Add paprika, rosemary leaves, and salt. Shake or toss to cover.

Place potatoes on baking sheet that has been coated with cooking spray. Bake for 30 minutes or until potatoes are nicely browned on all sides. Turn frequently for even browning. Preparation = 30 minutes. Serves 4.

Calories 61 (26% from fat); Fat 2g; Prot 1g; Carb 10g; Sod 6mg; Chol 0mg.

Potato Pancakes

These tasty little pancakes are great topped with applesauce.

2 cups grated potatoes
   (4 potatoes)
1 large egg, well beaten
2 tablespoons white rice flour
1 teaspoon baking powder

1 teaspoon salt
1/4 teaspoon white pepper
1/2 small onion, grated
1 tablespoon olive oil
cooking spray

Combine grated potatoes, egg, flour, baking powder, salt, pepper, and onion.

Heat a skillet or griddle and coat lightly with cooking spray. Add oil.

Drop batter onto hot griddle, using 1/4 cup of batter for each pancake. Cook about 5-7 minutes on each side, or until golden brown.

NOTE: Assemble all other ingredients before grating potatoes. Work quickly once potatoes are grated to prevent them from becoming discolored.

Preparation = 30 minutes. Serves 4.

Calories 101 (42% from fat); Fat 5g; Prot 3g; Carb 12g; Sod 710mg; Chol 53mg.

Scalloped Potatoes

This is another of those "comfort food" dishes, the kind we occasionally crave. Bake it in the oven while the Meat Loaf (See Index) cooks or add ham for a meal in itself.

4 medium russet potatoes
  (peeled, sliced)
3/4 teaspoon gf onion salt
1/4 teaspoon white pepper
1 tablespoon gf onion flakes
1/8 teaspoon ground nutmeg
1/2 teaspoon dried mustard
1 tablespoon canola oil

2 tablespoons potato starch
  or sweet rice flour
2 cups skim or 1% milk (or
  rice or soy milk)
1 tablespoon Parmesan cheese
  (cow, rice, or soy - optional)
1 tablespoon butter or oleo, in
  1/4-inch cubes
paprika for garnish

Preheat oven to 350 degrees. Toss potatoes with salt, pepper, and onion flakes in 1 1/2-quart casserole or baking dish. Combine remaining ingredients (except butter) in jar with screw top lid. Shake thoroughly until ingredients are blended. Or, blend in blender until smooth.

Pour milk mixture over potatoes. Dot with butter cubes. Lightly sprinkle with paprika. Bake for 1 hour or until sauce is bubbly and potatoes are lightly browned.

SCALLOPED POTATOES WITH HAM: Add 1 cup cubed ham and reduce onion salt to 1/2 teaspoon.

Preparation = 1 1/4 hours. Serves 4.

Calories 205 (29% from fat); Fat 7g; Prot 7g; Carb 30g; Sod 399mg; Chol 10mg.

Grilled Vegetables &
Quinoa or Brown Rice

One of the greatest flavor combinations is fresh vegetables and the smoky, charcoal flavor from the grill. If grilling is not possible, I've successfully stir-fried these vegetables in a skillet. Celiacs may substitute brown rice for the quinoa.

2 tablespoons olive oil
1/3 cup balsamic vinegar
1/3 cup green onions, chopped
1/2 teaspoon dried oregano
1 garlic clove, minced
1/2 teaspoon ground coriander
1/4 teaspoon ground cumin
1/4 teaspoon salt
1/4 teaspoon black pepper
2 teaspoons molasses
4 carrots, halved lengthwise

1 large red pepper
1 large yellow pepper
4 red new potatoes, halved
2 medium zucchini, sliced
     1/4-inch thick
1 large onion, halved
2 small yellow squash, sliced
     1/4-inch thick
2 cups cooked quinoa or
     brown rice
cooking spray

Combine first 10 ingredients (oil through molasses) in a large bowl to make vinegar mixture. Set aside. Cut vegetables into large pieces, keeping thickness to about 1/4 inch. You want them thin enough to cook thoroughly, yet thick enough to remain whole during the process. Let vegetables stand in vinegar mixture for about 30-45 minutes. Stir occasionally.

Drain the vegetables and arrange in grill basket that has been coated with cooking spray. Save vinegar mixture.

Cook on grill over medium-hot coals with lid down about 15-20 minutes, turning every 5 minutes.
Meanwhile, warm the vinegar mixture over medium heat.

Remove vegetables from grill basket and toss with vinegar mixture. Serve warm with cooked quinoa or rice. Makes 6 cups. Preparation = 45 minutes. Serves 6.
Calories 162 (26% from fat); Fat 5g; Prot 4g; Carb 28g; Sod 207mg; Chol 0mg.

POULTRY

Grilled Chicken

Grilled Chicken & Ancho
  Chiles 207
Grilled Chicken w/ Peach
  Salsa 208
Grilled Chicken w/ Spicy
  Glaze 206
Grilled Chicken w/ Teriyaki
  Glaze 209
Grilled Chipotle Chicken 209
Red Chile Barbecued
  Chicken 210

Stove-Top Chicken

Chicken Cacciatore 192
Chicken Curry 193
Chicken Paprika's w/ Egg
  Noodles 195
Creamed Chicken on
  Buttermilk Biscuits 194
Lemon Chicken 200
Lemon-Tarragon Chicken 201
Tostadas 236

Baked Dishes

Chicken & Broccoli
  Quiche 187
Chicken Breasts w/
  Mushrooms 188
Chicken Peanut Mole 191
Chile Relleno Casserole w/
  Chicken 196
Chicken Shepherd's Pie 190
Chicken Tandoori 189
Coq Au Vin 197
Cornish Game Hens w/
  Fruit Glaze 199
Enchiladas 198
Mexican Chicken
  Casserole 202
Oven-Fried Chicken 203
Spicy Oven-Fried Chicken 203
Tarragon-Dijon Chicken 204
Thai Chicken 205
Turkey Mole 191

See pages 261-263 for menus with Poultry as the main dish.

Poultry, especially chicken, is one of the most versatile foods in our diets. It can take on a variety of different personalities depending on how it's prepared—grilled, roasted, or baked—and the sauces we put on it can vary from hot and spicy to mellow and creamy.

In this section, chicken is prepared in a variety of ways for the wheat-sensitive person. There are several ethnic dishes such as Thai Chicken, Lemon Chicken (a Chinese favorite), and Chicken Tandoori. There are classic, elegant dishes such as Coq Au Vin and Chicken Cacciatore. And, of course, there are numerous Southwestern versions of chicken such as Grilled Chipotle Chicken and Mexican Chicken Casserole. And even turkey becomes Turkey Mole, a traditional Mexican dish.

Skinless, boneless chicken breasts are featured in many of these dishes. They are extremely low in fat and very easy to prepare because there are no skin or bones to remove. You can substitute other chicken pieces in most of these recipes, however, bear in mind that the fat and calorie content will increase.

Chicken & Broccoli Quiche

Looking more like a custard than a quiche, this dish eliminates the traditional pastry crust. Fat content is further reduced by using ricotta cheese and yogurt, with a minimal amount of Swiss cheese. This recipe is dairy-based.

1 cup light ricotta cheese
1/2 cup low-fat yogurt
2 medium eggs
1/4 cup brown rice flour
1/2 teaspoon baking powder
1/8 teaspoon ground nutmeg

1/2 teaspoon celery salt
1/4 cup Parmesan cheese
10 ounces frozen broccoli,
  (thawed, drained)
1 1/2 cups cooked chicken
1/4 cup grated Swiss cheese
cooking spray

Preheat oven to 350 degrees. Spray a 9-inch pie plate with cooking spray.

Combine ricotta, yogurt, eggs, flour, baking powder, nutmeg, celery salt, and Parmesan cheese in blender and puree until smooth. In large bowl, combine pureed mixture with chicken and broccoli. Spoon into prepared pie plate and top with grated Swiss cheese.

Bake for 30-45 minutes or until toothpick comes out clean. Let stand 10 minutes before serving.

Preparation = 1 hour. Serves 6.

Calories 252 (45% from fat); Fat 12g; Prot 22g; Carb 11g; Sod 349mg; Chol 131mg.

Chicken Breasts with Mushrooms

I've been making this recipe for 20 years, having converted it from one given to me by my friend, Pat Grantier. Thanks, Pat.

4 boneless, skinless chicken
   breast halves
3/4 cup dried gf bread crumbs
1/2 teaspoon dried thyme
2 tablespoons brown rice flour
3 large eggs, lightly beaten
1/2 teaspoon salt
1/4 teaspoon black pepper

2 tablespoons olive oil
1 cup fresh sliced mushrooms
1/2 cup Provolone or Muenster
   cheese (or non-dairy cheese of
   your choice)
1/2 cup gf dry white wine
1/3 cup fresh lemon juice
cooking spray

Wash chicken breasts and pat dry with paper towels. Cut into thin slices.

Combine bread crumbs (a good way to use up your leftover gf bread), thyme, and flour in pie plate. Dip chicken pieces into eggs, then bread crumbs. Season with salt and pepper.

Preheat oven to 350 degrees.

In heavy skillet, brown chicken slices in olive oil until golden brown. Coat 8 x 8-inch baking dish with cooking spray. Layer chicken slices on bottom, top with mushrooms, and lay cheese slices on top. Pour white wine on top.

Bake for 30-40 minutes or until cheese is melted and liquid is bubbly. Before serving, drizzle fresh lemon juice over casserole. Preparation = 45 minutes. Serves 4.

Calories 349 (37% from fat); Fat 13g; Prot 30g; Carb 21g; Sod 35mg; Chol 61mg.

Chicken Tandoori

The tangy flavors of this dish remind one of faraway, exotic places. And, its brilliant red-orange color looks gorgeous on your plate.

4 chicken hind quarters
1 tablespoon olive oil
1 medium onion, diced
1 minced garlic clove
2 teaspoons ground coriander
2 teaspoons ground cumin
2 teaspoons ground turmeric
2 teaspoons paprika
1 tablespoon grated fresh
   ginger root

1 tablespoon red wine vinegar
1 teaspoon salt
1/4 teaspoon cayenne pepper
8 ounces low-fat plain yogurt
   or 1/2-2/3 cup non-dairy liquid
2 teaspoons grated lemon peel
1 small lemon, sliced
1/4 cup chopped fresh parsley
cooking spray

In small, heavy skillet over medium heat, combine olive oil with onion and sauté for 1 minute. Add garlic, coriander, cumin, turmeric, paprika, ginger root, vinegar, salt, and pepper. Cook for about 10 minutes, stirring frequently until onion is tender and well coated with spices. Remove from heat; cool for 5 minutes.

In large bowl, combine cooled onion mixture with yogurt and lemon peel. Wash and pat dry chicken pieces. Add to yogurt mixture and marinate in refrigerator up to 4 hours.

Preheat oven to 425 degrees. Spray shallow baking dish with cooking spray. Remove chicken from marinade and arrange in baking pan. Bake, uncovered, for 45 minutes, turning once. Brush with reserved marinade during last 5 minutes of baking. Garnish with lemon slices and parsley.

Preparation = 1 hour. Serves 4.

Calories 431 (31% from fat); Fat 15g; Prot 60g; Carb 12g; Sod 967mg; Chol 228mg.

Chicken Shepherd's Pie

This dish is a great way to use up leftover chicken (or turkey), mashed potatoes, and vegetables.

1 pound skinless cooked chicken or turkey, cubed
1 cup green peas
1/4 cup corn
1 cup chopped carrots
1 tablespoon canola oil
1 small chopped onion
2 chopped celery stalks
1 minced garlic clove
2 1/2 cups low-sodium chicken broth
2 tablespoons tapioca flour
3 tablespoons water
1/2 cup fresh sliced mushrooms
1/2 teaspoon celery salt
1/2 cup gf dry white wine
1 teaspoon dried thyme
1/3 cup chopped fresh parsley
2 cups mashed potatoes
2 tablespoons Parmesan cheese (cow, rice, or soy)

If not using leftover cooked chicken and vegetables, blanch peas, carrots, and corn in small amount of boiling, salted water, and brown the chicken in canola oil. Set aside.

Place onion, celery, and garlic in skillet and cook in canola oil until onion is transparent. Add the chicken broth and bring to a boil. Reduce heat and simmer until mixture is reduced by one-third, about 5 minutes.

Mix tapioca flour with 3 tablespoons water until paste forms, then stir into skillet slowly. Simmer until thickened. Add all remaining ingredients, except potatoes, and Parmesan cheese.

Preheat oven to 450 degrees. Spoon mixture into four individual soup bowls. Mound the mashed potatoes on top, covering the surface entirely. Sprinkle with the Parmesan cheese.

Bake for about 35 minutes, until the potatoes are browned. Preparation = 1 hour. Serves 4.

Calories 452 (21% from fat); Fat 10g; Prot 41g; Carb 4g; Sod 1753; Chol 72mg.

Turkey Mole

There are many different versions of Mole (Mo-lay). It's unusual, but definitely carries a flavor of the Southwest.

1 cup low-sodium chicken broth
1 cup slivered almonds
1 cup chopped onion
1 small minced garlic clove
1/2 teaspoon ground cinnamon
1/2 teaspoon ground cloves
1/2 teaspoon ground coriander
1/4 teaspoon crushed red pepper

2 medium chopped tomatoes
1/2 cup chopped fresh cilantro
1/4 teaspoon black pepper
4 ounces diced green chiles (1 can)
1/4 cup raisins
1/8 teaspoon fennel seed, crushed
1 ounce unsweetened chocolate, melted
2 pounds cooked turkey breast

In blender, combine all ingredients except turkey breast and chocolate. Blend until nearly smooth. Add melted chocolate. Pour sauce over turkey breast in heavy skillet or pan. Cover and simmer for 20 minutes or until turkey breast is heated through.

To serve, arrange turkey breast on serving plate. Slice diagonally and spoon mole sauce on top.

Preparation = 30 minutes. Serves 6.

Calories 392 (47% from fat); Fat 21g; Prot 25g; Carb 30g; Sod 378mg; Chol 45mg

CHICKEN PEANUT MOLE: Substitute 4 cooked boneless skinless chicken breasts for the turkey breast. Add 2 tablespoons creamy gf peanut butter and follow directions above. Preparation = 30 minutes. Serves 4.

Calories 318 (50% from fat); Fat 19g; Prot 23g; Carb 19g; Sod 165mg; Chol 34mg

Chicken Cacciatore

The aroma of this dish wafting through the house on a cold, winter day is intoxicating. Your own homemade egg Pasta (See Index) and a crisp lettuce salad complete the dinner.

4 boneless skinless chicken breast halves
1 tablespoon olive oil
3 cups fresh mushrooms, halved
1 small green bell pepper, chopped
1 large onion, sliced
1 minced garlic clove
1/2 cup gf dry red wine
28 ounces canned tomatoes
2 tablespoons gf tomato paste
2 tablespoons lemon juice
2 teaspoons dried basil
1 teaspoon sugar
1 teaspoon dried thyme
1/4 teaspoon crushed red pepper
1/2 teaspoon salt
1/4 teaspoon black pepper
2 tablespoons tapioca flour
2 tablespoons water
1 recipe gf Pasta (made into noodles) (See Index)

In large, heavy skillet or Dutch oven, brown chicken on all sides in olive oil. Add mushrooms, green bell peppers, onion, and garlic to skillet. Cook until vegetables are tender. Add wine, bring to boiling and simmer, uncovered, until liquid is nearly evaporated. Add undrained canned tomatoes, tomato paste, lemon juice, basil, sugar, thyme, crushed red pepper, salt, and pepper.

Return chicken to pan and simmer, uncovered, for 15 minutes. To thicken sauce, stir 2 tablespoons tapioca flour with 2 tablespoons water and add to sauce, stirring until thickened. Preparation = 45 minutes. Serves 4.

Calories 189 (20% from fat); Fat 4g; Prot 17g; Carb 18g; Sod 533; Chol 40mg.

Chicken Curry

The many spices and apricots lend this dish a very interesting combination of flavors.

1 small chopped onion
1 minced garlic clove
1 tablespoon canola oil
4 boneless, skinless chicken
   breast halves
1/2 cup water
1 1/2 teaspoons ground
   coriander
1 teaspoon ground ginger
1/2 teaspoon ground
   cardamom

3/4 teaspoon ground cumin
1/4 teaspoon cayenne pepper
1/2 cup golden raisins
1/4 cup apricot preserves
2 tablespoons cornstarch
2 tablespoons cold water
1/2 teaspoon salt
1/4 teaspoon black pepper
1 cup low-fat plain yogurt or
   2/3 cup non-dairy milk
paprika for garnish

In large, heavy skillet sauté garlic and onion in canola oil until lightly browned. Add chicken and sauté until browned. Add water, coriander, ginger, cardamom, cumin, cayenne pepper, raisins, and apricot preserves. Simmer, covered, for 10-15 minutes stirring occasionally.

Stir cornstarch and water together until blended. Gradually stir mixture into skillet along with salt and pepper. Simmer gently, stirring constantly until sauce thickens. Gently stir in yogurt and bring to serving temperature. Do not boil. Serve alone or over cooked rice. Garnish each serving with paprika.

Preparation = 30 minutes. Serves 4.

Calories 293 (15% from fat); Fat 5g; Prot 25g; Carb 37g; Sod 519mg; Chol 52mg.

Creamed Chicken
on Buttermilk Biscuits

Save those leftover biscuits and top them with this flavorful sauce. Leftover chicken works great, too! This recipe is dairy-based.

4 boneless, skinless chicken breast halves, cut in 1-inch cubes
1 tablespoon canola oil
1 minced garlic clove
4 cups fresh mushrooms, halved
1/2 cup chopped onion
1/2 cup low-sodium chicken broth
1/2 teaspoon gf celery salt
1/4 teaspoon white pepper
2 tablespoons cornstarch
1 cup skim milk (cow, rice, soy)
1 cup low-fat gf sour cream or sour cream alternative
8 Buttermilk Biscuits (See Index), baked
4 tablespoons green onions or chives, finely chopped

In large, heavy skillet sauté chicken in canola oil over medium heat for 5-7 minutes. Remove chicken. Set aside.

Add garlic, mushrooms, and onion. Cook, uncovered, for 5-7 minutes or until liquid evaporates.

Add all but 2 tablespoons chicken broth, celery salt, and white pepper to skillet. Over medium heat, stir cornstarch into 2 remaining tablespoons of broth to form paste. Add to skillet and cook, stirring, until bubbly and thickened. Cook 1 minute more.

In a bowl, stir together the sour cream and milk. Stir gently into skillet. Heat to serving temperature.

Serve over biscuits. Garnish with chopped green onion or chives.

Preparation = 30 minutes. (Biscuits already made) Serves 4.

Calories 444 (35% from fat); Fat 17g; Prot 33g; Carb 36g; Sod 1253mg; Chol 113mg.

Chicken Paprika's with Noodles

This dish has a rich, bold flavor that fills the house with a wonderful aroma. Use noodles from your own Pasta (See Index).

4 boneless, skinless chicken breast halves
2 tablespoons canola oil
1 large onion, finely chopped
1 minced garlic clove
2 tablespoons Hungarian paprika
16 ounces canned tomatoes, drained
1/4 teaspoon cayenne pepper
1/2 teaspoon sugar or honey
1 teaspoon dried thyme

1/2 teaspoon salt
1/4 teaspoon black pepper
1 cup sliced mushrooms
1 cup low sodium chicken broth
2 tablespoons tapioca flour
2 tablespoon water
1/2 cup gf sour cream or sour cream alternative or Yogurt Cheese (See Index)
4 cups gf noodles from Pasta recipe (See Index)
1 teaspoon dried parsley

In large, heavy Dutch oven, brown chicken pieces on all sides in canola oil over medium heat. Remove from pan.

Add onion and sauté for 5 minutes over medium heat. Add garlic and paprika and cook, stirring constantly, for 1 minute. Stir in tomatoes, cayenne pepper, sugar, thyme, salt, and pepper.

Return chicken to pan, add mushrooms and chicken broth, and bring to a boil. Reduce heat, cover, and simmer for 20 minutes. (Can be prepared up to this point, then refrigerated for up to 24 hours.)

Stir flour into water to form paste. Stir mixture into sauce and cook for 3 minutes or until sauce thickens. Gently stir in sour cream. Serve over hot noodles. Garnish with parsley.

Preparation = 45 minutes. Serves 4.

Calories 500 (22% from fat); Fat 12g; Prot 42g; Carb 56g; Sod 840mg; Chol 123mg.

Chile Relleno Casserole with Chicken

This is a favorite at our house, combining the delicious flavors of chiles, eggs, and cheese. Omit the chicken for a meatless dish. This recipe is dairy-based.

1 cup Mozzarella cheese, shredded
1 cup Colby cheese, shredded
1 cup cooked chicken, cubed
4 ounces diced green chiles (1 can)
4 large eggs, beaten
1 cup gf light sour cream
1/2 teaspoon dried oregano
1/4 teaspoon ground cumin
1/8 teaspoon chili powder
paprika, for garnish
1/4 cup chopped fresh cilantro
cooking spray

Spray an 8 x 8-inch glass dish with cooking spray. Preheat oven to 350 degrees.

In dish, alternately layer cheeses, then chicken, then chiles in dish, ending with the cheese.

Beat together the eggs, sour cream, oregano, cumin, and chili powder. Pour over cheese mixture. Sprinkle generously with paprika.

Bake for 30-45 minutes, or until top is puffy and golden.

Serve immediately, topped with chopped cilantro.

Preparation = 45 minutes. Serves 4.

Calories 370 (60% from fat); Fat 25g; Prot 28g; Carb 8g; Sod 435mg; Chol 283mg.

MEATLESS CHILE RELLENO CASSEROLE: Omit chicken.

Calories 332 (63% from fat); Fat 23g; Prot 23g; Carb 8g; Sod 420mg; Chol 267mg.

Coq Au Vin

This is an elegant blend of flavors and the dish cooks slowly on its own, leaving you free to do other things.

1 bacon slice, uncooked
1 teaspoon olive oil
4 skinless chicken legs
4 skinless chicken thighs
1 package frozen pearl
  onions, thawed
3 garlic cloves, peeled
1/2 pound fresh mushrooms
1 cup low-sodium chicken broth
1/2 cup gf dry red wine
1 teaspoon dried thyme

1 teaspoon sugar or honey
1 teaspoon dried rosemary,
  crushed
1 teaspoon paprika
1/2 teaspoon gf celery salt
1/2 teaspoon black pepper
1 pound small new potatoes
1 pound baby carrots
1/4 teaspoon salt
1/2 cup chopped fresh parsley

In heavy, ovenproof Dutch oven, brown the bacon slice until crisp. Remove from pan and remove pan from heat.

Wash chicken and pat dry with paper towels. Return Dutch oven to medium heat. Add 1 teaspoon olive oil to bacon fat. Cook chicken pieces until browned on all sides. Remove chicken from pan and set aside.

In same Dutch oven, brown onions and garlic for about 5 minutes. Add the mushrooms and sauté 5 minutes more. Slowly pour in the chicken broth and wine. Add the thyme, sugar, rosemary, paprika, celery salt, and black pepper. Return chicken to the pan and add potatoes and bacon slice.

Bake, covered, for 30 minutes in 400 degree oven. Reduce heat to 350, add carrots and continue cooking for another 30 minutes. Check doneness of chicken. It should be nearly falling off the bone. Garnish with parsley.

Preparation = 1 1/4 hours. Serves 4.

Calories 339 (25% from fat); Fat 9g; Prot 23g; Carb 39.g; Sod 514mg; Chol 65mg.

Enchiladas

Enchiladas are a classic, Mexican dish. There are many versions of Enchiladas, so try this one and then improvise as you wish. This recipe is dairy-based.

4 boneless, skinless chicken breast halves, cooked, cut in 8 strips
1 cup chopped onion
1 minced garlic clove
16 ounces canned tomatoes, chopped
8 ounces gf tomato sauce
4 ounces diced green chiles (1 can)
1/2 teaspoon dried basil
1/2 teaspoon dried oregano
1/2 teaspoon gf celery salt
1/2 teaspoon ground cumin
1 teaspoon sugar or honey
1/2 cup chopped fresh cilantro
8 Corn Tortillas (See Index) or use purchased tortillas
1 cup Monterey jack cheese, shredded
1 cup Cheddar cheese, shredded
1 cup gf light sour cream
cooking spray
2 tablespoons fresh cilantro, for garnish

In a heavy, medium saucepan sauté onions and garlic in olive oil about 4 minutes. Add tomatoes, tomato sauce, chiles, basil, oregano, salt, cumin, sugar, and cilantro. Bring to a boil, reduce heat and simmer, covered, for 15 minutes. Remove from heat.

Preheat oven to 350 degrees. Dip each corn tortilla into tomato mixture to soften. Place a strip of chicken and 2 tablespoons of shredded cheese on each tortilla. Roll up and place seam side down in a 13 x 9-inch pan that's been sprayed with cooking spray.

Blend sour cream into remaining tomato mixture and pour over enchiladas. Top with remaining cheese.

Bake for 35 minutes, or until heated through. Garnish with additional chopped cilantro, if desired.

Preparation = 1 hour. Serves 4.

Calories 633 (46% from fat); Fat 33g; Prot 42g; Carb 44g; Sod 1231; Chol 131mg.

BEEF ENCHILADAS: Substitute 1/2 pound browned ground beef for chicken.

Calories 682 (56% from fat); Fat 43g; Prot 43g; Carb 44g; Sod 1211mg; Chol 123mg.

MEATLESS ENCHILADAS: Omit chicken and fill each tortilla with 4 tablespoons of Monterey jack and cheddar cheese.

Calories 588 (54% from fat); Fat 36g; Prot 25g; Carb 44g; Sod 1253mg; Chol 94mg.

Cornish Game Hens with Fruit Glaze

The glaze on these game hens is delicious and causes them to brown beautifully.

2 Cornish game hens, halved	1/4 teaspoon dried tarragon
1/2 teaspoon salt	1 teaspoon olive oil
1/4 teaspoon black pepper	1/4 cup red wine vinegar
1/2 cup raspberry jam	1 minced garlic clove
1/4 teaspoon dried thyme	cooking spray

Wash game hens and pat dry. Season with salt and pepper. Arrange game hens skin side up in roasting pan that has been coated with cooking spray. If possible, place hens on roasting rack in pan so they do not sit in fat while roasting.

Combine remaining ingredients in small bowl and microwave until jam is melted. Stir mixture thoroughly.

Bake hens, covered, in 400 degree oven for 45 minutes to 1 hour, brushing frequently with glaze.

Preparation = 1 hour. Serves 4.

Calories 784 (46% from fat); Fat 39g; Prot 77g; Carb 27g; Sod 1169mg; Chol 248mg.

Lemon Chicken

I often avoided this dish in Chinese restaurants because I wasn't sure how it was prepared. Now, you can enjoy your own wheat-free version.

4 boneless, skinless chicken
   breast halves
5/8 cup cornstarch
3/4 cup water
2 large egg yolks
2 tablespoons canola oil
3 tablespoons brown sugar,
   firmly packed

1 tablespoon fresh
   ginger root, grated
1 cup low-sodium chicken
   broth
1/3 cup fresh lemon juice
1 teaspoon grated lemon peel
1/2 cup green onions, finely
   chopped diagonally

Wash the chicken breasts and pat dry.

In medium-size bowl, combine 1/2 cup of the cornstarch, 1/4 cup of the water, and the egg yolks. Whisk until batter is smooth. Dip each chicken breast in batter to coat thoroughly.

Heat canola oil in large, heavy skillet. Brown chicken breasts on all sides. Remove to drain on paper towels; keep warm.

In same skillet, place remaining cornstarch, brown sugar, and ginger root. Stir in remaining 1/2 cup water and the chicken broth. Cook over medium heat, stirring frequently, until mixture thickens and comes to a boil. Remove from heat. Stir in lemon juice and lemon peel.

Cut each chicken breast into 4 pieces, slightly at a diagonal. Arrange on a plate and pour sauce over chicken. Sprinkle with chopped green onion.

Preparation = 30 minutes. Serves 4.

Calories 321 (32% from fat); Fat 11g; Prot 25g; Carb 28g; Sod 463mg; Chol 158mg.

Lemon-Tarragon Chicken

Skinless, boneless chicken breasts are a real time-saver in the kitchen. Here, they team up with lemon and tarragon in a creamy sauce served over noodles.

4 boneless, skinless chicken
  breast halves
1 tablespoon canola oil
1 cup fresh mushrooms, halved
1 minced garlic clove
1 1/2 teaspoons dried tarragon
1/2 teaspoon black pepper
14 1/2 ounces low-sodium
  chicken broth (1 can)

2 tablespoons cornstarch
1 teaspoon grated lemon peel
2 tablespoons gf light sour
  cream (or sour cream
  alternative)
1 recipe Pasta (See Index)
  made into noodles, cooked
2 tablespoons chopped fresh
  parsley

In a large, heavy skillet heat canola oil over medium-high heat. Add chicken, mushrooms, garlic, tarragon, and pepper. Cook, uncovered for 15 minutes—until chicken is no longer pink—turning once. Remove chicken and mushrooms with slotted spoon.

Combine 2 tablespoons of the chicken broth with cornstarch to form paste. Add cornstarch mixture to skillet along with remaining chicken broth, stirring over medium-high heat until thickened and bubbly. Remove about 1/2 cup of mixture and stir into sour cream.

Return to skillet along with chicken and mushrooms. Stir in lemon peel. Heat to serving temperature, but do not boil. Serve over hot noodles. Garnish with chopped parsley.
Preparation = 30 minutes. Serves 4.
Calories 356 (24% from fat); Fat 9g; Prot 31g; Carb 33g; Sod 805mg; Chol 91mg.

Mexican Chicken Casserole

I've served this dish for nearly 20 years, but modified it to exclude cream soup (which contains wheat flour). It features all the classic Mexican flavors in a creamy casserole topped with cheese. You may use non-dairy versions of the jack and cheddar cheeses, if you wish.

1 cup low-sodium chicken broth
1 cup gf Mexican tomatoes
1 medium onion, finely diced
1/2 cup gf light sour cream or sour cream alternative
4 ounces diced green chiles (1 can)
1/2 teaspoon dried oregano
1/4 teaspoon ground cumin
1/4 teaspoon ground sage
1/4 teaspoon chili powder
1/4 teaspoon garlic powder
1/2 teaspoon salt
2 cups cooked chicken, cubed
2 cups corn tortilla chips
1 cup grated cheddar cheese
1 cup grated Monterey jack cheese
cooking spray
2 tablespoons fresh chopped cilantro

Preheat oven to 350 degrees. Mix chicken broth, tomatoes, onions, sour cream, green chiles, spices, and salt together in bowl to form sauce. Set aside.

Coat a 10 x 14-inch casserole dish with cooking spray. Layer 1/2 of the chicken, then 1/2 of the sauce, cheese, and corn tortilla chips. Repeat layers, ending with cheese. Bake for 35-40 minutes, or until casserole is bubbly. To serve, garnish with chopped cilantro.

Preparation = 50 minutes. Serves 6.

Calories 310 (50% from fat); Fat 17g; Prot 26g; Carb 12g; Sod 699mg; Chol 73mg.

Oven-Fried Chicken

This favorite is wheat-free and low in fat. Try the spicy version if you like your fried chicken with a little heat.

4 skinless chicken thighs
1/2 cup buttermilk (or plain
   milk - dairy or non-dairy)
1/4 teaspoon cayenne pepper
1/4 teaspoon gf garlic powder
1/4 cup brown rice flour

3 tablespoons cornmeal
1/2 teaspoon salt
1/4 teaspoon white pepper
1/4 teaspoon paprika
cooking spray

Preheat oven to 400 degrees. Coat baking sheet with cooking spray. Wash the chicken thighs and pat them dry.

In pie plate, mix buttermilk, cayenne pepper, and garlic powder.

In another pie plate, mix together the dry ingredients. Dip each chicken thigh into the buttermilk mixture, then the flour mixture. Place on prepared baking pan. Gently spray with cooking spray.

Bake 45 minutes to 1 hour, or until chicken is crispy.

NOTE: Other chicken pieces may be substituted for the chicken thighs, however, darker meat will be juicier.

Preparation = 1 1/4 hours. Serves 4.

Calories 161 (20% from fat); Fat 4g; Prot 17g; Carb 14g; Sod 363mg. Chol 62mg.

SPICY OVEN-FRIED CHICKEN: Add these herbs to flour mixture: 1 teaspoon each dried oregano, dried basil, dried thyme, and 1/4 teaspoon cayenne pepper.

Tarragon-Dijon Chicken

This dish has never failed to please—and even impress—my guests! The tarragon and thyme blend nicely with the pineapple juice to create a delectable sauce.

4 boneless skinless chicken
  breast halves
1/2 teaspoon salt
1/4 teaspoon black pepper
2/3 cup pineapple juice
1/2 cup gf dry white wine
1 tablespoon Dijonnaise mustard
1 tablespoon gf Worcestershire
  sauce

1/2 teaspoon dried tarragon
1/4 teaspoon dried thyme
1 teaspoon cornstarch
1 tablespoon water
2 tablespoons chopped fresh
  parsley
cooking spray

Preheat oven to 375 degrees. Spray 8 x 8-inch square baking pan with cooking spray. Wash chicken breasts and pat dry with paper towels. Arrange chicken breasts in pan.

In small bowl, combine remaining ingredients (except cornstarch) and pour over chicken. Cover and bake for 45-50 minutes. Uncover, turn chicken over and bake another 10 minutes.

Transfer juices from baking pan to a saucepan, leaving chicken in oven to stay warm. (A turkey baster works well to remove juices.) Mix cornstarch with water to form paste. Over medium heat, stir cornstarch or arrowroot mixture into juices and cook until mixture thickens.

To serve, pour 1/3 of mixture over chicken breasts. Garnish with parsley. Serve remaining sauce on the side.

Preparation = 1 hour. Serves 4.

Calories 152 (12% from fat); Fat 2g; Prot 21g; Carb 7g; Sod 378; Chol 51mg.

Thai Chicken

Ethnic dishes provide great variety for our taste buds. This one features the creamy taste of peanut butter and peppery spices.

3/4 cup gf teriyaki sauce
1/4 cup creamy gf peanut
    butter (not fresh ground)
1 tablespoon sugar
1 teaspoon fresh ginger root,
    grated
1/4 cup water

1/2 teaspoon crushed red
    pepper
2 tablespoons chopped
    fresh cilantro
4 boneless, skinless chicken
    breast halves
cooking spray

Combine all ingredients, except chicken, in top of double boiler over simmering water. Stir until smooth, then cook until mixture thickens—about 20 minutes. Cool.

Preheat oven to 350 degrees.

Coat 8 x 8-inch baking dish with cooking spray. Arrange chicken breast halves in dish; brush sauce generously over chicken. Baste once again while baking.

Bake for 25-30 minutes or until chicken is cooked through.

Preparation = 45 minutes. Serves 4.

Calories 270 (31% from fat); Fat 10g; Prot 28g; Carb 18g.; Sod 2899mg; Chol 51mg.

Grilled Chicken with Spicy Glaze

This is delicious and very easy. Make the sauce the night before, light the grill when you get home from work the next day, and prepare the remainder of the meal while the chicken cooks.

8 pieces skinless chicken legs
  and thighs
1/2 teaspoon salt
1/4 teaspoon black pepper
2 tablespoons Dijonnaise mustard
2 tablespoons molasses

2 tablespoons orange juice
1 tablespoon gf soy sauce
1 tablespoon fresh ginger
  root, grated
1 teaspoon orange zest

Season chicken with salt and pepper. Arrange chicken on grill over hot coals.

While chicken is cooking, mix remaining ingredients together (if you haven't prepared sauce the night before). When chicken starts to brown, baste with glaze and continue basting until chicken is done.

Preparation = 30 minutes. Serves 4.

Calories 209 (25% from fat); Fat 5g; Prot 29g; Carb 8g; Sod 607mg; Chol 113mg.

Grilled Chicken & Ancho Chiles

Ancho chiles are dried poblanos and provide a mild, yet definite "heat" to the sauce. If anchos are unavailable locally, try Mail-Order sources (See Index).

4 boneless, skinless chicken
   breast halves
1/2 teaspoon salt
1/4 teaspoon black pepper
1 1/2 cups water
1 dried ancho chile

1 garlic clove, peeled
1 teaspoon salt
1/2 teaspoon dried thyme
1/2 cup fresh orange juice
1 tablespoon sugar or honey
1 teaspoon olive oil

Season chicken breasts with salt and pepper. Grill or broil chicken until cooked through.

While the chicken is cooking (or up to 1 day before serving), boil water, ancho chile, garlic, salt, and thyme for about 5 minutes. Using slotted spoon, remove ancho chile from cooking liquid. Reserve cooking liquid. Discard stem from chile and remove seeds. Puree chile and garlic clove in blender or food processor. With machine running, add 1/2 cup of the cooking liquid, orange juice, sugar, and olive oil and blend until mixture is smooth. Serve sauce with chicken.

Preparation = 30 minutes. Serves 4.

Calories 138 (18% from fat); Fat 3g; Prot 20g; Carb 7g; Sod 863mg; Chol 51mg.

Grilled Chicken with Peach Salsa

Fresh peaches combine with fragrant spices to top this grilled chicken. A great way to get extra fruit into your diet!

4 boneless, skinless chicken
  breast halves
1/2 teaspoon salt
1/4 teaspoon black pepper
4 medium ripe peaches
1 tablespoon lemon juice
1/4 teaspoon gf celery salt
1 cup chopped red bell pepper

1 small chopped onion
1/4 teaspoon cayenne pepper
1 teaspoon ground cumin
1/3 cup brown sugar, packed
1/3 cup cider vinegar
2 tablespoons diced green
  chiles
1/3 cup chopped fresh cilantro

Season chicken breasts with salt and pepper. Grill or broil chicken until cooked through.

While chicken is cooking, peel, pit, and cut peaches into thin wedges. Toss with lemon juice and celery salt. Set aside.

In heavy skillet coated with cooking spray, sauté red bell pepper and onion until vegetables are crisp-tender, about 5 minutes. Add cayenne pepper and cumin and stir for 1 minute. Add brown sugar and cider vinegar and heat for about 3 minutes. Add peach mixture (including juices) and green chiles and heat through. Stir in chopped cilantro. Serve at room temperature over grilled chicken.

Preparation = 30 minutes. Serves 4.

Calories 210 (8% from fat); Fat 2g; Prot 22g; Carb 27g; Sod 572mg; Chol 51mg.

Grilled Chicken with Teriyaki Glaze

This dish is easy and very tasty—great for summertime grilling.

4 boneless, skinless chicken
  breast halves
1/2 teaspoon salt
1/4 teaspoon black pepper
1/2 cup gf teriyaki sauce

2 teaspoons balsamic vinegar
1/2 teaspoon fennel seed,
  toasted
1/2 teaspoon grated orange peel

Season chicken with salt and pepper. Grill or broil chicken until cooked through.

Meanwhile, combine remaining ingredients. Brush chicken frequently with the sauce while it is cooking.

Preparation = 30 minutes. Serves 4.

Calories 132 (10% from fat); Fat 2g; Prot 22g; Carb 6g; Sod 1707mg; Chol 51mg.

Grilled Chipotle Chicken

Chipotles are dried, smoked jalapenos and are very hot!!! If not available in your area, check Mail-Order Sources (See Index).

4 boneless, skinless chicken
  breast halves
1/4 cup fresh orange juice
1 teaspoon chipotle pepper
  in adobo sauce

1 tablespoon cider vinegar
1 teaspoon Dijonnaise mustard
1 tablespoon molasses
1/4 teaspoon salt

Grill chicken breasts over hot coals. Combine remaining ingredients and baste chicken breasts twice during cooking.

Preparation = 30 minutes. Serves 4.

Calories 144 (10% from fat); Fat 2g; Prot 20g; Carb 10g; Sod 211mg; Chol 51mg.

Red Chile Barbecued Chicken

This sauce is bold and powerful. It can be made the night before, then refrigerated until you grill the chicken the next day.

4 boneless, skinless chicken breast halves
2 tablespoons canola oil
1 minced garlic clove
1 small onion, finely chopped
1 tablespoon red chile powder (New Mexico)
1 bay leaf
1/2 teaspoon fresh ginger root, grated
1/2 teaspoon curry powder
1/4 teaspoon black pepper
1 teaspoon dry mustard
1 teaspoon dried thyme
1/4 teaspoon crushed red pepper
8 ounces gf tomato sauce
1/2 cup fresh orange juice
2 tablespoons molasses
1 tablespoon gf Worcestershire sauce
1 tablespoon gf soy sauce

Wash chicken and pat dry. Combine canola oil, garlic and finely chopped onions in heavy skillet and sauté over medium-high heat until onions become transparent. Add remaining ingredients and simmer over low heat for 15 minutes. Sauce should be reduced to approximately 1 1/2 cups.

Prepare barbecue grill. Cook chicken pieces, turning once, until done. Brush sauce on chicken frequently.

Preparation = 45 minutes. Serves 4.

Calories 237 (33 % from fat); Fat 8g; Prot 22g; Carb 18g; Sod 794mg; Chol 51mg.

FISH & SEAFOOD

Fish

Cod Baked w/ Vegetables 213
Halibut w/ Papaya Salsa 214
Orange Roughy in
   Parchment 215
Red Snapper in Parchment 216
Red Snapper w/ Tomato-
   Lime Salsa 219
Salmon & Vegetables in
   Parchment 217
Salmon w/ Asian Sauce 218
Salmon w/ Maple Glaze 218

Shellfish

Cajun Shrimp on Noodles 222
Crab Zucchini Casserole 223
Oven-Baked Crab Cakes 220
Shrimp Creole 224
Shrimp Curry 225
Southwestern Crab Cakes 221
White Clam Sauce w/ Linguine 226

See pages 257-258 for menus featuring Fish & Seafood as entrees.

Fish is a great component of wheat-free, gluten-free diets because there are so many varieties of fish and because fish can be prepared in so many different ways, ranging from old favorites to light, contemporary cuisine. And, it's typically low in fat, too.

In this section, you'll find shellfish featured in dishes such as Shrimp Creole, Oven-Baked Crab Cakes, and White Clam Sauce with Linguine. Fish is featured with mouth-watering fruit salsas and glazes such as Salmon with Maple Glaze and Halibut with Papaya Salsa.

There are a variety of cooking methods in these recipes ranging from grilling to baking to parchment cooking (baking fish in parchment paper at high temperatures for short periods of time). You're sure to find several dishes to add to your repertoire of meals.

Cod Baked with Vegetables

Prepare this dish the night before, refrigerate, then bake when you get home from work. Fix the remaining dishes while it cooks. You'll be ready for dinner in about 30 minutes.

1 pound cod or sole fillets
1 tablespoon olive oil
1/3 cup carrot (peeled, diced)
1/3 cup finely chopped celery
1/3 cup green onion, chopped
1 small garlic clove, minced
1/2 teaspoon gf celery salt
1/4 teaspoon gf lemon pepper

1/2 teaspoon dried rosemary
1 large tomato, chopped
1 tablespoon fresh parsley, chopped
1/2 teaspoon lemon zest
2 tablespoons Parmesan cheese (cow, rice, or soy)
cooking spray

Preheat oven to 350 degrees. Coat 11 x 7-inch baking dish with cooking spray.

Arrange fish in single layer on bottom of dish. Set aside. Sauté carrots, celery, green onion, and garlic in 1 tablespoon olive oil over medium heat for about 3 minutes. Stir in celery salt, lemon pepper, rosemary, tomato, parsley and lemon zest. Spoon mixture over fish. Sprinkle with Parmesan cheese. Bake 20-25 minutes or until fish flakes easily.

Preparation = 25 minutes. Serves 4.

Calories 156 (30% from fat); Fat 5g; Prot 22g; Carb 5g; Sod 348mg; Chol 51mg.

Halibut with Papaya Salsa

The colors in this salsa are absolutely beautiful. And the jalapeno adds a little heat. This dish makes a wonderful summertime dinner entree, but we like it so much that I prepare it year-round.

1 ripe papaya, peeled	1/2 teaspoon minced garlic
1/4 cup red bell pepper	1/4 cup chopped fresh cilantro
1/4 cup yellow bell pepper	1 jalapeno pepper, 1/8-inch
1/4 cup red onion	top cut off
2 tablespoons fresh lime juice	1/4 teaspoon salt
1/4 cup frozen apple juice	1/8 teaspoon white pepper
concentrate, thawed	4 halibut steaks

Finely chop papaya, peppers, and red onion. Combine all ingredients except halibut. Cover and chill in refrigerator up to 4 hours. Remove jalapeno before serving. Makes 2 cups.

Meanwhile, grill halibut steaks (or broil) until cooked through. To serve, top each halibut steak with 1/2 cup salsa. Preparation = 15 minutes. Serves 4.

Calories 295 (12% from fat); Fat 4g; Prot 37g; Carb 29g; Sod 237mg; Chol 54mg.

Orange Roughy in Parchment

Fish cooked in parchment comes out very moist, tender and flavorful. It can be assembled the night before, then baked while you prepare the remainder of the meal.

4 orange roughy fillets,
(about 1 1/2 pounds)
1/4 cup sun-dried tomatoes
in oil, chopped
1/4 cup fresh lemon juice
1/2 teaspoon lemon zest
2 teaspoons dried rosemary,
crushed

1 small garlic clove, minced
1/4 cup chopped green onions
1/2 teaspoon gf lemon pepper
1/2 teaspoon salt
cooking spray
parchment paper

Cut 4 pieces of parchment paper into 13-inch squares. Preheat oven to 425 degrees. Combine all ingredients in small bowl, except orange roughy.

Arrange parchment squares on counter top. Place one orange roughy fillet on center of each square. Top with tomato mixture. Fold parchment paper together, crimping or folding edges attractively. Twist ends tightly to seal. Spray with cooking spray.

Bake at 425 degrees for about 15 minutes or until packages puff up and are lightly browned. Place on individual serving plates. Cut open carefully to avoid steam burns.

NOTE: Aluminum foil can be substituted for parchment paper. Do not spray with cooking spray.

Preparation = 30 minutes. Serves 4.

Calories 159 (46% from fat); Fat 8g; Prot 17g; Carb 4g; Sod 452mg; Chol 23mg.

Red Snapper in Parchment

Cooking in parchment produces a very tasty, low-fat dish. This red snapper is delightfully seasoned and very colorful.

4 red snapper fillets, about
   1 1/2-pounds
1 tablespoon olive oil
1/2 cup chopped fresh cilantro
2 medium tomatoes, chopped
2 tablespoons grated onion
1 teaspoon dried rosemary
1 teaspoon dried basil

1/4 cup gf dry white wine
1/4 cup black olives, sliced
1/2 teaspoon lemon zest
1/2 teaspoon salt
1/4 teaspoon black pepper
cooking spray
parchment paper

Cut 4 pieces of parchment paper into 13-inch squares. Set aside. Preheat oven to 425 degrees.

Combine olive oil, cilantro, tomatoes, onions, rosemary, basil, white wine, olives, lemon zest, salt, and pepper.

Place a red snapper fillet in the center of each parchment square. Evenly divide the tomato mixture on top of each fillet. Fold parchment paper together, crimping or folding edges attractively. Twist ends tightly to seal. Spray with cooking spray.

Bake at 425 degrees for about 15 minutes or until packages puff up and are lightly browned. Place on individual serving plates. Cut open carefully to avoid steam burns.

NOTE: Aluminum foil can be substituted for parchment paper. Do not spray with cooking spray.

Preparation = 25 minutes. Serves 4.

Calories 290 (24% from fat); Fat 7g; Prot 45g; Carb 5g; Sod 509mg; Chol 81mg.

Salmon & Vegetables in Parchment

This is an easy way to serve salmon and vegetables. Assemble the night before, refrigerate, and then bake while you prepare the remainder of dinner. This makes an excellent company dish, too.

4 salmon fillets
1/2 teaspoon salt
1/4 teaspoon black pepper
1 teaspoon dried dill weed
1 carrot, julienned
1 zucchini, julienned

1 red bell pepper, julienned
1 tablespoon grated onion
1 teaspoon lemon zest
1 tablespoon olive oil
parchment paper
cooking spray

Preheat oven to 425 degrees. Cut 4 pieces of parchment paper into 13-inch squares. Lay each piece flat on the counter top and lay a salmon fillet on each. Combine remaining ingredients and divide evenly on each salmon fillet.

Fold parchment paper together, crimping or folding edges attractively. Twist ends tightly to seal. Spray with cooking spray.

Bake at 425 degrees for about 15 minutes or until packages puff up and are lightly browned. Place on individual serving plates. Cut open carefully to avoid steam burns.

NOTE: Aluminum foil can be substituted for parchment paper. Do not spray with cooking spray.

Preparation = 30 minutes. Serves 4.

Calories 247 (34% from fat); Fat 9g; Prot 35g; Carb 4g; Sod 398mg; Chol 88mg.

Salmon with Asian Sauce

The light, yet slightly spicy sauce is a great companion for salmon.

1 cup low sodium gf soy sauce
1 tablespoon cornstarch
1 tablespoon fresh ginger root, grated
1 tablespoon rice vinegar
1 tablespoon olive oil

2 teaspoons corn syrup or honey
1/4 teaspoon cayenne pepper
1/4 teaspoon black pepper
1 garlic clove, minced
4 salmon fillets

Combine all ingredients, except salmon, in blender or food processor. Puree until almost smooth. Makes about 1 cup.

Meanwhile, grill (or broil) salmon fillets. Baste frequently with sauce. Serve immediately.

Preparation = 30 minutes. Serves 4.

Calories 280 (31% from fat); Fat 9g; Prot 37g; Carb 9g; Sod 2048mg; Chol 88mg.

Salmon with Maple Glaze

The sweet maple syrup produces a glaze that truly complements the salmon flavor.

1/2 cup fresh lemon juice
1/4 cup pure maple syrup
1/4 teaspoon gf maple extract
1 garlic clove, minced
1/2 teaspoon crushed red pepper
1 teaspoon olive oil

2 tablespoons fresh gingerroot, grated
1/4 teaspoon salt
4 salmon fillets, 1-inch thick
cooking spray

In a small, heavy saucepan mix together the lemon juice, maple syrup, maple extract, garlic, red pepper, olive oil, ginger root, and salt. Simmer until mixture is reduced to about 1/2 cup. Remove from heat and cool.

Meanwhile, preheat broiler or light grill. If broiling, spray broiler pan with cooking spray. If grilling, coat rack with cooking spray. While salmon is broiling or grilling, baste with sauce.

Preparation = 30 minutes. Serves 4.

Calories 268 (24% from fat); Fat 7g; Prot 34g; Carb 16g; Sod 250mg; Chol 88mg.

Red Snapper with Tomato-Lime Salsa

Tomatillos (they're not tomatoes) produce a slightly tart taste that combines beautifully with other flavors in this salsa.

4 red snapper fillets
1 tablespoon olive oil
2 Roma tomatoes, finely
  chopped
8 medium tomatillos
  (husked, chopped)
1/4 cup yellow bell pepper,
  finely chopped

2 tablespoons red onion,
  finely chopped
1 teaspoon lime zest
1 tablespoon fresh lime juice
1 tablespoon honey
1/4 teaspoon ground cumin
1/4 cup chopped fresh cilantro

Combine all ingredients, except snapper and olive oil. Cover and chill up to 4 hours. Makes about 1 cup.

Grill red snapper for approximately 10 minutes, per side, or until done. To serve, put about 1/4 cup of salsa on top of each red snapper fillet.

Preparation = 30 minutes. Serves 4.

Calories 155 (31% from fat); Fat 5g; Prot 18g; Carb 8g; Sod 6mg; Chol 31mg.

Oven-Baked Crab Cakes

Crab cakes are great as appetizers or as a main entree. Use your leftover slices of gf White Bread or French Bread (See Index).

1 celery stalk, finely chopped
1 tablespoon gf onion flakes
2 large egg whites
1 tablespoon Durkee shrimp spice
1 tablespoon fresh parsley, finely chopped
1/4 teaspoon cayenne pepper
1 tablespoon Parmesan cheese (cow, rice, or soy)

1 tablespoon gf Worcestershire sauce
1 teaspoon gf Italian Seasoning
1/2 cup low-fat plain yogurt or 1/4 cup milk of your choice
1 tablespoon baking powder
1 cup dried gf bread crumbs
1 pound crab meat, picked over
cooking spray

Preheat oven to 400 degrees. Combine all ingredients except crab and bread crumbs. Add bread crumbs to mixture and stir thoroughly. Gently stir in crab meat. Shape mixture into 8 crab cakes.

Arrange on baking sheet that has been generously coated with cooking spray. Bake for about 25 minutes: 15 minutes on the first side; 10 minutes on the other—or until both sides are gently browned.

Preparation = 30 minutes. Serves 4. (2 cakes each)

Calories 257 (11% from fat); Fat 3g; Prot 30g; Carb 25g; Sod 940mg; Chol 102mg.

Southwestern Crab Cakes

This is a Southwestern version of crab cakes. Serve with the Avocado Chile Sauce. Use your leftover gf White Bread or French Bread for the bread crumbs. (See Index for recipes).

1 tablespoon gf onion flakes
1 celery stalk, finely chopped
2 large egg whites
2 tablespoons low-fat plain yogurt (or 1 1/2 tablespoons milk of choice)
1 cup Monterey jack cheese with jalapeno, shredded (or non-dairy cheese of choice)
1/2 cup red bell pepper, finely minced
1/2 cup chopped fresh cilantro, chopped
1 teaspoon gf Italian Seasoning
1 cup dried gf bread crumbs
1 pound crab meat, picked over
cooking spray

Combine all ingredients except crab and bread crumbs. Add bread crumbs to mixture and mix thoroughly. Gently stir in crab meat.

Shape mixture into 8 patties.

Preheat oven to 400 degrees. Arrange patties on cookie sheet that has been coated with cooking spray. Bake for 25 minutes: 15 minutes on one side, 10 minutes on the other side—or until both sides are golden brown.

Preparation = 30 minutes. Serves 4.

Calories 354 (30% from fat); Fat 12g; Prot 36g; Carb 23g; Sod 763mg; Chol 126mg.

Cajun Shrimp on Noodles

This dish has a delightful spiciness and its colorful display looks great on your plate. You can use purchased rice noodles or your own homemade Pasta (See Index).

8 ounces snow peas (fresh or frozen)
1 medium red bell pepper, cut in thin strips
1 tablespoon canola oil
1 medium garlic clove, minced
1 tablespoon cornstarch
1 cup low-sodium chicken broth
1/2 cup gf dry white wine
1/2 teaspoon paprika
1/2 teaspoon dried thyme
1/2 teaspoon dried basil
1/4 teaspoon cayenne pepper
1/4 teaspoon black pepper, freshly ground
1/4 teaspoon crushed red pepper
1 pound medium shrimp
1 tablespoon chopped fresh parsley
1 teaspoon grated lemon peel
8 ounces Pasta (See Index) or purchased pasta
1/2 cup Parmesan cheese, for garnish (cow, rice, or soy)
cooking spray

Coat a heavy large skillet with cooking spray. Over medium heat, sauté snow peas and red bell pepper until crisp-tender —about 3 minutes. Remove vegetables.

Add canola oil to skillet and sauté minced garlic for 1 minute. Add cornstarch to 1/4 cup chicken broth and stir to form paste. Add cornstarch mixture, wine, and remaining chicken broth to skillet and cook another minute until sauce thickens. Stir in paprika, thyme, basil, cayenne pepper, black pepper, and crushed red pepper. Bring mixture to boil and add shrimp.

Reduce heat and cook 5 minutes. Return vegetables to skillet and cook 1 minute longer. Set aside.

Cook purchased pasta according to package directions. Or, if using Pasta recipe (See Index), cook according to recipe directions.

Just before serving, toss with lemon peel and parsley. Serve over hot noodles. Sprinkle with Parmesan cheese.
Preparation = 30 minutes. Serves 6.
Calories 289 (28% from fat); Fat 8g; Prot 24g; Carb 24g; Sod 698mg; Chol 159mg.

Crab Zucchini Casserole

This Italian-flavored dish makes a great lunch or light supper.

2 tablespoons olive oil
1 small onion, finely chopped
1 small garlic clove, minced
3 small zucchini (unpeeled, sliced)
3 large tomatoes (seeded, chopped)
1 1/3 cups low-fat Swiss cheese, diced (or non-dairy cheese of choice)
1 cup toasted gf bread crumbs
1 teaspoon salt
1 teaspoon black pepper
1 teaspoon dried basil
1/2 pound crab, cut in small pieces
1/2 cup Parmesan cheese (cow, rice, or soy)

Preheat oven to 375 degrees. In heavy skillet over low to medium heat, sauté onion and garlic in olive oil until onion is transparent. Add zucchini and sauté, stirring frequently, for 3 minutes. Remove from heat.

Combine tomatoes, 1 cup of the Swiss cheese, 3/4 cup of the bread crumbs, salt, black pepper, and basil in bowl. Add onion, garlic, zucchini, and crab. Mix lightly, but thoroughly.

Turn mixture into a 2-quart casserole that's been coated with cooking spray. Sprinkle top with remaining bread crumbs, Swiss cheese, and the Parmesan cheese.

Bake, uncovered, for 30-40 minutes.
Preparation = 1 hour. Serves 4.
Calories 376 (34% from fat); Fat 15g; Prot 30g; Carb 31g; Sod 1321mg; Chol 65mg.

Shrimp Creole

I've been making this recipe for over 20 years and it's still on our list of favorites. The sauce can be made earlier in the day and then reheated just before serving. Add shrimp just before serving.

1 tablespoon olive oil
1/2 cup onion, chopped
1/2 cup celery, chopped
1 garlic clove, minced
16 ounces canned tomatoes,
8 ounces gf tomato sauce
1 tablespoon gf Worcestershire sauce
1 teaspoon sugar
1 teaspoon salt
1/2 teaspoon gf celery salt

3/4 teaspoon gf chili powder
1/8 teaspoon cayenne pepper
2 teaspoons cornstarch
1 tablespoon cold water
1 pound shrimp (peeled, deveined)
1/2 cup green bell pepper, chopped
2 cups cooked white rice
1/4 cup chopped fresh parsley
4 cups cooked rice

In large, heavy Dutch oven, cook onion, celery, and garlic in olive oil until tender, but not brown. Add tomatoes, tomato sauce, Worcestershire sauce, sugar, salt, celery salt, chili powder and cayenne pepper. Simmer, uncovered, for 30 minutes.

Mix cornstarch with cold water until smooth. Stir into sauce. Cook, stirring until bubbly. Add shrimp and green bell pepper. Cover, simmer another 5 minutes. Serve over cooked rice. Garnish with chopped fresh parsley.

Preparation = 40 minutes. Serves 4.

Calories 744 (8% from fat); Fat 6g; Prot 35g; Carb 130g; Sod 1570mg; Chol 173mg.

Shrimp Curry

This is a very spicy, flavorful version of Shrimp Curry.

1 large onion, chopped
1 medium red bell pepper, chopped
1 teaspoon canola oil
1 garlic clove, minced
1 tablespoon gf curry powder
1 teaspoon ground cumin
1 teaspoon ground coriander
1/4 teaspoon ground cardamom
12 ounces evaporated skim milk (1 can) or soy or rice milk

1/4 cup coconut milk, unsweetened
1 1/2 pounds shrimp (peeled, deveined)
2 tablespoons fresh lime juice
1 tablespoon cornstarch
1/3 cup chopped fresh cilantro
1/2 teaspoon salt
1/4 teaspoon black pepper
4 cups white rice, cooked

In large, heavy saucepan sauté the onions and bell peppers in canola oil until softened, about 5 minutes. Add garlic, curry powder, cumin, coriander, and cardamom. Sauté until fragrant, or about 2 minutes more. Reduce heat to low and pour in evaporated skim milk and coconut milk. Bring to simmer, stirring constantly to prevent scorching. Simmer for 5 minutes. Add shrimp and cook, uncovered, until shrimp are pink and curled, about 10-12 minutes.

In a small bowl, combine lime juice and cornstarch, stirring until smooth. Add to the shrimp mixture and cook, stirring constantly until thickened. Stir in cilantro, salt and pepper. Serve over cooked rice.

Preparation = 30 minutes. Serves 4.

Calories 740 (8% from fat); Fat 7g; Prot 35g; Carb 130g; Sod 767mg; Chol 262mg.

White Clam Sauce with Linguine

This is wonderful served over noodles made from the Pasta recipe (See Index). Try it with the spinach noodle version.

15 ounces clams with liquid
(2 cans)
1/4 cup gf dry white wine
1 garlic clove, minced
1 teaspoon olive oil
1/4 teaspoon dry mustard
1/8 teaspoon ground ginger
1/2 teaspoon gf onion salt
1/4 teaspoon white pepper
1 teaspoon onion flakes

1 tablespoon cornstarch
1 cup milk (cow, rice, or soy)
2 tablespoons fresh lemon juice
1/4 cup chopped fresh parsley
1/4 cup Parmesan cheese (cow,
rice, or soy)
paprika, for garnish
2 cups noodles gf Pasta (See
Index)

In large, heavy saucepan over medium heat, simmer clams (uncovered) with their juices, wine, garlic, and olive oil together for 5 minutes to reduce liquid slightly. Stir in the mustard, ginger, salt, pepper, and onion flakes and cook for another 3 minutes.

Combine cornstarch with 1/4 cup of the milk to form smooth paste. Add to clam mixture along with remainder of the milk. Cook over low-medium heat, stirring constantly, until mixture thickens.

Remove from heat and stir in lemon juice and parsley. Serve over noodles made from Pasta (See Index). Garnish with Parmesan cheese and paprika.

Preparation = 15 minutes. Serves 4.

Calories 417 (24% from fat); Fat 10g; Prot 12g; Carb 63g; Sod 909mg; Chol 132mg.

MEATS: BEEF & PORK

Beef

Beef Burgundy 230
Beef Paprika's w/ Noodles 229
Beef Stroganoff 231
Enchiladas 198
Meat Loaf 232
Mexican Beef Pie 233
Sloppy Joes 234
Stir-Fry Ginger Beef w/ Rice 235
Tostadas 236

Mixed Meats

Sausage 248
Chorizo Sausage 247
Lasagna 251
Meatless Lasagna 251
Spaghetti & Meatballs 249
Swedish Meatballs 250
White Bean Cassoulet w/
   Sausage 252

Pork & Ham

Baked Ham w/ Wine
   Sauce 246
Pork Chops in Mushroom
   Sauce 237
Pork w/ Apples &
   Cabbage 242
Pork Chops w/ Dried Fruit 238
Pork Chops w/ Mustard
   Sauce 239
Pork Chops w/
   Maple Glaze 241
Pork Tenderloin w/ Apple
   Chutney 241
Pork Tenderloin w/ Brandy
   Sauce 240
Spareribs w/ Chile Glaze 243
Sweet-Sour Pork 244
Thai Pork Noodle Bowl 245

See pages 259-260 for menus featuring Beef or Pork as the main dish.

Growing up on a farm in Nebraska, I ate plenty of meat and never gave much thought to how it was prepared—fried, baked, roasted, or grilled.

When I began a wheat-free diet, I was dismayed to learn how many meat dishes have hidden wheat in them in the form of breading, sauces, gravies, stuffing, and marinades. Now I pay careful attention to how my meat is prepared.

The recipes in this section were selected either because they didn't require flour at all or because the dish could be prepared using acceptable alternatives to wheat flour without sacrificing quality and taste.

You'll find family favorites such as Meat Loaf, Sloppy Joes, and Sausage. You'll also find lighter, more contemporary cuisine such as Pork Tenderloin with Apple Chutney or Pork Tenderloin with Brandy Sauce. Ethnic favorites are also included such as Sweet-Sour Pork, Thai Pork Noodle Bowls, and Swedish Meatballs. Southwestern cuisine is featured in Mexican Beef Pie, Enchiladas, and Chorizo (Mexican sausage).

Beef Paprika's with Noodles

This is similar to the Hungarian dish, Chicken Paprika's (See Index). It makes a wonderful dinner for cold winter nights.

1 tablespoon olive oil
1 large onion, chopped
1 pound beef tenderloin,
   cut in 1/2-inch cubes
1/2 cup chopped green bell pepper
1 pound fresh sliced mushrooms
2 cups low-sodium beef broth
1 tablespoon gf tomato paste
1 tablespoon Hungarian paprika
2 tablespoons cornstarch
2 tablespoons fresh dill
   (2 teaspoons, dried)

2 tablespoons gf white wine
1/2 cup sour cream or sour
   cream alternative
1/2 teaspoon celery salt
1/4 teaspoon black pepper
4 tablespoons fresh parsley,
   chopped
cooking spray
1 recipe Pasta, made into
   noodles (See Index)

In a heavy Dutch oven over medium heat, sauté onion, beef cubes and bell pepper in olive oil until vegetables are tender and meat is browned, about 10 minutes. Add mushrooms and sauté for another 2-3 minutes. Mix in broth (reserving 1/4 cup), tomato paste and paprika and simmer, covered, for 8-10 minutes.

Stir cornstarch into reserved 1/4 cup of broth to form paste, then stir into sauce. Cook until sauce thickens, about 3-5 minutes. Stir in dill, wine, Yogurt Cheese, celery salt, and pepper. Bring to serving temperature. Serve over hot cooked noodles. Garnish with fresh parsley.

Preparation = 25 minutes. Serves 4.

Calories 528 (53% from fat); Fat 32g; Prot 33g; Carb 29g; Sod 766mg; Chol 108mg.

Beef Burgundy

This is a favorite company dish at our house, especially now that I make my own wheat-free noodles. But you can use purchased noodles, if you wish.

1 bacon slice, uncooked
2 pounds beef sirloin
    steak, cut in 1-inch cubes
2 cups onion, chopped
4 medium carrots, cut into
    1-inch pieces
1 small garlic clove, minced
1 teaspoon gf brandy extract
3 cups gf Burgundy wine
1 1/2 cups low-sodium beef
    broth
2 teaspoons salt

1/4 teaspoon black pepper
2 tablespoons gf tomato paste
2 bay leaves
1 teaspoon dried thyme
1 pound mushrooms, halved
2 cups small white onions
1 tablespoon cornstarch
2 tablespoons water
1/2 cup chopped fresh parsley
1 recipe Pasta, made into
    noodles (See Index)

Sauté bacon in large, heavy Dutch oven until brown. Remove with slotted spoon, leaving drippings in pan. Brown beef and chopped onion in bacon oil over medium heat, about 5 minutes. Add carrots and garlic; sauté another 2 minutes. Add browned bacon slice, brandy extract, Burgundy, beef broth, salt, pepper, tomato paste, bay leaves, thyme, mushrooms and small white onions to pan. Stir thoroughly and bring to boil.

Cover and bake in 325 degree oven for 1 hour or until meat is very tender. If mixture needs thickening, stir cornstarch into 2 tablespoons water to form paste. Stir into Beef Burgundy over medium heat until thickened. Serve over hot cooked noodles. Preparation = 1 1/3 hours. Serves 6.

Calories 452 (50% from fat); Fat 21g; Prot 28g; Carb 19g; Sod 1887mg; Chol 92mg.

Beef Stroganoff

The rich, creamy texture of this dish suggests lots of fat. However, when made with Yogurt Cheese the amount of fat is substantially reduced—but without any loss of flavor or creamy texture. You may use a sour cream alternative, if you wish.

2 tablespoons canola oil
1 pound beef sirloin steak, cut in 1/2-inch cubes
1 small can mushrooms
1/2 cup chopped onion
1/2 teaspoon salt
1/4 teaspoon black pepper
1 small garlic clove, minced
10 1/2 ounces low-sodium beef broth

2 tablespoons gf tomato paste
3 tablespoons brown rice flour
1 cup Yogurt Cheese (See Index) or sour cream or sour cream alternative
2 tablespoons gf dry white wine
1 recipe Homemade Egg Pasta , made into noodles, (See Index)
2 tablespoons fresh parsley, chopped

Heat 2 tablespoons canola oil in large, heavy skillet and brown meat quickly on all sides. Add mushrooms, chopped onions, salt, pepper, and garlic. Cook 5 minutes over low-medium heat or until onion is crisp-tender. Remove mixture to plate.

Add all but 1/4 cup of beef broth to skillet over medium heat, making sure to scrape all drippings from bottom of skillet.

Combine brown rice flour with remaining 1/4 cup of the beef broth and stir until mixture becomes a paste. Add to skillet and stir over medium heat until mixture is thickened and bubbly.

Return meat, mushrooms, and onions to skillet. Reduce heat to low and stir in sour cream or Yogurt Cheese. Heat to serving temperature, but do not boil. Serve over noodles. Garnish with chopped parsley.

Preparation = 30 minutes. Serves 4.

Calories 420 (46% from fat); Fat 21g; Prot 30g; Carb 25g; Sod 610mg; Chol 100mg.

Meat Loaf

This makes a very flavorful Meat Loaf. The sauce on top and inside the Meat Loaf add extra moisture. Use those leftover gf bread crumbs from your rice flour breads. You may use all beef in this recipe if you wish, but the fat content may increase.

8 ounces gf tomato sauce	3/4 pound lean ground beef
1/4 cup brown sugar, packed	1/4 pound ground turkey
1/2 teaspoon dry mustard	1 large egg, beaten
1/2 teaspoon gf chili powder	1 cup dried gf bread crumbs
1/4 teaspoon ground cloves	(crushed)
1 garlic clove, minced	1/2 teaspoon salt
1 teaspoon gf Worcestershire	1/4 teaspoon black pepper
sauce	1 tablespoon gf onion flakes

Preheat oven to 350 degrees. In small bowl, combine tomato sauce, brown sugar, mustard, chili powder, cloves, garlic, and Worcestershire sauce. Mix well.

In large bowl, put one half of the tomato mixture. Add ground beef and turkey, egg, bread crumbs, salt, pepper, and onion flakes. Mix well with hands.

Shape into loaf, either rounded or rectangular, and place in baking pan. If desired, place loaf on metal rack (I use a round, perforated rack which allows fat to drip through to the bottom of the pan, yet the Meat Loaf does not sit in this fat during baking). Make indentation in center of loaf and pour remaining tomato mixture into this indentation.

Bake for 45 minutes, or until Meat Loaf is nicely browned. Preparation = 1 hour. Serves 4.

Calories 429 (42% from fat); Fat 20g; Prot 26g; Carb 34g; Sod 918mg; Chol 134mg.

Mexican Beef Pie

This is a good dish for casual entertaining. It looks pretty and inviting and tastes great. You may use non-dairy cheddar and jack cheeses, if you wish.

1 cup onion, chopped
1/2 pound lean ground beef
1 garlic clove, minced
1 tablespoon gf chili powder
1/2 teaspoon ground cumin
1/2 teaspoon ground oregano
1/4 teaspoon salt
1/4 teaspoon black pepper
1/8 teaspoon cinnamon
1/8 teaspoon ground cloves
1 teaspoon sugar
1 cup canned tomatoes, undrained

1/2 cup chopped fresh cilantro
4 ounces mild green chiles, diced (1 can)
8 ounces corn tortilla chips, unsalted
1 cup pinto beans, cooked
1 cup black olives, sliced
1/2 cup cheddar cheese, grated
1 cup monterey jack cheese, grated
1/4 cup chopped green onion, for garnish

Preheat oven to 400 degrees. In large, cast-iron skillet (or oven-proof skillet) brown ground beef and onion. Add garlic and cook for 1 more minute. Stir in spices (chili powder through cloves) and sugar and cook another 2 minutes to blend spice flavors. Stir in undrained tomatoes, cilantro, and chiles. Reduce heat to low and simmer, stirring occasionally, for 10 minutes.

Transfer mixture to a large bowl. Wipe skillet clean with paper towels and coat with cooking spray.

Place half of the tortilla chips on bottom of skillet. Spoon half of the meat sauce over them and then half of the beans and all of the black olives. Sprinkle with half of the cheeses. Top with remaining chips and spread remaining meat sauce on top and then remaining beans. Sprinkle remaining cheeses on top.

As mixture is assembled, use spatula to press down chips. Bake for 20 minutes, or until mixture is bubbly and cheeses are browned. Garnish with chopped green onion. (Guacamole and sour cream can be used as additional garnishes.)
Preparation = 35 minutes. Serves 6.
Calories 478 (42% from fat); Fat 23g; Prot 23g; Carb 46g; Sod 716mg; Chol 59mg.

Sloppy Joes

You can make this the night before. Reheat for a quick supper.

1 **pound lean ground round**	1/2 **teaspoon dry mustard**
1 **small onion, finely chopped**	1/4 **teaspoon gf chili powder**
1 **teaspoon gf celery salt**	1/4 **teaspoon dried thyme**
1 **teaspoon cornstarch**	1/8 **teaspoon ground cloves**
1/2 **teaspoon sugar or honey**	1 **teaspoon gf Worcestershire**
6 **ounces gf tomato paste**	**sauce**
1/4 **teaspoon gf garlic powder**	1 1/4 **cups water**

Brown ground round and onion in heavy skillet. Drain fat and extra juices. Mix cornstarch and sugar together and add to skillet, along with remaining ingredients. Simmer for 10-15 minutes.
Preparation = 20 minutes. Serves 4.
Calories 318 (56% from fat); Fat 20g; Prot 23g; Carb 11g; Sod 654mg; Chol 78mg.

Stir-Fry Ginger Beef with Rice

This is a tasty, colorful Chinese dish that's fun to prepare while your guests watch.

2 tablespoons gf low-sodium soy sauce
1 teaspoon sesame oil
2 garlic cloves, minced
1 1/2 teaspoons brown sugar, packed
1/2 teaspoon crushed red pepper
1 pound lean beef sirloin steak, cut in thin strips
1 cup fresh mushrooms
3 tablespoons fresh ginger-root (peeled, julienned)
1 small onion, chopped
3 tablespoons peanut oil
1 pound broccoli flowerets
1 large red bell pepper, cut in thin strips
1 1/4 cups water
2 teaspoons cornstarch
4 cups white cooked rice

In a medium bowl, combine 1 tablespoon of the soy sauce with the sesame oil, the garlic, sugar, and crushed red pepper. Add meat and marinate at room temperature for 15 minutes. In large, heavy skillet or wok stir fry the mushrooms (washed and halved) and ginger in 1 tablespoon of the peanut oil over high heat for about 1 minute.

To same skillet, add another tablespoon of peanut oil and stir-fry the beef and its marinade and the onion over medium heat until just browned, about 2 minutes. Transfer beef to plate.

Return skillet to high heat and add remaining tablespoon of peanut oil and remaining soy sauce. Sauté the broccoli and bell pepper for 1 minute.

Stir in the cornstarch which has been mixed with the water to form a paste. Cover and cook for another 2 minutes.

Return beef to skillet and heat to serving temperature. Serve over cooked rice.

Preparation = 30 minutes. Serves 4.

Calories 599(17% from fat); Fat 11g; Prot 36g; Carb 86g; Sod 918mg; Chol 66mg.

Tostadas

Tostadas are easy, fun and delicious. You can vary the toppings as you wish. You may use non-dairy cheese and jack cheese, if you wish.

8 Corn Tortillas (See Index) or use purchased tostada shells, 6-inch size
3 tablespoons canola oil
1/2 pound ground beef or chicken
4 ounces diced green chiles (1 can) or to taste

2 cups shredded lettuce
2 small Roma tomatoes, diced
1 cup shredded Monterey jack cheese
1/2 cup shredded cheddar cheese
1 cup Mexican tomato salsa, warmed

In heavy skillet, heat the canola oil. Fry Corn Tortillas, one at a time, in the hot oil about 20-40 seconds on each side, or until crisp and golden. Drain on paper towels and keep warm wrapped in foil in 250 degree oven.

Brown the ground beef (or the chicken which has been cut into 1/2-inch cubes) and stir in chiles.

Top each tostada shell with layers in this order: meat, tomato, lettuce, and cheese. Top with Mexican tomato salsa.

Guacamole and sour cream are additional options.

Preparation = 20 minutes. Serves 4 (2 tostadas per serving).

BEEF TOSTADAS: Calories 600 (62% from fat); Fat 42g; Prot 25g; Carb 33g; Sod 553mg; Chol 88mg.

CHICKEN TOSTADAS: Calories 492 (28% from fat); Fat 28g; Prot 29g; Carb 33g; Sod 555mg; Chol 74mg.

Pork Chops in Mushroom Sauce

The pork chops rest in a creamy, onion-flavored mushroom sauce. Served with cooked white rice, this also makes a wonderful company dish. You may use fresh grated onion and minced garlic to taste in place of the onion powder and garlic powder.

4 pork chops, center-cut
1 tablespoon canola oil
1 cup fresh mushrooms, sliced
1/4 teaspoon gf onion powder
1/8 teaspoon gf garlic powder
1/4 teaspoon salt
1 tablespoon gf onion flakes
1/4 teaspoon dried sage

1/4 teaspoon white pepper
1/2 cup gf dry white wine
1/2 cup low-sodium chicken broth
1 teaspoon tapioca flour
2 tablespoons water
1/2 cup sour cream or sour cream alternative
2 tablespoons fresh parsley, chopped

Trim fat from pork chops. Wash and pat dry with paper towels.

In heavy skillet over medium heat, brown pork chops in canola oil. Remove from pan.

Add mushrooms and brown lightly. Stir in onion and garlic powders, salt, onion flakes, sage, and white pepper. Add wine and chicken broth. Return pork chops to pan, cover, and simmer for 20 minutes.

Mix tapioca flour with 2 tablespoons water to form paste. Stir slowly into juices around pork chops, continuing stirring until mixture thickens slightly. Add sour cream and heat gently to serving temperature. Serve with cooked rice. Garnish with chopped parsley.

Preparation = 40 minutes. Serves 4.

Calories 358 (64% from fat); Fat 24g; Prot 26g; Carb 4g; Sod 277mg; Chol 86mg.

Pork Chops with Dried Fruit

The flavors of dried fruit complement the pork.

4 pork chops, center-cut
   (about 1 pound)
salt and pepper to taste
2 tablespoons canola oil
1 small onion, chopped
2 1/2 cups low-sodium
   chicken broth
3/4 cup gf red wine

1/2 teaspoon dried thyme
1/2 cup chopped pitted prunes
1/4 cup dried cranberries
1/4 teaspoon salt
1/4 teaspoon black pepper
4 tablespoons fresh parsley,
   chopped

Wash pork chops and pat dry with paper towels. Trim excess fat. Season with salt and pepper.

In heavy Dutch oven over medium heat, brown pork chops in canola oil. Remove pork chops from Dutch oven; keep warm. Add chopped onion to Dutch oven and brown onions, about 5 minutes.

Place pork chops on onions; add chicken broth, wine, thyme, prunes, and cranberries. Bring to simmer, cover, and cook for about 30 minutes.

Using slotted spoon, transfer pork chops to platter. Using same spoon, transfer fruit to top of pork. Keep warm.

Boil remaining cooking liquid until thickened slightly, stirring occasionally, about 15-20 minutes. Add salt and pepper. Spoon sauce over pork and garnish with fresh parsley.

VARIATION: Substitute dried apricots for the cranberries.

Preparation = 1 hour. Serves 4.

Calories 403 (42% from fat); Fat 18g; Prot 25g; Carb 28g; Sod 648mg; Chol 56mg.

Pork Chops with Mustard Sauce

This is a quick, easy dish to prepare and the sauce adds bold flavor..

1 large onion, chopped
1 teaspoon olive oil
4 pork chops, center-cut
  (about 1 pound)
2 tablespoons Dijonnaise mustard
1 tablespoon pure maple syrup
1/2 teaspoon dried rosemary

1/2 teaspoon dried thyme
1/4 teaspoon salt
1/4 teaspoon black pepper
2 tablespoons cider vinegar
4 tablespoons fresh parsley,
  chopped

In large, heavy skillet over medium heat, sauté onions in olive oil until slightly transparent, about 8-10 minutes. Push onions to one side in skillet.

Wash pork chops and pat dry with paper towels. Brown pork chops in same skillet alongside onions, about 10 minutes, turning once.

In small bowl, stir together mustard, maple syrup, rosemary, thyme, salt, pepper, and vinegar. Add to skillet and heat to boiling, stirring until mixture is slightly reduced. Remove pork chops to serving plate, drizzling remaining sauce on top.
Garnish with fresh parsley.
Preparation = 30 minutes. Serves 4.
Calories 217 (53% from fat); Fat 12g; Prot 18g; Carb 6g; Sod 415mg; Chol 56mg.

Pork Tenderloin with Brandy Sauce

This makes a wonderful fall or winter dinner entree and is especially good as a company dish—my guests always love it.

1 1/4 pounds pork tenderloin
1 tablespoon black pepper
1/2 cup low-sodium chicken
  broth
1 teaspoon gf onion flakes
1/2 teaspoon dried thyme
1 teaspoon gf brandy extract

1/4 cup Yogurt Cheese (See Index) or use plain yogurt or
2 tablespoons milk of choice
2 tablespoons butter or oleo
1 tablespoon fresh lemon juice
1/4 teaspoon salt
1/4 teaspoon white pepper
1/4 cup fresh chives, chopped

Wash pork tenderloin and pat dry with paper towels. Rub pork with black pepper. Place on rack in shallow baking pan and roast at 325 degrees until thermometer registers 160 degrees.

Meanwhile, to make sauce combine chicken broth and onion flakes in medium saucepan. Bring to boil; reduce heat. Cover and simmer 2 minutes. Add thyme and brandy extract and simmer, uncovered, over medium heat for 5 minutes.

Reduce heat to low. Add yogurt, then butter to sauce, one tablespoon at a time, stirring constantly with a wire whisk. Stir in lemon juice, salt, and white pepper.

To serve, slice pork tenderloins into 1 inch thick slices. Place 3 slices on each plate, top with sauce. Garnish with chopped chives (or use parsley).

Preparation = 1 1/4 hours. Serves 4.

Calories 475 (73% from fat); Fat 35g; Prot 26g; Carb 3g; Sod 326mg. Chol 118mg.

Pork Chops with Maple Glaze

An easy, really tasty way to prepare pork chops.

4 pork chops, center-cut	1/4 cup pure maple syrup
(about 1 pound)	1 teaspoon gf maple extract
1/2 teaspoon salt	3 tablespoons Dijonnaise mustard
1/4 teaspoon black pepper	1 teaspoon balsamic vinegar
1/2 teaspoon dried marjoram	

Wash pork chops and pat dry with paper towels. Season with salt and pepper. Grill over medium-hot coals.

While chops are grilling, combine remaining ingredients. Brush over chops during final 15 minutes of cooking time, coating both sides.

Preparation = 30 minutes. Serves 4.

Calories 295 (48% from fat); Fat 15g; Prot 24g; Carb 14g; Sod 480mg; Chol 74mg.

Pork Tenderloin with Apple Chutney

The chutney that accompanies this dish is spectacular. This dish was enthusiastically endorsed by my holiday guests.

1/4 cup olive oil	1 teaspoon ground cinnamon
4 garlic cloves, minced	3 pounds pork tenderloin
1 teaspoon dried thyme	1 1/2 cups Apple Chutney
4 teaspoons cumin powder	(See Index)
2 teaspoons cayenne pepper	

Combine olive oil, garlic, thyme, cumin, cayenne, and cinnamon. Rub over pork and refrigerate for at least 4 hours or overnight.

Preheat oven to 400 degrees. Season pork with salt and pepper. In large nonstick skillet, brown pork on all sides. Transfer pork to large baking pan and roast for about 30 minutes, or until meat thermometer registers 155 degrees in thickest part of meat.

Cut pork into 1/2 to 3/4-inch slices. Serve with Apple Chutney. Preparation = 1 hour. Serves 6.

Calories 539 (69% from fat); Fat 42g; Prot 26g; Carb 15g; Sod 206mg. Chol 109mg.

Pork with Apples & Cabbage

This is an easy, very tasty casserole that goes great with a crusty, hearty bread, such as Fennel or Pumpernickel (See Index).

1 pound pork loin, cubed
1 1/2 teaspoons dried
    rosemary, crushed
1/2 cup chopped onion
2 cups cabbage, coarsely
    chopped

1 apple (peeled, chopped)
1/2 cup gf dry white wine
1/2 cup apple juice
1/2 teaspoon gf celery salt
    cooking spray

Wash pork cubes and pat dry with paper towels.

In heavy, large skillet that has been coated with cooking spray, combine pork, rosemary, and onion and sauté for 5 minutes. Make sure pork is browned on all sides.

Add cabbage and remaining ingredients. Bring to boil, cover, reduce heat and simmer for 30 minutes, stirring occasionally. Preparation = 40 minutes. Serves 4.

Calories 241 (46% from fat); Fat 11g; Prot 18g; Carb 11g; Sod 251mg; Chol 56mg.

Spareribs with Chile Glaze

This glaze is slightly spicy due to the combination of chile and chili powders. The addition of maple syrup and orange juice further complements this spicy glaze.

4 pounds spareribs
1 1/2 teaspoons New Mexico
   red chile powder
1/2 cup fresh orange juice
1/4 cup olive oil
1 garlic clove, minced

1 1/2 teaspoons gf chili powder
2 tablespoons pure maple syrup
2 teaspoons dried oregano
1 teaspoon gf celery salt
cooking spray

Preheat oven to 350 degrees. Wash spareribs and pat dry with paper towels. Arrange in baking pan on metal rack that has been coated with cooking spray. Combine remaining ingredients and spread chile glaze on both sides.

Bake for 30 minutes with meaty side of ribs down. Turn ribs and cook another 30 minutes. Slice between ribs and serve.

If you wish, you can grill the spareribs instead, basting them frequently with the glaze.

Preparation = 1 hour. Serves 4.

Calories 883 (72% from fat); Fat 70g; Prot 48g; Carb 11g; Sod 624mg; Chol 220mg.

Sweet-Sour Pork

This has been a family favorite for the past 20 years.

1 tablespoon gf low-sodium
  soy sauce
1 teaspoon ground ginger
1 tablespoon corn starch
1 garlic clove, minced
1 tablespoon pineapple juice
1 pound pork, cubed
1 tablespoon canola oil
1 small onion, diced
1 medium carrot, sliced
  1/4-inch thick
1 small green bell pepper,
  chopped

1/2 cup red bell pepper,
  chopped
8 ounces pineapple chunks
  in juice
2 tablespoons brown sugar
3 tablespoons cider vinegar
2 tablespoons gf low-sodium
  soy sauce
1 tablespoon fresh ginger-
  root, grated
1/8 teaspoon white pepper
1 tablespoon cornstarch
2 tablespoons water
4 cups cooked rice

Combine first 5 ingredients in bowl. Rinse pork cubes and pat dry with paper towel. Add pork cubes to bowl and marinate while chopping the vegetables.

In a heavy skillet over medium heat, brown onion, carrots, and pork cubes in canola oil until lightly browned, stirring frequently. Remove from skillet. Sauté red and green bell peppers for 3 minutes, stirring frequently. Remove from skillet. Set aside.

To skillet, add pineapple chunks (including juice and water to equal 2/3 cup liquid), brown sugar, vinegar, soy sauce, ginger root, and white pepper over medium heat. Stir cornstarch with 1 tablespoon water until paste forms. Stir slowly into skillet, continuing to stir until mixture thickens slightly.

Return pork, onions, and carrots to skillet. Cover and simmer gently for 10 minutes. Add red and green bell peppers and

bring to serving temperature. Serve over hot cooked rice.
Preparation = 30 minutes. Serves 4.
Calories 505 (8% from fat); Fat 4g; Prot 11g; Carb 105g; Sod 773mg; Chol 5mg.

Thai Pork Noodle Bowl

You can find this dish in Thai or Vietnamese restaurants. It's easy to make and fun to eat—very colorful, with varied textures.

1/2 pound pork, cut in 1/2-inch cubes	6 tablespoons brown sugar, firmly packed
1/4 cup green onions	4 teaspoons paprika
1 garlic clove, minced	1 teaspoon Reese anchovy paste
1 tablespoon canola oil	3/4 teaspoon cayenne pepper
1/2 cup red bell pepper, chopped	2 cups mung bean sprouts
1/4 cup gf rice vinegar	1 cup fresh chopped cilantro
3 tablespoons gf-low sodium soy sauce	12 ounces rice noodles (cooked, drained)
	1/4 cup peanuts, chopped

In large, heavy skillet over medium heat, sauté pork, green onions, and garlic in canola oil until pork is lightly browned and cooked through. Add red bell peppers to skillet and cook for another minute. Set aside.

In a small bowl, combine vinegar, soy sauce, brown sugar, paprika, anchovy paste, and cayenne pepper. Add mixture to skillet and toss, along with cilantro until heated through.

Place cooked noodles in individual serving bowls and top with meat mixture, bean sprouts, and sauce. Garnish with chopped peanuts.

Preparation = 25 minutes. Serves 6.
Calories 420 (30% from fat); Fat 14g; Prot 18g; Carb 55g; Sod 457mg; Chol 80mg.

Baked Ham with Wine Sauce

This makes a wonderful Easter entree or the main dish for a special Sunday dinner.

5 pounds ham (fully cooked)
2 cups low-sodium chicken broth
1/2 cup gf red wine
1 bay leaf
1/4 cup orange juice concentrate, thawed

1/2 teaspoon dried thyme
1/8 teaspoon ground cloves
1 cup golden raisins
1 tablespoon cornstarch or arrowroot
2 tablespoons water

Bake ham at 325 degrees for 1 hour, or until heated through. Meanwhile, in heavy medium saucepan combine the chicken broth, wine, bay leaf, orange juice concentrate, thyme, and cloves. Bring to boil, then remove from heat to cool. Add raisins.

When ready to serve, return sauce to medium heat. Cook for about 10 minutes, or until sauce is slightly reduced.

Stir cornstarch with 2 tablespoons water, then stir into sauce. Continue stirring constantly until mixture thickens slightly. Makes about 2 cups of sauce. Serve sauce over sliced ham. Preparation = 1 hour. Serves 10.

Calories 611 (46% from fat); Fat 30g; Prot 51g; Carb 26g; Sod 3938mg; Chol 162mg.

Chorizo (Mexican Sausage)

Chorizo is a traditional Mexican sausage—hot and spicy, so a little goes a long way. Although sausage is typically a high-fat item, you can control the fat content by grinding your own lean meat, rather than buying it already ground. Also, I often just brown the sausage without shaping it into links or patties if I'm in a hurry.

1 pound ground round	2 teaspoons dried oregano
2 pounds ground pork	3 garlic cloves, minced
1 tablespoon paprika	1 teaspoon ground coriander
1/3 cup cider vinegar	1 teaspoon ground cumin
1 teaspoon salt	1/2 teaspoon ground cloves
1 teaspoon crushed red pepper	cooking spray

In a large bowl, mix together the ground meats. Add remainder of ingredients. Mix thoroughly, using a spatula or your hands. Shape into a large ball or log and refrigerate for at least 4 hours.

Shape meat mixture into sausage patties, about 1/2-inch thick and 2 inches in diameter. (If you prefer link sausage, shape into links about 3 inches long and 3/4-inch in diameter).

In non-stick pan that has been coated with cooking spray, fry sausages until nicely browned on both sides. You can freeze sausages for up to 2 weeks. Makes about 12-16 sausages, depending on how big you make them.

Preparation = 30 minutes. (Longer if you grind your own meat).

Serves 12. (1 sausage per serving)

Calories 319 (64% from fat); Fat 22g; Prot 26g; Carb 1g; Sod 259mg; Chol 97mg.

Sausage

Now you can enjoy sausage, knowing that there's no wheat-bread filler. And, this version excludes unnecessary fat. If you grind your own meat, you can really control the fat content! If you'd like, you can just brown the sausage without shaping it into links or patties.

1 pound ground round
1 pound ground pork
1 pound ground turkey
4 garlic cloves, minced
6 green onions, minced
1/2 cup green bell pepper
1/2 cup red bell pepper
2 teaspoons fresh cilantro, chopped

2 teaspoons ground cumin
2 teaspoons dried thyme
2 teaspoons fennel seed
1/4 teaspoon ground nutmeg
1/2 teaspoon crushed red pepper
1 teaspoon salt
cooking spray

In large bowl, mix together by hand the beef, pork, and turkey. Finely chop red and green bell peppers and add to meat mixture. Add remaining ingredients. Mix thoroughly. Shape into large ball or log and refrigerate for at least 4 hours.

Shape meat mixture into sausage patties, about 1/2-inch thick and 2 inches in diameter. (If you prefer link sausage, shape into links about 3 inches long and 3/4-inch in diameter).

In non-stick pan that's been coated with cooking spray, fry sausages until nicely browned.

Preparation = 30 minutes. (Excludes chill time) Serves 12.

Calories 289 (55% from fat); Fat 17g; Prot 25g; Carb 7g; Sod 279mg; Chol 92mg.

Spaghetti & Meatballs

This dish has been a family favorite for over 20 years. I reduce the fat by browning the meatballs in the oven rather than in a skillet. Be sure to use lean beef and pork. The meatballs freeze well for up to one month.

1 pound ground round
1/4 pound ground pork
1/2 teaspoon salt
1 teaspoon black pepper
1/2 cup dried gf bread
   crumbs, crushed
2 large eggs
3 tablespoons dried parsley
1 tablespoon basil

1 teaspoon oregano
1 clove garlic, minced
3 tablespoons Romano cheese
1/2 teaspoon crushed red
   pepper flakes
Spaghetti Sauce (See Index)
gf homemade Pasta, made
   into spaghetti (See Index) or
   use gf purchased spaghetti

Preheat oven to 350 degrees. Combine all ingredients (except Spaghetti Sauce and pasta) in large bowl and mix well. Shape into 1 1/2-inch balls and place on cookie sheet. Bake for 20 minutes. Remove from oven and cool on cookie sheet for 15 minutes.

Add cooled meatballs to Spaghetti Sauce. Serve over cooked spaghetti.

Preparation = 30 minutes for Meatballs. Serves 12.

Calories 242 (44% from fat); Fat 12g; Prot 13g; Carb 22g; Sod 1059mg; Chol 37mg.

Swedish Meatballs

So easy to make and so wonderful to eat. You can brown the meatballs the night before (I brown mine in the oven). Then, make the sauce when you get home from work. You'll have a meal in less than 30 minutes.

1/2 pound ground round
1/2 pound ground pork
1/4 cup dry gf bread crumbs
1 small onion, finely chopped
1 large egg, slightly beaten
2 garlic cloves, minced
1/2 teaspoon ground allspice
1/4 teaspoon ground nutmeg
1/2 teaspoon salt

1/4 teaspoon black pepper
1 cup low-sodium beef broth
1 tablespoon cornstarch
1 1/2 tablespoons dried dill weed
1 tablespoon gf brandy extract
1 cup Yogurt Cheese (See
   Index) or low-fat sour cream or
   sour cream alternative
cooking spray

Preheat oven to 350 degrees. Combine first 10 ingredients (ground round through black pepper) in bowl, reserving 2 teaspoons dill weed. Shape into 24 1-inch meatballs.

Coat baking sheet with cooking spray and place meatballs on sheet. Bake for 20 minutes or until browned.

Combine cornstarch with 3 tablespoons of the beef broth. Heat remaining beef broth and 1 teaspoon of the dill in large saucepan. Add cornstarch mixture and stir over medium heat until thickened. Add meatballs to pan and simmer gently for 10 minutes. Stir in yogurt (or sour cream) and brandy extract.

Serve hot over cooked white rice, mashed potatoes, pasta, or Wild Rice Pancakes (See Index). Sprinkle with remaining dill. Preparation = 30 minutes. Serves 4.

Calories 391 (54% from fat); Fat 23g; Prot 33g; Carb 10g; Sod 602mg; Chol 147mg.

Lasagna

You can enjoy Lasagna, when it's made with gf pasta. You can make your own Pasta or use the purchased variety found in health food stores (or see Mail Order Sources). If you use fresh Pasta, you don't have to cook it first. This recipe is dairy-based.

1/2 pound ground round,
    browned
12 gf lasagna noodles (made
    of rice flour or made from
    Pasta, See Index)
1 pound low-fat ricotta cheese
1/2 cup low-fat cottage cheese

1 large egg, slightly beaten
1/2 cup Parmesan cheese
1 pound low-fat mozzarella
    cheese, shredded
2 cups Spaghetti Sauce
    (See Index)
cooking spray

Preheat oven to 350 degrees. While pasta is cooking in lightly salted water, brown meat in frying pan. Set aside.

Add cottage cheese, egg, and Parmesan cheese to ricotta cheese. Mix well.

Lightly coat 13 x 9-inch pan with cooking spray. Reserve 3/4 cup spaghetti sauce and 1 cup mozzarella cheese for top of Lasagna.

Spread 1/2 cup Spaghetti Sauce on bottom of pan. Arrange 4 lasagna noodles over tomato mixture. Spread half of ricotta mixture over noodles, then half of meat, then half of the mozzarella cheese and half of the Spaghetti Sauce. Repeat layers, ending with noodles. Top with 3/4 cup Spaghetti Sauce and 1 cup mozzarella.

Bake for 30-40 minutes, or until cheese is melted and sauce bubbles around edge of pan. Cut into squares.

Preparation = 45 minutes. Serves 10.

Calories 709 (27% from fat); Fat 21g; Prot 39g; Carb 88g; Sod 692mg; Chol 79mg.

MEATLESS LASAGNA: Omit the ground round.

Calories 656 (24% from fat); Fat 17g; Prot 35g; Carb 88g; Sod 677mg; Chol 63mg.

White Bean Cassoulet with Sausage

Fix this on a cold winter day when you want a hearty, hot meal—but don't want to spend a lot of time in the kitchen. Cook the beans in your crock pot while you're at work. Assemble the cassoulet when you get home and bake it while you prepare the remainder of the meal.

3 cups white beans
6 cups water
1 bay leaf
1 teaspoon salt
1/2 pound gf Sausage (See Index)
1/2 pound pork, cut in
   1/2-inch cubes
1 large onion, chopped
2 garlic cloves, minced

28 ounces canned tomatoes
   (whole, drained)
1/3 cup chopped fresh parsley,
1 teaspoon dried rosemary
1 teaspoon dried thyme
1/2 teaspoon black pepper
1/2 teaspoon celery salt
cooking spray

Rinse and pick over white beans. Cook in 6 cups water, with salt bay leaf in crock pot all day.

Preheat oven to 400 degrees. In large, heavy ovenproof skillet over medium heat, brown sausage, pork cubes, and garlic over medium-high heat. Remove meat from skillet and drain on paper towels.

Combine meat mixture with remaining ingredients and cooked beans (bay leaf removed) in 4 individual oven-proof dishes that have been coated with cooking spray.

Cover with aluminum foil and bake for 20 minutes. Uncover, and bake another 20 minutes. Serve.

Preparation = 45 minutes. Serves 6.

Calories 592 (29% from fat); Fat 19g; Prot 37g; Carb 70g; Sod 758mg; Chol 55mg.

MENUS

"What's for dinner?" For the cook, this means not only deciding on the entree—but also choosing other dishes that taste good and look good served alongside the entree. These decisions are hard, but for the wheat-free, gluten-free cook they're even more challenging.

The following 100 menus contain dishes that have compatible flavors, complement one another, look appealing on your plate and—above all—taste good in your mouth.

These menus will also help you prepare grocery lists and be more efficient in the kitchen because you can plan ahead. You should consult with your physician or nutritionist for specific dietary information.

You'll find the following categories of menus in this chapter. An asterisk indicates the recipe is not included in this book, however, it either requires minimal preparation (such as steamed broccoli) or it is easily found in other cookbooks.

Quick & Easy Dinners   **Poultry Menus**
Reduced Fat, Low Calorie Meals   **Southwestern Menus**
Fish & Seafood Menus   **Meatless Meals**
Meat (Beef & Pork) Menus

Quick & Easy Dinners

Each entree requires 10 or fewer ingredients and minimal last-minute preparations. Some dishes can be assembled the night before.

Chicken	Fish
Cornish Game Hens w/Fruit Glaze Fruit Salad* Steamed Broccoli* Herbed Brown Rice Butterscotch Pudding	Oven-Baked Crab Cakes Carrots in Maple Syrup* Whipped Potatoes* Bananas w/ Rum Sauce*
Grilled Chicken & Ancho Chiles Jicama, Orange & Avocado Salad* Mexican Rice Corn Bread Mexican Flan	Red Snapper in Parchment Lettuce w/ Citrus Dressing Green Bean* Cooked White Rice* Fresh Cantaloupe w/ Cinnamon*
Chicken w/ Spicy Glaze Fruit Salad* Steamed Snow Peas* White Cooked Rice* Butterscotch Pudding	Orange Roughy in Parchment Lettuce w/ Buttermilk Dressing Broiled Tomatoes* White Cooked Rice* Pineapple Upside-Down Cake
Grilled Chicken w/ Teriyaki Glaze Steamed Snow Peas* White Cooked Rice* Yellow Cake w/ Strawberries	Salmon w/ Asian Sauce Fruit Salad* Linguine w/ Pine Nuts Easy Chocolate Cheesecake
Grilled Chipotle Chicken Lettuce w/ Lime Cilantro Dressing Baked Potato* Spoonbread Mexican Flan	Salmon w/ Maple Glaze Jicama & Mandarin Oranges* Broiled Tomatoes* Oven-Fried Potatoes Lemon Bars

Quick & Easy Dinners

Chicken	Fish
Lemon Chicken Steamed Asparagus* Cooked White Rice* Clafouti	Red Snapper w/Tomato-Lime Salsa Steamed Broccoli* Linguine w/ Pine Nuts Butterscotch Pudding
Tarragon-Dijon Chicken Spinach Salad w/ Fruit* Carrots in Maple Syrup* Herbed Rice Easy Chocolate Cheesecake	White Clam Sauce w/ Linguine Lettuce w/ Citrus Dressing Steamed Asparagus* White Cooked Rice* Vanilla Custard
Thai Chicken Lettuce w/ Asian Vinaigrette Asian Soba Noodles Broiled Tomatoes* Cherry-Apricot Crisp	Southwestern Crab Cakes Lettuce w/Southwestern Dressing Buttered Corn* Corn Tortillas w/ Honey Butterscotch Pudding
Miscellaneous	**Meat**
Bean Soup* Raw Vegetable Sticks* Fennel Bread Clafouti	Pork Chops w/ Maple Glaze Baked Acorn Squash* Rice Pilaf w/ Dried Fruits & Nuts French Bread Chocolate Pudding
Cheese Soup Raw Vegetable Sticks* Pumpernickel Bread Fresh Fruit*	Pork w/ Apples & Cabbage Green Beans* Russian Black Bread Ice Cream w/ Fresh Fruit*

Reduced Fat, Low Calorie Meals

Per serving, these main dishes have fewer than 400 calories and the calories from fat are 35% or less. Side dishes are also low in fat.

Cod Baked w/ Vegetables White Cooked Rice* Steamed Broccoli* Dilly Bread Bananas w/ Rum Sauce*	Salmon & Vegetables in Parchment Herbed Brown Rice Popovers Fresh Fruit w/ Vanilla Wafers
Red Snapper in Parchment Green Beans* Saffron Rice Pilaf Green Salad* Pavlova*	Red Snapper &Tomato Lime Salsa Green Peas* Homemade Egg Pasta Noodles Poached Pears*
Grilled Chicken w/ Spicy Glaze Orange and Avocado Salad* Steamed Snow Peas* Corn Bread Clafouti	Tarragon-Dijon Chicken Spinach Salad* Green Peas & Pearl Onions* Rice Pilaf w/ Fruits & Nuts Broiled Pineapple*
Coq Au Vin French Bread Yellow Cake	Grilled Chicken w/ Peach Salsa Steamed Asparagus* White Cooked Rice* Baked Apples*
Lemon-Tarragon Chicken Steamed Green Beans* Breadsticks Chocolate Pound Cake	Thai Chicken Fruit Salad* Creamed Corn White Cooked Rice Sponge Cake w/ Fruit

Fish & Seafood

These entrees contain limited spices and have fairly mild flavors.

Cod Baked w/ Vegetables Lettuce w/ Hazelnut Vinaigrette Steamed Broccoli* White Cooked Rice* Dilly Bread Banana Cream Pie	Salmon & Vegetables in Parchment Lettuce w/ Herb Vinaigrette Carrots in Maple Syrup* Popovers Biscotti
Sole in White Dill Sauce Snow Peas w/Butter* White Cooked Rice* Popovers Coconut Cream Pie	Oven-Baked Crab Cakes Lettuce w/ Citrus Dressing Buttered Corn* French Bread Banana Cream Pie
Grouper w/ Apricot Sauce* Lettuce w/ Pine Nut Dressing Broiled Tomatoes* Saffron Rice Pilaf Cheesecake	Crab Zucchini Casserole Lettuce w/ Herb Vinaigrette French Bread Cherry-Apricot Crisp
New England Clam Chowder Fresh Vegetable Plate* Dilly Bread Boston Cream Pie	Orange Roughy in Parchment Fruit Salad* Broiled Tomatoes* Risotto w/ Mushrooms & Herbs Butterscotch Pudding
White Clam Sauce w/ Linguine Lettuce w/ Pine Nut Dressing Focaccia Crepes w/ Fresh Fruit	Grilled Yellowfin Tuna* Lettuce w/Avocado Dressing Baked Potatoes* Green Peas* Yellow Cake

Fish & Seafood

These fish and seafood entrees have several spices and bold flavors.

Salmon w/ Asian Sauce Fruit Salad* Asian Soba Noodles Steamed Asparagus* Vanilla Wafers	Salmon w/ Tomatillo-Apple Salsa Lettuce w/ Southwestern Dressing White Cooked Rice* Sautéed Zucchini* Clafouti
Shrimp Creole White Rice* Lettuce w/ Herb Vinaigrette Green Peas* French Bread Cheesecake w/ Blueberries	Salmon w/ Maple Glaze Lettuce w/ Asian Vinaigrette Oven-Fried Potatoes Carrots in Maple Syrup* Carrot Cake
Halibut w/ Honey Mustard Sauce Lettuce w/ Citrus Dressing French Bread Boston Cream Pie	Southwestern Crab Cakes w/ Avocado Chile Sauce Jicama, Orange & Avocado Salad* Flour Tortillas Mexican Flan
Shrimp Curry Steamed Snow Peas* White Cooked Rice* Coconut Cream Pie	Halibut w/ Papaya Salsa Lettuce w/ Citrus Dressing Broiled Tomatoes* Baked Potatoes* Lemon Pudding
Cajun Shrimp on Noodles Lettuce w/ Asian Dressing Buttered Corn* French Bread Yellow Cake w/ Strawberries	Red Snapper &Tomato Lime Salsa Lettuce w/ Red Chile Dressing Steamed Broccoli* White Cooked Rice* Butterscotch Pudding

Meat: Beef & Pork

These beef and pork entrees have few spices and mild flavors.

Meat Loaf Scalloped Potatoes Green Peas in Cream Sauce Buttermilk Biscuits Chocolate Brownies	Pork Chops in Mushroom Sauce Lettuce w/ Walnut Oil* Broiled Tomatoes* White Cooked Rice* Pineapple Upside-Down Cake
Beef Paprika's w/ Egg Noodles Lettuce w/ Herb Vinaigrette Steamed Broccoli* Russian Black Bread Chocolate Pound Cake	Baked Ham w/ Wine Sauce Fruit Salad* Whipped Potatoes* Creamed Corn Vanilla Custard
Sloppy Joes Hamburger Buns Raw Carrot Sticks* Potato Chips* Chocolate Wafer Cookies	Swedish Meatballs Homemade Egg Pasta Noodles Green Peas* Pumpernickel Bread Gingerbread w/ Lemon Sauce
Pork Chops* Spinach Salad w/ Fruit Butternut Squash* Spiced Red Crab Apples* Flourless Chocolate Torte	Pork Tenderloin w/ Brandy Sauce Lettuce & Pear Salad* Herbed Brown Rice Sautéed Fennel* Easy Chocolate Cheesecake
Roast Beef* Baked Acorn Squash* Green Peas w/ Pearl Onions* Dilly Bread Chocolate Souffle	Smoked Pork Chops* Potato Pancakes Applesauce* Spiced Red Cabbage* Spice Cake

Meat: Beef & Pork

(continued)

These beef and pork entrees have several spices and bold flavors.

Pork Chops w/ Mustard Sauce Fruit Salad* Sautéed Zucchini* Whipped Potatoes* Shortbread w/ Sliced Fruit	Pork Ribs w/ Maple Glaze Coleslaw* Boston Baked Beans Baked Potatoes* Rhubarb Meringue Dessert
Pork Chops w/ Apples & Cabbage Steamed Green Beans* Fennel Bread Gingerbread w/ Lemon Sauce	Pork Tenderloin w/Apple Chutney Lettuce w/ Walnut Oil Vinaigrette Brussels Sprouts in Walnut Oil* Linguine w/ Pine Nuts Cream Puffs
Mexican Beef Pie Raw Vegetable Sticks* Corn Bread Chocolate Chip Cookies	Stir-Fry Ginger Beef w/ Rice Fruit Salad* Popovers Fresh Cantaloupe w/ Cinnamon*
White Bean Cassoulet w/ Sausage Lettuce w/ Herb Vinaigrette Breadsticks Chocolate Pound Cake	Spareribs in Chili Sauce Coleslaw* Boston Baked Beans Spoonbread Ice Cream & Vanilla Wafers
Pork Chops w/ Red Wine Sauce Lettuce & Pear Salad* Steamed Broccoli* White Cooked Rice* Lemon Pudding	Spaghetti & Meatballs Green Salad w/ Herb Vinaigrette French Bread Chocolate Brownies

Poultry

These chicken entrees contain few spices and have mild flavors.

Chicken Paprika's Green Beans* Homemade Egg Pasta Noodles French Bread Chocolate Pudding	Oven-Fried Chicken Green Peas w/ Pearl Onions* Hash Brown Casserole Buttermilk Biscuits Apple Pie*
Creamed Chicken on Buttermilk Biscuits Fresh Fruit* Steamed Asparagus* Gingersnaps	Oven-Fried Chicken Potato Salad* Boston Baked Beans Buttermilk Biscuits Watermelon*
Lemon Chicken Steamed Asparagus* Cooked White Rice* Cream Puffs	Tarragon-Dijon Chicken Mixed Green Salad* Green Peas* Herbed Rice Lemon Pudding
Chicken Shepherd's Pie Lettuce w/ Hazelnut Vinaigrette* Fruit Salad w/Balsamic Dressing* French Bread Boston Cream Pie	Roast Chicken* Waldorf Salad* Creamed Corn Baked Potatoes* Dilly Bread Cherry Pie*
Chicken & Broccoli Quiche Fruit Salad* French Bread Carrot Cake	Chicken Breasts w/ Mushrooms Risotto w/ Mushrooms & Herbs Carrots in Maple Syrup* French Bread Pavlova*

261

Poultry

These chicken entrees have more spices and bold flavors.

Chicken Tandoori Cucumber Salad* Curried Rice Pilaf w/ Raisins Popovers Fresh Blueberries*	Grilled Chicken w/ Peach Salsa Lettuce w/ Avocado Dressing Green Peas* French Bread Pineapple Upside-Down Cake
Chicken Curry Green Peas* White Cooked Rice* French Bread Fruit Plate w/ Berry Sauce*	Chicken Cacciatore on Noodles Lettuce w/ Buttermilk Dressing Brussels Sprouts in Walnut Oil Popovers Chocolate Pound Cake
Grilled Chicken w/ Spicy Glaze Sautéed Fennel Spinach Salad* Clafouti	Chicken Curry Steamed Broccoli* Saffron Rice Pilaf Poached Pears*
Coq Au Vin Lettuce w/ Herb Vinaigrette* Green Peas* French Bread Chocolate Pound Cake	Thai Chicken Ambrosia Salad* Green Peas* Asian Soba Noodles Pavlova*
Grilled Chicken w/ Teriyaki Glaze Mixed Green Salad* Orange-Glazed Carrots* Wild Rice w/ Dried Fruit Lemon Pudding	Spicy Oven-Fried Chicken Waldorf Salad* Creamed Corn Oven-Fried Potatoes Buttermilk Biscuits Gingerbread w/ Lemon Sauce

Southwestern Menus

These menus feature many flavors from the Southwest.

Grilled Chicken & Ancho Chiles Black Bean Salad* Buttered Corn* Buttermilk Biscuits Vanilla Custard w/ Fresh Fruit*	Chicken Burritos* with Sauces: Red Chile Sauce Tomatillo Sauce Green Chile Sauce Southwestern Beans Mexican Flan
Grilled Chipotle Chicken Jicama & Mandarin Oranges* Green Peas* Corn Bread Mexican Flan	Red Chile Barbecued Chicken Coleslaw* Baked Potatoes* Spoon Bread Lemon Bars
Turkey Mole Fresh Fruit* Spoonbread Mexican Rice Mexican Chocolate Cake	Chile Relleno Casserole Fruit Salad* Flour Tortillas Mexican Wedding Cakes
Enchiladas Mexican Rice Refried Beans Flour Tortillas Anise - Pine Nut Cookies	Mexican Chicken Casserole Lettuce w/ Lime Cilantro Dressing French Bread Lemon Bars
Grilled Chicken w/ Peach Salsa Grapefruit & Avocado Salad* Green Peas* White Rice w/ Pine Nuts* Coconut Macaroons	Mexican Tortilla Casserole Jicama, Orange & Avocado Salad* Southwestern Beans Corn Bread Natillas

Meatless Meals

Here are ideas for those who enjoy an occasional meal without meat.

Huevos Rancheros Fresh Fruit* Refried Beans Mexican Wedding Cakes	Veggiburgers Hamburger Buns Carrot Sticks* Oven-Fried Potatoes Butterscotch Pudding
Mexican Tortilla Casserole Lettuce w/ Southwestern Dressing Southwestern Beans Mexican Rice Natillas	Eggplant Parmesan Lettuce w/ Herb Vinaigrette Steamed Asparagus* Breadsticks Biscotti
Southwestern French Onion Soup Raw Vegetable Sticks* Corn Bread Mexican Flan	Grilled Vegetables & Quinoa Lettuce w/ Citrus Dressing Buttermilk Biscuits Cherry-Apricot Crisp
Red Beans & Rice Raw Vegetable Sticks* Corn Bread Chocolate Pudding	Cheese Enchiladas Southwestern Beans Mexican Rice Sopaipillas Lemon Bars
Quiche Lorraine Fruit Salad* Steamed Broccoli* Popovers Lemon Pudding	Chile Relleno Casserole Lettuce w/ Red ChileDressing Mexican Rice Corn Tortillas w/ Honey Margarita Pie*

APPENDICES

Wheat Flour Equivalents

Use the following amount of flour in place of **1 cup of wheat flour**.

Kind of Flour	Amount
Amaranth Flour*	1 cup
Barley Flour*	1 1/3 cup
Bean Flour (garbanzo/fava)	1 cup
Buckwheat Flour*	7/8 cup
Corn Flour	1 cup
Cornmeal	3/4 cup
Cornstarch	3/4 cup
Garbanzo (Chick-Pea) Flour	3/4 cup
Nuts (any kind–ground fine)	1/2 cup
Oat Flour*	1 1/3 cup
Potato Starch	3/4 cup
Quinoa Flour*	1 cup
Rice Flour (Brown or White)	7/8 cup
Rye Flour*	1 1/4 cups
Soybean Flour	1/2 cup + 1/2 cup potato starch flour
Spelt Flour*	1 cup
Sweet Rice Flour	7/8 cup
Tapioca Flour	1 cup
Teff Flour*	7/8 cup

Flours from reputable sources will usually measure consistently, although differences in flour milling processes may affect the texture and texture. As you become more experienced with these flours, you'll be able to judge if the dough is dry, too moist, or just right.

*Amaranth, Barley, Buckwheat, Oats, Quinoa, Rye, Spelt, and Teff are included in this chart for your information since some wheat-sensitive persons can eat these flours. However, the Celiac Sprue Association recommends avoiding these flours. If you're not sure whether you can tolerate these flours, it's best to avoid them.

Substitutes for Wheat As a Thickener

Many of us learned to cook using wheat flour as a thickener—in gravies, soups and sauces. Other starches and flours can thicken certain foods but each alternative has certain strengths and weaknesses, so use the following information in choosing among them.

In place of **1 tablespoon of wheat flour**, use the following:

Ingredient and Suggested Amount	Characteristics	Suggested Uses
Agar (Kanten) – 1 1/2 teaspoons	Follow package directions. Colorless and flavorless. Sets at room temperature. Gels acidic liquids. Thin sauces need less.	Puddings, pie fillings, gelatin desserts, ice cream, glazes, cheese. Holds moisture and improves texture in pastry products.
Arrowroot – 1 1/2 teaspoons	Mix with cold liquid before using. Thickens at a lower temperature than wheat flour or cornstarch, so it's better for eggs or sauces that shouldn't be boiled. Add during last 5 minutes of cooking. Serve immediately after thickening. Clear, shiny. Semi-soft when cool.	Any food requiring clear, shiny sauce, but good for egg or starch dishes where high heat is undesirable. Gives appearance of oil when none used. Don't overcook or sauce will become thin.
Bean Flour – 1 tablespoon	Produces yellowish, rich-looking sauce.	Soups, stews, gravies. Slight bean taste.
Cornstarch – 1 1/2 teaspoons	Mix with cold liquid before using. Stir just until boiling. Makes transparent, shiny sauce. Slight starchy flavor. Thicker and rigid when cool.	Puddings, pie fillings, fruit sauces, soups. Gives appearance of oil when none used.

Ingredient and Suggested Amount	Characteristics	Suggested Uses
Gelatin Powder –1 1/2 teaspoons	Dissolve in cold water, then heat until liquid is clear before using. Won't gel acid.	Jello puddings, aspics, cheesecakes
Guar Gum – 1 1/2 teaspoons	Mix with liquid before using. Has high fiber content and may act as laxative.	Especially good for rice flour recipes.
Kudzu (kuzu) Powder – 1 1/2 teaspoons	Dissolve in cold water before using. Odorless, tasteless. Produces transparent, smooth sauces with soft consistency.	Puddings, pie fillings, and jelled preparations. May need to experiment with exact amount to use.
Oat Flour – 1 tablespoon (not for celiacs)	Mix with liquid before adding to sauce. Tendency to turn "gray."	Sauces where additional color is added, to overcome "gray" of oat flour.
Sweet Rice Flour – 1 tablespoon	Excellent thickening agent.	Sauces such as vegetable sauces.
Rice Flour (brown or white) – 1 tablespoon	Mix with cold liquid before using. Somewhat grainy texture. Consistency the same hot or cold.	Soups, stews or gravies.
Tapioca Flour – 1 1/2 tablespoons	Mix with cold or hot liquid before using. Add during last 5 minutes of cooking to avoid rubberiness. Produces transparent, shiny sauce. Thick, soft gel when cool.	Soups, stews, gravies, potato dishes.
Quick-Cooking Tapioca (pre-cooked) – 2 teaspoons	Mix with fruit, let stand 15 minutes before baking.	Fruit pies, cobblers, and tapioca pudding.
Xanthan Gum – 1 teaspoon	Mix with dry ingredents first, then add.	Puddings, salad dressings, and gravies.

Wheat-Free Flours

Here we discuss baking characteristics, color and flavor, and storage recommendations for wheat-free flours (and grains) used in this book. General comments are also offered.

Flour	Characteristics
Amaranth	**Not recommended for Celiac Sprue patients.**
Baking	Excellent. Especially good in dark-colored baked goods or those with spices such as chocolate cakes or cookies, spice cakes and dark breads. Tends to brown quickly. Use alone or with other flours.
Color and Flavor	Mild, grain-like, nutty. Color varies from beige to nearly black, but usually light tan.
General Comments	Not related to wheat or other grains. Color varies depending on origin. Cost is higher due to labor-intensive harvesting—grain is size of poppy seed and difficult to grind. Higher in protein and fiber than any other grain.
Storage	Air-tight container in cool, dry, dark place. Refrigeration preferred since flavor may intensify or turn rancid during prolonged storage. Buy in small quantities to avoid aging.
Arrowroot	
Baking	Good in baking because it adds no flavor of its own and lightens baked goods. If used as breading, produces golden brown crust.
Color and Flavor	Snow white in color—looks like cornstarch. Flavorless.
General Comments	Silky, fine powder. Often used to replace cornstarch or tapioca flour.
Storage	Air-tight containers in cool, dry, dark place.

Flour	Characteristics (continued)
Bean	
Baking	Two kinds of bean flour: 1) pure garbanzo or chickpea flour, and 2) flour made from a combination of garbanzo and fava (broad) beans (available from Authentic Foods - See Mail Order Sources). Both flours provide protein that is beneficial in baking. Use combination with other flours to totally (or partially) replace rice flour.
Color and Flavor	Light tan or yellowish. Slight "beany" flavor, especially if flour is pure chickpeas or garbanzo bean –less so if using garbanzo/fava bean combination. The latter imparts a slightly sweet taste to baked goods.
General Comments	Adds important protein to otherwise "starchy" gluten-free flour blends. Not widely available in stores, but can be ordered. (See Mail-Order Sources.)
Storage	Air-tight contains in cool, dry, dark place.
Corn	
Baking	Excellent in corn bread , muffins, and waffles —especially when blended with cornmeal. This is not corn meal. Principle ingredient in Corn Tortillas.
Color and Flavor	Light yellow in color. Tastes like corn.
General Comments	Smooth flour from corn. Make sure it's wheat-free.
Storage	Air-tight container in cool, dry, dark place.
Cornmeal	
Baking	Excellent in corn bread , muffins, and waffles– especially when blended with corn flour. Blue cornmeal can be substituted in muffins and waffles.

Flour	Characteristics (continued)
Color and Flavor	White or yellow. Tastes like corn. Blue cornmeal is grayish-blue and has a somewhat stronger flavor.
General Comments	Coarser than corn flour; often used in Mexican dishes. Used in Polenta. Blue cornmeal can substitute for white or yellow cornmeal in some dishes. Make sure cornmeal does not contain wheat.
Storage	Air-tight container in cool, dry, dark place.
Oat	**Not recommended for Celiac Sprue patients.**
Baking	Especially good in cookies or breakfast items such as pancakes, waffles, or muffins.
Color and Flavor	Light tan in color, browns baked goods. Flavor is mild and doesn't dominate baked goods.
General Comments	Somewhat heavy, so use with rice flours in baking. Produces "sticky" feel in the mouth. May turn sauces "gray" unless other coloring is used such as paprika or curry powder.
Storage	Air-tight container in cool, dry, dark place.
Potato Starch	
Baking	Excellent baking properties, especially when combined with eggs. Lumps easily, so stir before measuring.
Color and Flavor	Very white. Bland flavor.
General Comments	Very fine, powdery texture. Not the same as potato flour, which is made from dried and ground potatoes. Potato flour is heavy and used very little in wheat-free cooking.

Flour	Characteristics (continued)
Storage	Air-tight container in cool, dry, dark place.
Quinoa (keen-wah)	**Not recommended for Celiac Sprue patients.**
Baking	Excellent in all types of baking, including cakes, cookies, breads, and biscuits. Best if blended with other flours and used in highly-spiced or flavored foods.
Color and Flavor	Grain looks like sesame seeds. Flour color ranges from hues of red-yellow-orange to pink-purple-black, although flour tends to be tan. Flavor is somewhat nutty and can dominate baked goods.
General Comments	Not actually a cereal grain, but a member of the Chenopodiaceae family (related to beets and spinach). It is a complete protein.
Storage	Air-tight container in cool, dry, dark place. Keeps well.
Rice–White	
Baking	A bit gritty by itself, but works fine when combined with other flours. Should be about 2/3 of total flour. The coarser the grind, the more liquid needed.

Color and Flavor	White color. Bland, pleasant-tasting flavor.
General Comments	Milled from broken hulls of rice kernel. Among least "allergenic" of all flours. Mostly starch and nutritionally inferior since bran and germ layers have been removed in milling.
Storage	Air-tight container in cool, dry, dark place.

Rice–Brown	
Baking	Excellent in baked goods such as cookies or pizza crusts. Produces off-white color in baked goods.
Color and Flavor	Off-white color. Mild flavor.
General Comments	Higher in nutrient value than white rice since brown rice still contains bran. Contains no gluten.
Storage	Air-tight container in cool, dry, dark place. Somewhat shorter shelf life due to higher oil content in bran. May want to refrigerate.
Soy	
Baking	Excellent. Works well in baked goods with nuts, fruits or chocolate. Best when combined with other flours such as rice.
Color and Flavor	Yellow in color. Bland, somewhat nutty flavor -- leans toward "beany". Can be camouflaged by mixing with spices, fruit, nuts, or chocolate.
General Comments	Makes crispy coating for breading. Higher in protein and fat than other flours. Short shelf life, so purchase in small amounts to avoid spoilage. A common allergen, so use soy cautiously.
Storage	Air-tight container in cool, dry, dark place. Best if refrigerated.
Sweet Rice	
Baking	Don't confuse with white rice flour. Manufacturers suggest using in muffins, breads, and cakes although some sources recommend using only small amounts.
Color and Flavor	White, bland in flavor. Easily confused with white rice flour because they look alike.

Flour	Characteristics (continued)
General Comments	Sometimes called sticky rice; often used in Chinese cooking. Contains more starch than rice flours, making it an excellent thickener. Helps inhibit separation of sauces when they're chilled or frozen.
Storage	Air-tight container in cool, dark, dry place.
Tapioca	
Baking	Excellent in baked products when it makes up 25-50% of total flour. Lightens baked goods and imparts "chewiness" to breads. Browns quickly and produces crispy coating in breading.
Color and Flavor	Snow-white, velvety powder. "Anonymous" flavor.
General Comments	Sometimes called cassava or cassava starch. Similar to arrowroot and can be used interchangeably
Storage	Air-tight container in cool, dark, dry place
Teff	**Not recommended for Celiac Sprue patients.**
Baking	A little gritty, but works well in baked goods such as cakes or breads—if used as 25-50% of total flour. Best in "dark" baked goods such as chocolate cake or brownies, pumpernickel bread, or gingerbread.
Color and Flavor	Brown color. Slightly strong-tasting.
General Comments	Belongs to a tribe of its own in the grain family.
Storage	Air-tight container in cool, dark, dry place

Hidden Sources Of Wheat

* Beverages: Avoid beer and ale, gin, whisky (bourbon, scotch and rye), vodka (if it's grain-based; potato and grape-based vodka are wheat-free), Postum and Ovaltine.

* Breads: Unless the label says "wheat-free", avoid any biscuits, breads, crackers, croutons, crumbs, doughnuts, tortillas or wafers. If you bake your own from recipes in this book, however, you can eat all these foods. (I also avoid breads made of spelt, kamut, barley and rye—just to be safe—because they are similar to wheat.)

* Candy: Wheat may be an ingredient (for example, licorice) or used in the shaping or handling of the candy.

* Caramel Color: This may contain malt syrup or wheat starch. However, when you make Butterscotch Pudding (See Index), the caramel flavor comes from the cooked brown sugar, not wheat.

* Cereal: Avoid those made from wheat, rye, oats, barley, spelt, and kamut or if they contain malt flavoring or malt syrup.

* Coffee: Some decaffeinated, flavored and instant coffees may cause distress for wheat-sensitive persons.

* Condiments and Baking Ingredients: Check labels, especially on mixed spices, ketchup, some prepared mustards, and most soy sauces. Look for wheat-free versions of these ingredients.

* Dairy Products: Some flavored yogurts contain modified food starch (which could be wheat). Look for those with pectin (this is fruit). Malted milk, processed cheese spreads, and chocolate milk may contain wheat.

* Desserts and Other Sweets: You'll bake your own pies, cakes and cookies—but also avoid commercial pudding mixes, marshmallow creme, cake decorations, and marzipan.

* **Distilled Vinegar**: Vinegars made from wine, rice or cider are usually safe for wheat-sensitive persons. Avoid those made from grain.

* **Flavorings and Extracts:** Grain alcohol is often an ingredient. Look for wheat-free or gluten-free flavorings.

* **Meat, Fish, and Eggs**: Avoid any meat that's been breaded or in which fillers might be used such as sausage, luncheon meats or hot-dogs. Avoid self-basting turkeys. Buy tuna in spring water rather than oil. Egg-substitutes are not pure eggs but often contain many other additional ingredients.

* **Modified Food Starch**. This could be corn or wheat or some other food starch. Since you can't tell from the label, it's best to avoid altogether.

* **Pastas**: Look for "wheat-free" on label. You can eat Oriental rice noodles, bean threads and commercial pasta made from rice, corn, tapioca or potato starch. Better yet, make your own from recipes in this book.

* **Soups and Chowders**: Many canned soups, soup mixes, and bouillon cubes or granules contain hydrolyzed vegetable protein (HVP) which may contain wheat.

* **Vegetables**: When you see "vegetable starch" or "vegetable protein" on the label, this could mean corn, peanuts, rice, soy, or wheat. Avoid vegetables that are breaded, creamed, or scalloped.

MAIL-ORDER SOURCES

If you don't have a health food or specialty food store nearby, the following companies take phone or mail orders. Contact them for a catalog.

Flours, Ingredients, Mixes
Ener-G-Foods, Inc.
P.O. Box 84487
Seattle, WA 98124-5787
(800) 331-5222
(206) 764-3398 - FAX
www.ener-g.com

Flours, Ingredients, Mixes
Gluten-Free Pantry
PO Box 881
Glastonbury, CT 06033
(203) 633-3826
(860) 633-6853 - FAX
http://www.glutenfree.com\
    pantry@glutenfree.com

Flours, Grains
Bob's Red Mill Natural Foods
5209 S.E. International Way
Milwaukie, OR 97222
(800) 553-2258
(503) 654-3215
(503) 653-1339 - FAX

Flours, Ingredients, Mixes
Miss Roben's
PO Box 1434
Frederick, MD 21702
(800) 891-0083
(301) 631-5954 - FAX
http://www.jagunet.com/~msrobensmi
    ssroben@aol.com

Gluten-Free Flavorings
Bickford Flavors
19007 St. Clair Avenue
Cleveland, OH 44117-1001
(800) 283-8322

Bean Flour, Mixes
Authentic Foods
1850 W. 169th, Suite B
Gardena, CA 90247
(800) 806-4737 (310) 366-7612
http: //pages.prodigy.com/AUTFOODS

Southwestern ingredients can be ordered from the Chile Shop, 109 East Water Street, Santa Fe, NM 87501 (505) 983-6080, FAX (505) 984-0737.

This list, offered for your convenience, was updated when this book was published and is not intended as an endorsement of any particular company. The author cautions that names, addresses, and phone (or fax) numbers of these companies may have changed as well as the product lines they carry.

BAKING WITH ALTERNATIVE SWEETENERS

This section presents information for those who prefer to use sweeteners other than white sugar. Some basic guidelines are presented below, but each individual recipe may require a little experimentation to achieve the desired results—especially the preferred sweetness.

SWEETENER	AMOUNT TO USE	WHEN TO USE/TIPS
Honey From bees. Color and taste depend on flower source. 20% to 60% sweeter than white sugar.	Use 2/3 to 3/4 cup for 1 cup white sugar. Reduce liquid 1/4 cup. Add 1/4 teaspoon baking soda per cup of honey to neutralize acids. Reduce oven 25°.	All baked goods. Some vegans avoid. Don't give honey to children under age 2, because of possible botulism.
Granulated Fruit Sweetener From grape juice concentrate and rice syrup (**Fruit Source™**). Light brown granules taste like brown sugar. Not as sweet as white sugar.	Use 1 1/4 cups for 1 cup white sugar. Reduce salt 30- 50%. Use plenty of cooking spray on pans or use parch-ment paper. Don't overmix batter. Keep oven tempera-ture at 350° or lower and adjust baking time.	Cookies, cakes, and pud-dings. Works better when dissolved in warmed liquid before adding to recipe. Company sources verify that the rice syrup is gluten-free.
Mixed Fruit Juice Concentrate (liquid) Usually made of peach, pear, grape, and pineapple juices plus rice syrup. (**Fruit Source™**). Fruity-tasting liquid. Light brown color. Refrigerate after opening.	Use 2/3 cup for 1 cup white sugar. Reduce liquid 1/3 cup per cup of sweetener. Add 1/4 teaspoon baking soda per cup fruit sweetener. Reduce oven temperature 25° and adjust baking time. More user-friendly than the granulated version of Fruit-Source™.	All baked goods and desserts, except white cakes and chocolate dishes. If using in fruit pies, drain canned fruit thoroughly since too much liquid produces soggy pie crust. Company sources verify that the rice syrup is gluten-free.

BAKING WITH ALTERNATIVE SWEETENERS

(continued)

SWEETENER	AMOUNT TO USE	WHEN TO USE/TIPS
Frozen Fruit Juice Concentrate (e.g., Apple, White Grape, Orange, Pineapple) Look for *pure* concentrate.	Same as for mixed fruit juice concentrate—but this is a thinner liquid, so use about 25% less. Add 1/4 teaspoon baking soda per recipe.	Homemade applesauce, cakes, cookies, bars
Fruit Puree Use baby food fruits or puree fruits in blender.	Prune, apple, apricot, bana-na, pear. Best if used as substitute for 1/2 (not all) of sugar (or fat).	Baked goods, e.g., banana in banana bread, prunes in "dark" colored foods, etc.
Dried Cane Juice (Suca-nat®) - *Sugar Cane Natural*) Made of sugar cane with water removed. Coarse, amber granulates. Mild molasses taste.	Use same amount as white sugar. Add 1/4 teaspoon baking soda per cup of dried cane juice. Sift before using. Store in dry, cool place.	Cookies, cakes, pies, and puddings, but not white cakes. May be grainy in baked goods unless first dissolved in warmed liquid ingredient.
Date Sugar Ground, dehydrated dates. Coarse, brown granules. Very sweet.	Use 2/3 as much as white sugar. Works well when used in combination with other sweeteners. Store in dry, cool place.	Dissolve in hot water or other liquid before adding to recipe. Works well as top-ping for fruit desserts. May burn in recipes that bake for a long time.
Brown Rice Syrup Made from brown rice and enzymes from barley. Half as sweet as white sugar. Refrigerate after opening. (Lundberg's new version is gluten-free, but others may not be—read label.)	Use 1 1/3 cups for 1 cup white sugar. Reduce liquid 1/4 cup per cup rice syrup. Add 1/4 teaspoon baking soda per cup of syrup.	Cookies, pies, puddings. Use with other sweeteners in cakes. Makes baked goods crisp. **Caution:** Celiacs must avoid brown rice syrup, unless its gluten-free status is verified.

BAKING WITH ALTERNATIVE SWEETENERS

(continued)

SWEETENER	AMOUNT TO USE	WHEN TO USE/TIPS
Maple Syrup (pure) From maple tree sap. Dark (Formerly Grade C) best for flavor in baking. Dark brown in color.	Use 2/3 to 3/4 cup maple syrup for 1 cup white sugar. Reduce liquid in recipe by 3 tablespoons. Add 1/4 tea- spoon baking soda per cup maple syrup. Refrigerate after opening.	All baked goods, especially cakes. Use only organic to avoid formaldehyde and other possible additives.
Maple Sugar From maple syrup that has been boiled down to gran- ular sugar. Light brown granules.	Use 1 cup maple sugar for 1 cup white sugar. Add 1/8 teaspoon baking soda for each cup maple sugar.	Dissolve in warmed liquid from recipe before using in batters, if possible.
Molasses (unsulphured) Made from concentrated sugar cane juice. Strong flavor.	Use 1/2 cup molasses for 1 cup white sugar. May com-bine with other sweeteners to minimize strong flavor. Reduce liquid by 1/4 cup.	All baked goods, especially when strong spices are used as in spiced cakes, muffins, cookies, etc.
Stevia Sweet-leafed herb from Paraguay. In leaf, tincture, or powder form.	30-40 times sweeter than sugar. Slight licorice after- taste.	Recipes require total modi-fication to successfully use stevia. Best used in recipes requiring little sugar.

Sweeteners for Diabetics: You may use your favorite sweetener in these recipes, but make sure the sweetener is designed for baking if you use it in baked goods. You may need to experiment a bit to achieve the desired results. NutraSweet will not work in baking.

BAKING WITH ALTERNATIVE SWEETENERS

(continued)

The following sweeteners are believed to be more highly refined than those on the previous pages. Nonetheless, they work quite well in baking. Here are some guidelines for successful results.

SWEETENER	AMOUNT TO USE	WHEN TO USE/TIPS
Brown Sugar Actually white sugar with molasses added for heartier flavor and color. May use light or dark version.	Use 1 cup brown sugar in place of 1 cup white sugar.	When heartier flavor and darker color in baked goods is desired.
Corn Syrup Produced by action of enzymes on cornstarch. Used in many commercial products.	Use 1 cup corn syrup in place of 1 cup white sugar. Reduce liquid by 1/4 to 1/3 cup.	Use in any baked item that can use honey. **NOTE:** High fructose corn syrup <u>may</u> contain gluten from a brewer's yeast ex-tract used in processing.
FructoseError! Bookmark not defined. Granular version usually refined from corn syrup, although sometimes from fruit sources. A bit sweeter than white sugar. Liquid version also derived from corn.	Use 1 cup of fructose in place of 1 cup white sugar. Use 1 cup liquid fructose in place of 1 cup white sugar. Reduce liquid by 1/4 to 1/3 cup.	Use in cakes, cookies, bars, breads, muffins, or any baked item where honey is also appropriate. Use liquid fructose in same way as corn syrup.
Turbinado Actually just raw sugar with the impurities removed.	Use 1 cup turbinado in place of 1 cup white sugar.	Use in any recipe, but works better in darker colored baked goods.

BAKING WITH DAIRY SUBSTITUTES

Milk is one of the easiest ingredients to make substitutions for in baking, although some milk substitutes lend a subtle flavor to baked goods and may affect the degree of browning while baking. In addition, read labels to avoid problem ingredients such as casein. Celiacs should avoid versions with brown rice syrup (which may be processed with barley malt).

In place of 1 cup of cow's milk, use:

SUBSTITUTE	AMOUNT TO USE	WHEN TO USE/TIPS
Rice Milk (rice beverage) Be sure to buy brands that are vitamin-fortified.	1 cup. Mild flavor, white color. Looks like skim milk from cows.	In any recipe, although it is slightly sweet-tasting. Make sure it's gluten-free.
Soy Milk (soy beverage) Be sure to buy brands that are vitamin-fortified.	1 cup. Slight soy flavor, light tan in color. Can buy in liquid or powder form (which must be mixed with water.) Powdered version makes lighter color milk. New, un-sweetened version.	Best in recipes with stronger flavors so soy taste is masked, if desired, and in baked goods with darker colors since soy milk darkens with heat. Make sure it's gluten-free.
Nut Milk (usually almond) Persons with nut allergies to nuts should use caution. Ener-G NutQuik is made of almond meal and guar gum.	1 cup. Mild, slightly nutty flavor. Light brown color.	Best in dessert recipes. Tastes slightly "off" in savory dishes.
Goat Milk Available in powdered and liquid form; also in low-fat liquid. Not recom-mended for those with true milk allergies.	1 cup. Most closely re-sembles cow's milk in color (pure white.)	In any recipe. Works especially well in ice cream, puddings and other milk-based dishes. Aseptic and powdered varieties have stronger flavor.

BAKING WITH DAIRY SUBSTITUTES

If the recipe calls for Dry Milk Powder: Use same amount of non-dairy milk powder, but read labels to make sure there are no problem ingredients such as casein. You may also use 3/4 as much goat's milk powder, if approved for your diet. Milk-allergic people should avoid goat's milk, but milk-intolerant people say they can use goat's milk. Or omit dry milk powder altogether and add same amount of rice flour or sweet rice flour. Baked goods won't brown as much without dry milk powder (not the same as Carnation instant dry milk). In yeast breads, rising and browning will diminish without milk powder.

In place of 1 cup evaporated skim milk, use:

SUBSTITUTE	AMOUNT TO USE	WHEN TO USE/TIPS
Ener-G NutQuik or SoyQuik or other non-dairy milk powders. Mix at double strength.	1 cup	Recipes using evaporated skim milk. Flavors will be stronger. Calories and nutrient values will be doubled.

In place of 1 cup buttermilk, use:

SUBSTITUTE	AMOUNT TO USE	WHEN TO USE/TIPS
Use 1 tablespoon fresh lemon juice or cider vinegar or reconstituted Ener-G gluten-free vinegar and enough rice, soy, or nut milk to make 1 cup.	1 cup (Some non-dairy milks produce a thinner buttermilk. If so, use 2 tablespoons less of non-dairy buttermilk per cup specified in recipe.)	Any recipe calling for buttermilk

Density of Milk: Whether you're using liquid non-dairy milks or mix your own from powder, the thinner the milk the less you'll need. For example, reduce the liquid by 1 tablespoon per cup if you use skim milk in place of whole milk. You may need to experiment a bit to achieve the desired results since liquid milk densities vary by brand and the ratio of powder to water will affect the density of milks made from non-dairy powders.

Lactose-Reduced Milk: You may use gf lactose-reduced milk in these recipes, however, you'll need to experiment to achieve desired results.

BAKING WITH DAIRY SUBSTITUTES

(continued)

In place of 1 cup yogurt, use:

SUBSTITUTE	AMOUNT TO USE	WHEN TO USE/TIPS
Goat Yogurt (Persons with true milk allergy should avoid all goat products.)	1 cup	Any recipe calling for yogurt. However, the tapioca in goat yogurt may make baked item "doughy".
Soy Yogurt	1 cup	Not well-suited to heat, but works well in dips, ice creams, and other non-baked items. Won't drain.
Non-Dairy Milk Liquid	2/3 cup	Any recipe calling for yogurt. Best to add liquid in 1/3 cup increments to avoid adding too much.

Cheese: Although there are several "non-dairy" cheeses such as Parmesan cheese made from rice, soy, or nuts, it is difficult to find one that doesn't have additional problem ingredients. For example, they may contain milk proteins called calcum caseinate, sodium caseinate, or casein. Others include oats (which is off-limits for celiacs) or texturized vegetable protein (which can have various sources, but is often soy.) Also, plain milk may contain one set of ingredients but flavored versions may contain different ingredients.

Sour Cream and Cream Cheese: Soyco makes a rice-based version, however, check the label to make sure it's right for your diet—the milk protein, casein, is present in both items. Soymage makes a casein-free sour cream alternative.
Keep in touch with your natural food store. New, non-dairy cheeses are being developed.

BAKING WITH EGG SUBSTITUTES

Eggs are one of the hardest ingredients to make substitutions for because they play such critical roles in baking. They can be used as binding agents (hold ingredients together), moisturizers (add moisture), or as leavening agents (make things rise) in baking. Generally speaking, egg-free baked goods rise less and have a denser texture than those made with eggs. Here are some general guidelines when modifying recipes to exclude eggs.

Eggs As Binders:
If the recipe has only one egg but contains a fair amount of baking powder or baking soda, then the egg is the binder.

In place of 1 egg as a binder, use:

SUBSTITUTE	AMOUNT TO USE	WHEN TO USE/TIPS
Tofu (soft silken) by Mori-Nu®	Use 1/4 cup for each egg and blend with recipe liquid in food processor until completely smooth before adding to recipe.	Cakes, cookies, breads— but light-colored baked goods won't brown as deeply. Makes very moist baked goods with a somewhat heavier texture.
Pureed fruits/vegetables Apples (or apple butter), apricots, prunes, or pears. Or, pureed vegetables such as corn. Baby foods (Gerber's 1st) have no additional fillers.	Use 3 tablespoons to replace each egg. Increase liquid in recipe by 1 tablespoon.	Especially useful in baked goods where the flavor of the fruit or vegetable puree complements or doesn't detract from the flavor of the dish (e.g., pureed prunes work fine in chocolate cakes but not in yellow cakes).

You may use liquid egg substitutes in place of real eggs. But please note that liquid egg substitutes actually contain eggs. The yolks have been removed to reduce the fat and cholesterol. *People with egg allergies cannot safely consume these products because they still contain eggs. Also, some egg substitutes contain other problem ingredients such as modified food starch which may or may not be wheat-based.* Read the label.

In place of 1 egg as a binder, use: (continued)

SUBSTITUTE	AMOUNT TO USE	WHEN TO USE/TIPS
Unflavored Gelatin Powder May use animal derived or vegetable-based (kosher) gelatin powder.	Mix 1 envelope of unflavored gelatin with 1 cup boiling water. Substitute 3 tablespoons of this liquid gelatin for each egg in your recipe. Refrigerate; then microwave to liquefy before use.	Baked goods such as cookies, cakes, breads
Arrowroot, Soy, Lecithin	Whisk together 1/4 cup warm water, 2 tablespoons arrowroot, 1 tablespoon soy flour, and 1/4 teaspoon lecithin liquid or granules.	All baked goods, but preferably those with stronger flavors since soy and lecithin may affect the overall taste of dish.
Flaxseed	Pulverize 1 teaspoon whole flax seeds in coffee grinder or blender. Combine with 1/3 cup water and bring to boil. Reduce heat and sim-mer for 3-5 minutes until mixture is consistency of egg whites.	Cool mixture before adding to baked goods. Best used in "dark" dishes since the brown color of flax may discolor baked goods. Mild flavor. **NOTE:** Some celiacs report discomfort due to a slight laxative effect.

BAKING WITH EGG SUBSTITUTES

(continued)

Eggs as Leavening Agents:
If there are no other ingredients that make the baked item rise, then the egg is the leavening agent.

In place of 1 egg as a leavener, use:

SUBSTITUTE	AMOUNT TO USE	WHEN TO USE/TIPS
Egg Replacer by Ener-G (a powder of potato starch, tapioca flour, calcium lactate, calcium carbonate, citric acid and a vegetable-derived gum) It may not be corn-free, however.	1 1/2 teaspoons Egg Replacer powder mixed in 2 tablespoons water. For double effect, double the Egg Replacer powder in same amount of water.	All baked goods. Flavorless, so won't affect taste of recipe. For added lightness, whip in food processor or blender for 30 seconds.
Buttermilk-Soda See page 156 for making dairy-free buttermilk.	Replace liquid in recipe with same amount of buttermilk (or thinned yogurt) Replace baking powder with same amount of baking soda–no more than 1 tsp. per cup flour.	All baked goods, but this technique works best in dishes that don't require a lot of "rising" to look good. such as cookies, bars and flatbreads.

Other Hints When Omitting Eggs (when used as leavening agents)
1. Add air to lighten the recipe by creaming the fat and sweetener together with your electric mixer. Then add dry ingredients
2. Whip the liquid ingredients in a food processor or blender for 30 seconds as another way of incorporating air into the recipe.
3. Add an extra 1/2 teaspoon baking powder per egg. Do not exceed 1 teaspoon baking powder per cup of flour or a bitter taste will develop. As an alternative to commercial baking powder (which contains corn), try the homemade version on page 141.
4. Recipes with acidic liquids such as buttermilk, molasses, lemon juice, or vinegar tend to rise better than those with non-acidic liquids such as water or milk.

BAKING WITH EGG SUBSTITUTES

(continued)

Eggs as Moisture:

The egg's purpose is to add moisture if there are leavening agents in the recipe, but not much water or other liquid in the recipe.

Generally speaking, baked goods without eggs are somewhat heavier and more dense than those with eggs. For that reason, slightly increase the leavening agent in your egg-free recipes to compensate for the egg's natural leavening effect. In addition, using liquid sweeteners such as honey or molasses for part of the sugar in a recipe helps compensate for the loss of the "binding" effect of eggs.

In place of 1 egg for moisture, use:

SUBSTITUTE	AMOUNT TO USE	WHEN TO USE/TIPS
Fruit juice, milk, or water	2 tablespoons. Increase leavening by 25-50%. May need to bake items slightly longer.	Baked goods such as cakes, cookies, bars
Pureed fruit such as bananas, applesauce, apricots, pears, prunes. (The natural pectin in fruits, especially prunes, traps air which helps "lighten" baked goods.)	1/4 cup. Increase leavening agent by 25-50%. May need to bake items slightly longer.	Baked goods where the fruit's flavor complements the overall dish such as applesauce in spice cakes, bananas in banana bread, apricots and pears in mild-flavored items, and prunes in dark, heavily-flavored items such as chocolate or spice cakes.

Index

—A—

Agar (Kanten), 266
Alfredo Sauce, 71
Altitude, 12
Amaranth, 64, 265, 268
  Recipes using Amaranth,
  15, 19, 25, 27, 29, 32, 45, 50,
  64, 99, 100, 103, 106, 110, 112
Anise-Pine Nut Cookies, 118
Apple
  Chutney, 163, 241, 260
  Pork Chops & Cabbage, 242,
  255, 260
Apricot
  Rum Balls, 115
  Cherry Crisp, 96, 255, 257,
  264
  Sauce, 149
Arrowroot, 266, 268
Asian Soba Noodles, 78, 255,
  258, 262
Asian Vinaigrette, 167, 255, 258
Ascorbic Acid, 7
Avocado
  Chile Sauce, 149, 258
  Dressing, 167, 262

—B—

Baby Foods, 7
Bagels, 49
Baked Doughnuts, 45
Baked Ham w/ Wine Sauce,
  246, 259
Baking Powder, 7
Banana Bread, 50
Banana Cream Pie, 119, 257
Bananas w/ Rum Sauce, 97, 254,
  256

Barbecue Sauce, 156
Barley, 265, 274, 278, 281
Bars
  Chocolate Brownies, 110, 259,
  260
  Lemon Bars, 117, 254, 263-64
Bean(s)
  Boston Baked Beans, 89, 260,
  261
  Cassoulet w/ Sausage, 252, 260
  Flour, 266
  Red, & Rice, 91, 264
  Refried, 90, 263, 264
  Southwestern, 90, 263, 264
Bean flour, 10, 39, 265, 267, 269,
  270, 277
Beef
  Burgundy, 230
  Paprika's w/ Noodles, 229, 259
  Stroganoff, 231
  Enchiladas, 198, 263, 264
  Meat Loaf, 232, 259
  Mexican Pie, 233, 260
  Sloppy Joes, 234, 259
  Stir-Fry Ginger, w/Rice, 235,
  260
  Sausage, 248
  Tostadas, 236
  Chorizo, 247
  Lasagna, 251
  Spaghetti & Meatballs, 249
  Swedish Meatballs, 250, 259
  White Bean Cassoulet w/
  Sausage, 252, 260
Biscotti, 33, 114, 257, 264
Biscuits (Buttermilk), 51, 194
Biscuits & Gravy, 56
Blackberry Cobbler, 95
Blue Corn Waffles, 55
Blueberry-Lemon Muffins, 47
Boston Baked Beans, 89, 260,
  261
Boston Brown Bread, 32

Huevos Rancheros, 59, 264

293

ABOUT THE AUTHOR

A former university professor and marketing executive with a Fortune 500 corporation, Dr. Fenster graduated from the University of Nebraska with a degree in home economics and was a home economics specialist with the Cooperative Extension Service in North Dakota for several years.

After discovering her own food sensitivities several years ago, Dr. Fenster studied extensively to find flavorful alternatives for problem ingredients. She understands the importance of a healthy diet and the desire for fine dining—which is all the more challenging when one has to avoid certain ingredients.

She serves as vice-president of her local asthma and allergy support group (affiliated with the Asthma and Allergy Foundation of America) and is a member of the Celiac Sprue Association of USA and the Gluten Intolerance Group of North America.

As a wheat-sensitive individual herself, Dr. Fenster understands the importance of a healthy diet and the desire for fine dining—which is all the more challenging when one has to avoid wheat or gluten. She wrote this book all of us can continue to enjoy eating a wide variety of dishes. She lives in Denver, CO.

THE SPECIAL DIET SERIES ORDER FORM

Enjoy the dishes you love . . .without ingredients you can't have

Name_____

Address_____

City/State/Zip_____

Telephone (   ) _____

Please send the following items to the address above:

	How Many?	PRICE (Canada & UK add $5)	TAX (Colorado Residents only)	TOTAL
Special Diet Solutions: *Healthy Cooking Without Wheat, Gluten, Dairy, Eggs, Yeast, or Sugar*	_____	$15.95	$.60 per book	_____
Wheat-Free Recipes & Menus *275 recipes for breads, desserts, entrees, sauces. Gluten-free.*	_____	$19.95	$.75 per book	_____
Bookmarks (laminated)				
Baking With Wheat-Free Flours	_____	$1.50 each	$.20	_____
Baking With Alternative Sweeteners	_____	$1.50 each	$.20	_____
Baking With Dairy Substitutes	_____	$1.50 each	$.20	_____
Baking With Egg Substitutes	_____	$1.50 each	$.20	_____

SUB-TOTAL _____

Shipping & handling ($3 per book) _____

(Canada: $5) _____

Total Amount Enclosed _____

Please allow 2 weeks for delivery

Check
(payable to Savory Palate, Inc.)

Money Order

Visa, MasterCard, Discover

Account Number_____

Expiration Date_____

Customer Signature_____

SAVORY PALATE, INC.
**8174 South Holly, Suite 404
Littleton, CO 80122-4004**

In Colorado	Outside Colorado
(303) 741-5408	(800) 741-5418 (orders only)

FAX (303) 741-0339